THE TOTAL
BOATING
MANUAL

BOATING
WORLD'S LARGEST POWERBOAT MAGAZINE

THE TOTAL BOATING MANUAL

KEVIN FALVEY
AND THE EDITORS OF **BOATING MAGAZINE**

weldon**owen**

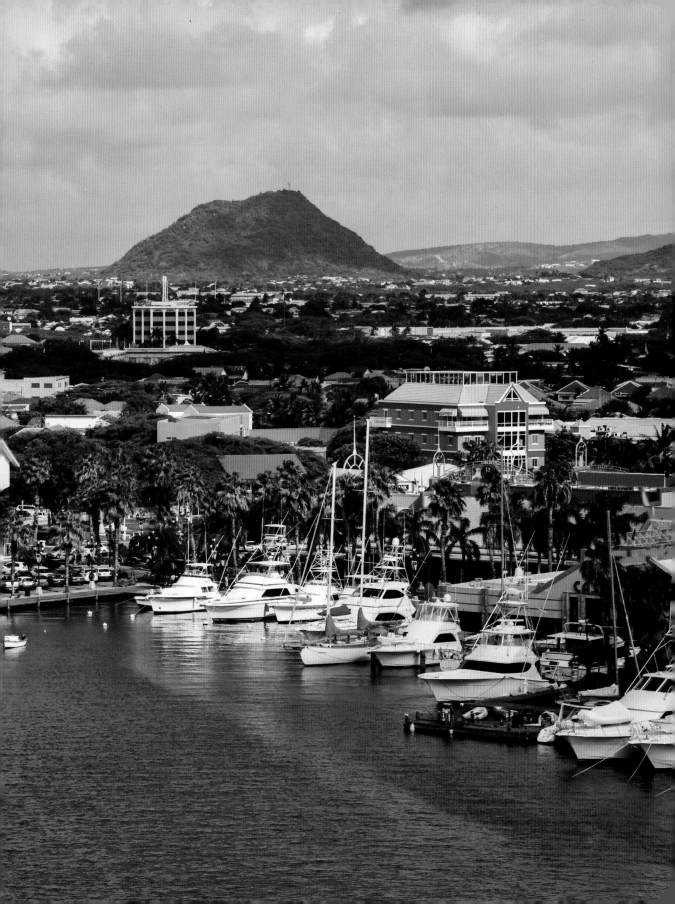

CONTENTS

Author Introduction

TOOLS & GEAR

REPAIR & MAINTENANCE

JUST ADD WATER

Ancient marine wisdom holds that the two happiest days in any boater's life are the day that the boat is bought and the day that the boat is sold.

Cynical? Sorta. But the statement doesn't lack for merit. Boating is an expensive, time-consuming, and skill-dependent activity. Joining the ranks of boat owners, one does more than just practice conspicuous consumption. One embarks upon a journey of fun, adventure, discovery—and potential frustration.

New boaters soon learn some hard lessons, like that a land-based weather forecast doesn't cut it and that a seeming tiny difference in wind speed can change how they dock, anchor, and cruise their boat. They learn that there is a bewildering array of equipment that can help ease their way or enhance their enjoyment on the water, but little reliable instruction for the use of this gear. New boaters also learn that anything that can break will, and usually at the worst time, and that furthermore, one cannot count on getting out and walking, hailing a cab or simply waiting idly after calling for a tow when Murphy rears his head.

This book will help with all of that, and do so in a way that other sources cannot. The publication of this *Total Boating Manual* just happens to coincide with *Boating* magazine's 60th anniversary. The editors at *Boating*, have collectively authored thousands of boat reviews and technical articles and produced hundreds of videos related to boat buying, boat ownership, boat use, and boat maintenance. Millions of boaters have placed their trust in Boating magazine's expertise, and we've brought that same level of care and passion to this book.

One of the great things about boating is the way that it rewards its devotees with a sense of accomplishment and of self-reliance and grants the avid practitioner the gift of mastery over a wide variety of disciplines. There is no price that can be placed upon such a bounty. The *Total Boating Manual* will help guide you to receipt of that prize and ensure that the happiest day of your life is any day you step aboard a boat you can call your own.

TOOLS & GEAR

Boats are often compared to automobiles. This is a mistake on too many levels to list. For one thing, a boat operates on a surface that can change from smooth to rough in minutes; highways never suddenly change from newly paved to being riddled with three-foot deep potholes.

Furthermore, most all boats are built and bought for pleasure while most all automobiles are built and bought for need. Because owning a boat is almost always entirely discretional and almost always entirely for pleasure, there are myriad more types of boats than there are automobiles. In fact, the number of boat categories is staggering—so much so that beginners often purchase the wrong boat for where and how the intend to use it. This holds true for the trailer, the gear and the accessories that the boat must be outfitted with as well.

To help you navigate the shoal-ridden water of boat buying, this first chapter of the *Total Boating Manual* provides clear, easy-to-understand guidance that you will find useful when buying and outfitting a boat, from the best boat for your needs to the gear to complete the package.

001 IDENTIFY THE BEST BOAT FOR YOU

If you're new to the wonderful world of boating, investigating options for your first purchase, or are a seasoned boater wanting to trade up, you may feel a bit overwhelmed by all the options available to you. Never fear! *Boating* magazine's experts have analyzed all of the most important factors to account for and assembled them in this one handy chart. Start at the top, figure out your needs and wants, and then see what the pros recommend.

WATER TYPE

Determining the type of water you intend to boat in most of the time drives a cascading series of decisions that can affect diverse characteristics, from which beach or cove you can explore to economy of operation. Hulls with deeper-V shapes ride smoother but draw more water and may require more power to achieve a given speed.

WET OR DRY?

Marinas are costly but convenient. A trailer requires maintenance and registration, yet provides self-sufficient freedom.

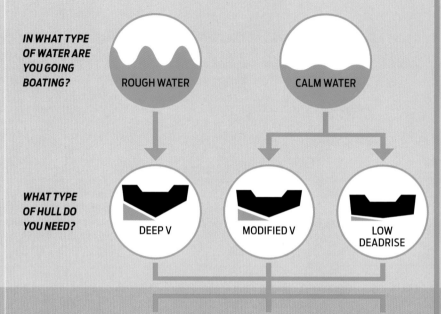

IN WHAT TYPE OF WATER ARE YOU GOING BOATING?

ROUGH WATER   CALM WATER

WHAT TYPE OF HULL DO YOU NEED?

DEEP V   MODIFIED V   LOW DEADRISE

GEOGRAPHY, ATTITUDE, AND BOAT SIZE AND TYPE ARE FACTORS TO CONSIDER.

DRY STACK   DOCK   TRAILER

CHOOSE ONE

A

P.W.C.
A far cry from the "stand-up" models some may think of, these jet-powered craft provide excitement, economy, and easy trailerability in trade for few onboard amenities.

B

DECK BOAT
Deck boats carry the width of their beam to the bow for maximized space. Generally they have less deadrise than bowriders, but the distinctions are now blurring.

C

BOWRIDER
The quintessential "day boats," bowriders provide maximum lounging topside. Most have a provision for an enclosed head, and larger versions sport berths and galleys.

D

DUAL CONSOLE
Self-bailing cockpits, standard fishing features, and hulls designed for open water differentiate these split-windshield boats from bowriders. As large as 30 feet (9.1 m).

E

CENTER CONSOLE
Complete 360-degree access around the boat and acres of cockpit make these the longtime darlings of anglers. Many are now equipped for day-tripping.

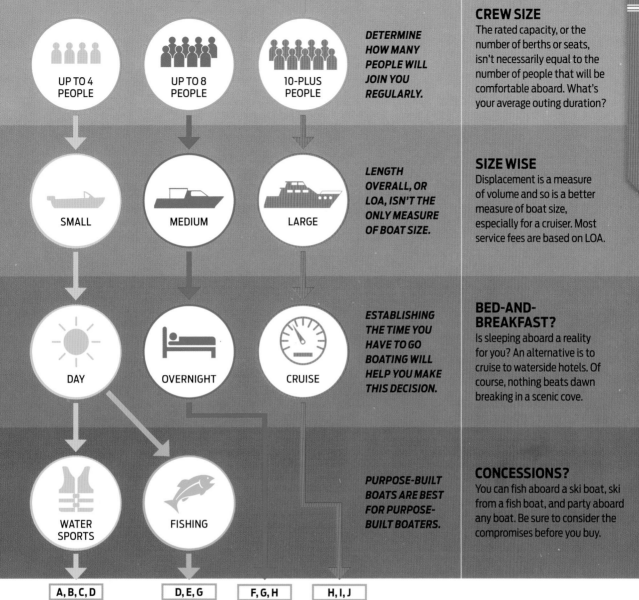

UP TO 4 PEOPLE

UP TO 8 PEOPLE

10-PLUS PEOPLE

DETERMINE HOW MANY PEOPLE WILL JOIN YOU REGULARLY.

CREW SIZE
The rated capacity, or the number of berths or seats, isn't necessarily equal to the number of people that will be comfortable aboard. What's your average outing duration?

SMALL

MEDIUM

LARGE

LENGTH OVERALL, OR LOA, ISN'T THE ONLY MEASURE OF BOAT SIZE.

SIZE WISE
Displacement is a measure of volume and so is a better measure of boat size, especially for a cruiser. Most service fees are based on LOA.

DAY

OVERNIGHT

CRUISE

ESTABLISHING THE TIME YOU HAVE TO GO BOATING WILL HELP YOU MAKE THIS DECISION.

BED-AND-BREAKFAST?
Is sleeping aboard a reality for you? An alternative is to cruise to waterside hotels. Of course, nothing beats dawn breaking in a scenic cove.

WATER SPORTS

FISHING

PURPOSE-BUILT BOATS ARE BEST FOR PURPOSE-BUILT BOATERS.

CONCESSIONS?
You can fish aboard a ski boat, ski from a fish boat, and party aboard any boat. Be sure to consider the compromises before you buy.

| A, B, C, D | D, E, G | F, G, H | H, I, J |

F — CUDDY CABIN
Also called "sport boats," a cuddy cabin provides a cushioned, crawl-in space for taking naps, hiding a head, and serving as lockable stowage. Racier looks than a bowrider.

G — WALKAROUND
The cabins aboard these fishing boats are smaller than express or midcabin boats due to the recessed, rail-protected walkways providing safer, easier access to the bow.

H — MIDCABIN
Really a subset of express cruisers less than 30 feet (9.1 m) LOA, midcabins offer a berth under the helm deck and maximum berth count in the shortest length. Any are trailerable.

I — EXPRESS
Express boats offer less windage while docking, eliminate ladders and stairs, and their lower top-hamper reduces rolling motion. The low, sleek looks garner points, too.

J — FLYBRIDGE
A flying-bridge boat means more living space than a similarly sized express. Visibility is generally better, though seeing the transom while docking can be hard.

002 KNOW YOUR OPTIONS

Many boat buyers know exactly what they want and why. First-timers, however, may not even know which questions to ask or where to get unbiased answers. Buying a boat means opening up a whole new world of fun, whether you're interested in fishing, watersports, or just enjoying a lazy day on the lake. It also means spending a lot of money, so you want to be sure you do it right. The first step is figuring out what basic type of boat is best for you. Your options can be divided into three general categories, with some crossover.

CRUISING If your primary interest is to have a fun day out or go on overnight trips with friends and family, look at cruising boats. This is a big category with a lot of variation, from bowriders, which are intended for day trips only, to luxurious crafts with seriously swanky accommodations.

FISHING While you can fish off of just about any boat, if fishing is your main interest, you'll want a model designed to maximize deck space, which means that the trade-off is for less seating and cabin space. A bigger fishing boat will still have its own overnight accommodations, but they will not be as roomy as those on a similarly sized cruiser.

WATERSPORTS Designed for waterskiing and wakeboarding, these boats are small and fast and are often purpose-designed for expert users. A basic waterski or sport-boat model is a good entry point for the enthusiastic hobbyist.

003 GET YOUR FEET WET

Once you've really thought about how you'll be enjoying your new boat and settled on a basic type (cruising, fishing, or watersports), you're ready to get serious! Here are your next steps.

DO YOUR HOMEWORK Read up on the best-rated boats in the class you're considering, and familiarize yourself with their features (as well as questions you might need answered). *Boating* magazine publishes tons of reviews; check out our website for details and inspiration.

HIT THE FLOOR Now you're ready to go to a boat show or to a reputable dealer's showroom and check out the boats you're interested in. Look at everything. Take the time to sit at the helm and test out the legroom and see how you like the control set-up, visibility, and comfort. Open the engine hatch and ask the dealer to walk you through common tasks, such as checking the oil, power-steering fluid, coolant, etc. How accessible is everything? If the boat has overnight accommodations, have a lie-down. You want to make sure your floating home-away-from-home is as comfortable as it looks. This is a big decision, so take your time.

SCHEDULE A TEST-DRIVE If everything checks out, it's time to take her for a spin. See items 022–023.

004 STUDY UP

Even in calm conditions, you need to feel comfortable handling wind, waves, tides, currents, weather, and other boat traffic, as well as tending to your passengers' safety. And if any unexpected events do come up, you will want to be ready. Most states require you to at least acquire a safe boating certificate before hitting the water, and you may want to look into some further training through the United States Power Squadron, the Coast Guard, or other sources. The more that you know, the safer you'll be, no matter what nature has in store.

005 CHOOSE BETWEEN NEW AND USED

Anyone who's ever bought a car will be familiar with the basic trade-offs. Buying from a dealer means the latest technology, a full warranty, and (hopefully) support for years to come. Buying used, of course, can save you a lot of money. That might mean an incredible deal, or a nightmare.

BUY NEW Buying new means going through a dealer. To find a good one, check out the tips in items 009–010. The boat you get should be factory-perfect with a good warranty covering any problems that may arise. A good dealer will be there for you over the years, so really ask around and do your research.

BUY USED A good used boat may come from a dealer who took it as trade-in, from a broker, or from a private owner. As is the case when you buy a used car, that used boat may have been lovingly cared for by a little old lady who only took it fishing on Sundays or by a dimwit who skimped on maintenance and "forgot" to mention accidents he'd been in. You can protect yourself and get a great deal by following the guidelines in item 021.

Unless you're mechanically inclined, have a lot of spare time, and love to tinker, you're probably best off with a new or relatively new (three years old or less) boat from a reputable dealer, especially for your first purchase.

006 START SMALL(ISH)

If you're just starting out, you'll want to start small. Smaller boats tend to be more affordable, but that's the least of your concerns in choosing one. As a relative novice, you will want a craft that is easy to handle and relatively painless to maintain. You will also want to find one that offers you maximum flexibility. For example, some larger boats may not be trailerable, which will seriously limit your options and increase storage costs.

It's true that bigger boats do have all kinds of cool amenities, like roomier cabins, a full galley (kitchen), and a much nicer head (bathroom). But the right 22- to 24-foot (6.7- to 7.3-m) boat can offer everything you need. If you fall in love with a bigger boat, be cautious. Only look at it seriously if it really is the best for your needs—for instance, if you're planning to carry a lot of passengers on a regular basis or go on long, multiday trips. And take your test-drive seriously. If you struggle to control the boat or are flummoxed by overly complex systems, you won't have as much fun. And fun is why you got into boating in the first place, right?

007 STUDY BOAT ANATOMY

A waterworthy vessel does have a fair amount of complex components, but here's a primer on some of the basic terms and structures to help you navigate your way around a boat.

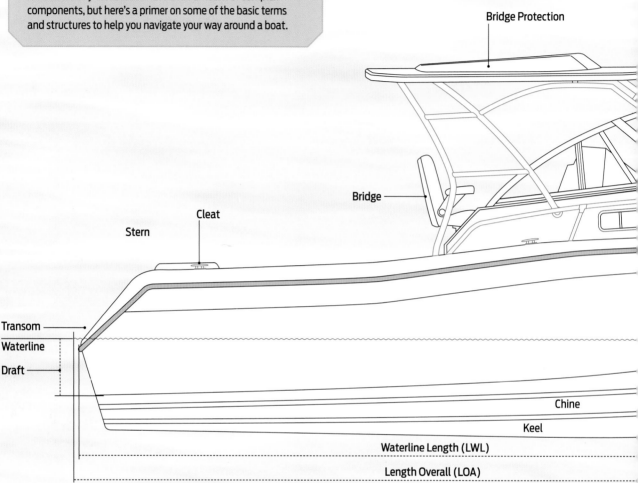

Bridge Protection

Bridge

Cleat

Stern

Transom

Waterline

Draft

Chine

Keel

Waterline Length (LWL)

Length Overall (LOA)

008

HAVE A PEEK AT YOUR PROPELLER

This is how your boat gets around, and it's no simple piece of metal. Depending on your boat type and the waters you travel in, there will be a propeller design for every vessel and occasion you can imagine. That said, they all share some common design features, as seen here.

Ribs

Exhaust Passage

Outer Hub

Inner Hub

Cup

Blade Face

Trailing Edge

Leading Edge

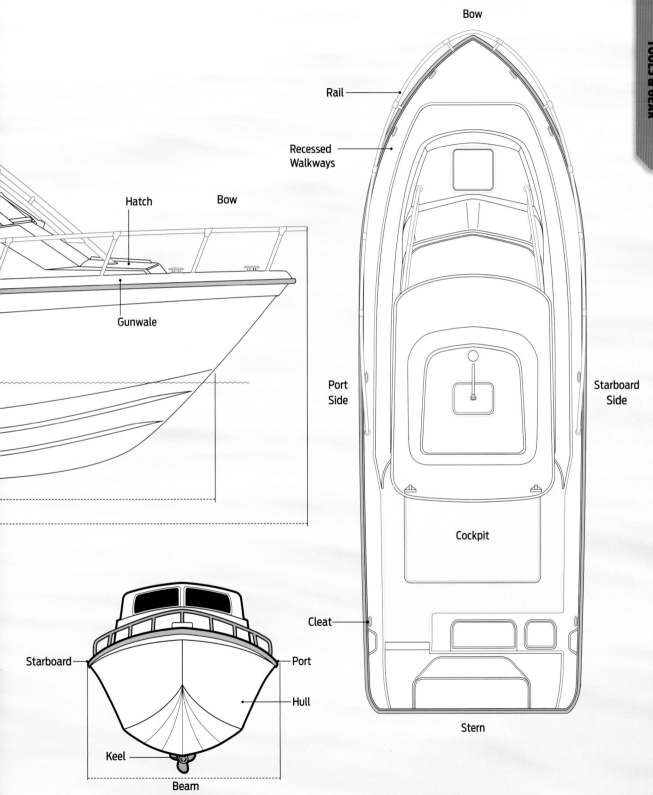

Bow

Rail

Recessed
Walkways

Port
Side

Starboard
Side

Cockpit

Cleat

Stern

Hatch

Bow

Gunwale

Starboard

Port

Hull

Keel

Beam

009 FIND THE BEST BOAT DEALER

Buying a new boat usually means going through a dealership, so here are some tips to ensure the dealer is as good as the vessel you want to purchase.

MAKE CONTACT Are any calls or emails to the staff promptly responded to? Or are they unwilling to work with you when not in person? It's not always possible to negotiate or get answers in-store, so get email confirmation of any deals made over the phone.

GET REVIEWS Search the Web for reviews of a dealer. One or two glowing reviews or a few critical posts shouldn't be an undue influence, so look to see which type of review outweighs the other. Ask a dealership about contacting existing customers for their own references as well.

PAY A VISIT Nothing beats real-life experience. Your very first encounter with the shop can tell you a lot. Is the store staff happy to see you? If no one greets you or asks if they can help you within

a few minutes of your showing up, don't count on some improved service in the future. Confused or annoyed looks when you ask for help are an even bigger red flag. If you've made an appointment with a salesperson and are kept waiting for a long time or if you're interrupted repeatedly by them taking calls, be wary.

CHECK THE SHOP How are the yard and showroom? Are they clean and organized or unkempt and cluttered? If you can, talk to the service manager or mechanics before closing the deal. A clean, well-managed shop with good equipment and knowledgeable staff is a good sign.

ASK FOR CERTIFICATIONS Does this dealership hold marine-industry certifications? Have they ever held a spot in the Boating Industry Top 100? (There are about 3,000 dealers in the United States, so earning a place is a serious achievement). Check with the service manager about any manufacturer certifications—the more they have, the better.

010 LOOK FOR FIVE STARS

A dealer can make or break your ownership experience. But how do you identify the best from the bilge crud?

The boating industry recognizes this problem. Specifically, the Marine Retailers Association of the Americas and the Grow Boating Initiative run a dealer-certification program designed to grant boat buyers the confidence they need to close a deal with a boat dealer they can trust.

The program is called Marine Five Star Dealer Certification (MFSDC). Launched in 2006 as one of the core strategic programs of Grow Boating, Inc., MFSDC has more than 300 certified boat dealers throughout North America. MFSDC is built on a stringent set of standards designed to enhance the sales and service experience, with the goal of promoting industry growth.

In early June 2013, MFSDC unveiled research results that demonstrate certified dealers outperformed noncertified dealers in every category of the Customer Satisfaction Index (CSI) surveys. Boat buyers were asked in a 2012 survey to rank their dealer's performance in a variety of sales and service areas. In every category, customers demonstrated that they were more satisfied with their experiences with certified dealers compared to their noncertified counterparts. Certified dealers must also publicly post the Marine Consumers Bill of Rights, which ensures compliance with industry-set standards.

011 GO TO SCHOOL

Few trailer-boaters are 100-percent confident and comfortable at the launch ramp, and everyone has nervous days on the water. Confidence around the docks is vital to a new owner's fun on the water, and a great dealer should be there when the boat is brought to port the first time.

Boating skills are really techniques, easily learned—with the right teacher. Too many boat dealers bypass this part of the sale; instead, they offer to hitch the trailer to the truck and just walk away after the sale. Some buyers resort to asking friends and family to teach them all about boating. Finding someone who has the information and the time to show the buyer is rare.

Continuing boater education is essential. Experienced dealers make great coaches and cheerleaders for new and existing boaters. At the very least, a dealer should know who in the community conducts classes in boating skills and safety,

where to find adult education courses, how to access training provided by the United States Power Squadrons, or other resources. Some dealers may even sponsor or host courses at their dealerships.

Be sure to go to school—uncertainty on the water can be intimidating. A dealer can serve as a committed mentor to help overcome the hurdles that a new buyer may not know about yet. They can teach the rules of the road, provide lessons on knots and other seamanship skills, and guide you on those all-important safety measures in a format that's efficient and enjoyable.

Given how important they are, the lessons aren't as hard as you might imagine—and there aren't an interminable number of them. Classes in local communities allow new owners to meet other new boaters, where they may find they have a lot in common. These are bonds that can last a lifetime.

012 KNOW YOUR MATERIALS

What goes into making a boat? That's a really simple question with some very complicated answers and a lot of debate around the best choices. There's no way we can give you more than a cursory introduction here, but you'll learn the basics and figure out what you still need to research in the rest of this book, on our website, and beyond.

FIBERS Most boat hulls are made with fabric created from glass fibers; fiberglass gives boats their stiffness. Carbon fiber and other newer fiber materials may be lighter, stiffer, and stronger than fiberglass, but are also expensive and experimental. Expect this to change quickly, as the dream of a lighter, stronger, more efficient, faster boat is almost universal.

CORE MATERIALS Fiberglass is a very light material, but use enough of it, and the weight does start to add up. For boats smaller than 30 feet (9.1 m) or so, this may not be a big deal. But with larger vessels, you can get the stiffness you need with less weight, by sandwiching a lighter material in between inner and outer layers of fiberglass laminate.

RESINS Your boat is quite literally held together by resin. This is some serious chemistry going on, and you'll be bombarded by a lot of terms. Take the time to know what the trade-offs between performance and price may mean, and what will be best for your specific boat's intended mission.

BACKING PLATES Backing plates are installed on the back side of fiberglass, beneath or behind hardware or fittings, such as cleats, hatch lids, and grab rails. In the past, backing plates were almost always plywood, but there are much better plastic materials available today that won't get soft and mushy when they get wet. Backing plates provide " bite" for screw threads, add crush-resistance to cored laminate, and spread loads over a wider area than fasteners alone.

014
CALL FOR REINFORCEMENTS

"Fiberglass" refers specifically to fabric made from glass fibers, but the term is used colloquially to describe any type of boat molded with resin and fabric. That's why boatbuilders use the term "reinforcement." In addition to glass fiber, there are other reinforcement products.

GET THE ORIGINAL Fiberglass itself is melted glass that has been extruded and woven or knitted, and provides a good all-around balance of strength and weight. It's inexpensive but not very stiff, and it must be used relatively thick and heavy to achieve desired stiffness.

TRY CARBON Seventy percent lighter than steel, carbon fiber is thin strands—thinner than human hair—of carbon that may be woven into cloth or knitted into yarns. While tough, it is also costly; carbon fiber exhibits an exceedingly high stiffness-to-weight ratio and is used with the highest level of engineering.

GO BULLETPROOF Kevlar (aramid) is another artificial fiber, resistant to heat, abrasion, and solvents. It's the stuff used to make bulletproof vests. While it provides an excellent strength-to-weight ratio, it's poor in compression and moderately expensive.

013
UNDERSTAND THOSE FIBERS

Most boat hulls are made using either knitted or woven fabric created from glass fibers set in resin. Woven fibers often translate to a lower-cost end-product, but as with so many cases in life, the way a material is used is as important as the choice of material itself. The knitted fabric lies almost flat when applied, whereas the woven one is bulkier, which can cause trouble down the line.

DEAL WITH SUN DAMAGE As the woven-fiber hull ages in the sun, it is more likely to develop "print-through," in which the fiber's texture shows through so that the finish is no longer smooth but appears slightly distorted in a crisscross pattern. This condition is seen in darker-color hulls (green, blue, or black) more often, because they absorb more light and can reach temperatures of more than 200º F (93º C) in the direct summer sun.

WATCH FOR WEAR Woven fabrics also will last a shorter period of time before the composites break down and fatigue from repeated stress (pounding and slamming) on the out-of-plane fibers (springs) formed by the weave. At the end of the day, a boat using knitted fabrics and an equivalent structural design would last longer and experience less cosmetic cracking.

KEEP YOUR INTEGRITY From a structural standpoint, builders that use knitted fabric as their primary reinforcement will make hulls, decks, and parts that are stronger and stiffer (given proper engineering) than those built with woven-fabric composites. The parts will also be lighter for the same or stronger strength, since it takes less resin to saturate less bulky fabric.

CONSIDER ALL ANGLES When fiber talk gets really nerdy, it turns to the angle at which the fibers cross, generally at 0- and 90-degree orientations (0/90) or plus and minus 45 degrees. The debate about "axial configurations" is as heated as it is incomprehensible to outsiders. There is no "best" axial fiber alignment. But there is proper fiber orientation for any given strength and direction of expected loads on a finished part (hull, deck, cabin, fishbox, and so on).

015 WORK YOUR CORES

In terms of a boat's performance, a cored or sandwich composite is better than a solid composite with respect to strength-to-weight ratio. Cored composites yield lighter, faster, and more fuel-efficient boats.

A good, long-lasting core can be made of either balsa wood or foam—what makes it truly good is not the materials, but the installation. Luckily, innovations in closed-molding techniques, such as resin infusion, have made installing a good core much easier than in the old days, when builders had to do everything by hand (and often by touch in areas out of the line of sight). The vacuum-infusion process has improved core installations, performance, and longevity.

Don't be afraid of buying a new boat that is made with core materials, but do your homework in selecting your brand and what is behind it. Most of those windmill blades you see spinning on the distant peaks are built using vacuum infusion with cored composites.

HONEYCOMB Formed from hexagonal shapes arranged in a matrix, the two common materials used in this type of core are Nomex and Nida Core. The former is relatively expensive and is mainly used on competitive sailing yachts. The latter is relatively inexpensive and well suited as a core for decks and superstructures.

END GRAIN BALSA Providing exceptionally high shear, tensile, compressive strengths, and stiffness for its weight, this material is available in a variety of panels and sheets. Like plywood, it must be kept dry or it may rot and turn soft. Fixtures and fittings must be expertly sealed and a regimen of checking those seals must be maintained.

DIVINYCELL A rigid PVC foam with a closed, inert gas–filled cellular structure, divinycell is produced in a wide range of densities and thicknesses to meet required specifications and is available in varying sheets or planks.

CORECELL This styrene-acrylonitrile (SAN) polymer offers the advantages of cross-linked foams, plus the impact tolerance of linear foam. Relatively new to the marine market, it has gained favor with high-end builders.

PLYWOOD Formerly used to core outboard boat transoms and form the "encapsulate" stringer systems of many boats, plywood is used less as a core material today. It is light, strong, and durable, but care must be taken to prevent water from reaching it. Water, often seeped past sloppily sealed fixtures and hardware, may cause plywood to rot and become soft or structurally unsound.

016 KEEP IT TOGETHER

The resin used to build your boat holds everything together—but how do you evaluate the best option or even understand the terminology? We can help you navigate these tricky waters.

POLYESTER RESINS This term covers an array of brands and types. The key difference is the type of acid used to make each variant. Orthophthalic acid is used to produce general-purpose marine resins; isophthalic acid gives a more chemical-resistant and slightly stronger grade. (There's a third variant, using terephthalic acid, but it's rarely seen in boats.)

DCPD-MODIFIED RESIN DCPD (dicyclopentadiene) helps shield polyester resin against damage as water breaks down its chemical bonds. It also reduces the cost of the resin. Its downfall is its brittleness, which lowers the crack resistance of your boat.

VINYLESTER RESINS Related to DCPD, these resins are more expensive, due to their great chemical and moisture resistance. They are also much tougher and more flexible than the others. This means that design stress levels can be higher in the composites. This also means a lighter, more durable boat that can take a beating and keep on ticking without cracking or breaking. Vinylester resins are the resins of choice if you're willing to pay a little extra for a trouble-free experience.

EPOXIES Fickle to use and more heat-sensitive (bad for dark hulls in the tropics), epoxies offer high performance similar to vinylesters. Mostly found in custom boats, epoxy resins also require a highly technically proficient labor force to use.

ECONOMY	HIGH QUALITY	CUSTOM
Orthopthalic	Vinylester, DCPD	Epoxy, Vinylester

017 GET GOOD BACKUP

From engines to cleats, problems that create the most headaches for owners are those associated with backing up hardware. There's no reason to buy a new boat that uses plywood in the stringers or floor, as backups for cleats, in handrails, around hatches, and, most of all, in the transom. Plywood will get wet and rot. You will never be able to sink another new screw into it. Your transom will need to be replaced eventually and so will your stringers, toe rails, etc. Don't go there.

There are numerous alternative materials, referred to as "boards," that are designed, engineered, and produced for this purpose. If they get wet, they will not rot or lose properties. They will last longer and make your life easier as an owner. Many quality boats used plywood for many years because it was cheap, available, and easy to cut and fit. Today, there is no excuse for it. Make sure a polymer backer board is used in your vessel. You will enjoy boating all the more for it. The risk of increased costs and lost time on the water associated with using plywood in a new fiberglass boat are far too high to buy one using them.

018 GO WITH THE GRAIN

Wood speedboats are nostalgic nods to the sport's golden era. Models such as a 1996 Riva Aquarama Special Hull 774 fetch premium prices at auctions (one Aquarama sold for nearly a million dollars in 2011), and inspire enthusiasts to sand and varnish till their knuckles bleed, all for the pleasure of simply gazing at—and sometimes cruising in—a piece of history. For a select few, owning a classic wooden boat represents one of boating's great joys. These boats are collectibles and works of art, cared for and displayed like classic cars in showrooms. Many of their builders (such as the maker of the 1929 Hickman Sea Sled) were ahead of their time, pioneering engine technology such as oil coolers now popular several decades later. These boats are links to the past, and their owners prize them for their uniqueness as well as their beauty.

BEHOLD THESE BEAUTIES Wood is the obvious constant in the creation of these old boats; it's both beautiful and functional. Enthusiasts praise the architecture and regard these boats as almost alive thanks to this material. The most coveted boats—especially pre–World War II models such as the Gar Wood Triple Cockpit Runabout—show wood in all its glory; they're incredibly rare, full of history, and pursued by plenty of high-end collectors.

Some buyers pay for full restoration, from wooden hull to vintage engine, while others find joy in paying even more to get their hands dirty—more than 60 percent of buyers are DIY types. Antique boat clubs are full of boaters who share events, information, and interests, and run educational workshops in the off-season for everything from woodworking, varnishing, and painting, to engines and electronics.

THINK IT OVER If you're looking for one of these wooden wonders, resources (such as Antique Boat America, Freedom Boat Service, and Mecum Auctions) are easily located on the Internet and elsewhere. This isn't a newcomer's activity, though; wood boats demand not only high prices and extensive knowledge, but also passion and respect for the culture and its traditions. If these ideas appeal, then vintage wood may be just right for you!

019 BUY A BOAT AT AUCTION

Jeff Henderson owns Harrison Marine, a Michigan company that repossesses and sells boats, splitting the proceeds with the bank. If a boat owner misses out on payments, Henderson heads out to pick up the vessel and will resell it to make back part of the value.

The boats range in condition: Sometimes they're stripped—by the owner, or by vandals because the owners have abandoned them. Naturally, what Henderson wants is a boat that's in good condition, fueled and ready to go, and an owner who is fine with seeing it repossessed.

A boat spends its first day or so on the lot getting cleaned up and inspected, to give the bank an idea of what it has in lieu of monthly payments. "There's no sense advertising that it will pass a marine survey if it won't," Henderson says. "Sometimes we'll ask the bank to fix things to get a better resale value, but their position is, 'Why lose more money?'"

The vast majority of boats head directly to auction. "The banks and credit unions don't know about people like myself," Henderson explains. "They take boats to auctions a lot of times only because that's where they take their repossessed cars. They're only doing what they know."

The largest auctions are held regularly on the coasts, but every good-size city holds them. Boats are auctioned "as is, where is"; that is, no repairs or deliveries. Today's auctions now often place minimum reserve prices, so no longer can you buy a twin-engine boat for $50. You may have just minutes to make an inspection, so you have to keep it quick and simple.

Remember: You're buying distressed property. Some boats are neglected; some aren't winterized; worse, the engine block is cracked, or a fast boat used for drug-running is stripped of seats, running lights, and more. Some bidders buy two or three boats to build one—a good option if you are mechanically inclined.

020 INSPECT THE GOODS

You've just walked inside the auction house and spotted the repossessed boat of your dreams. But you won't get to talk to the guy who used to own it, and you won't get to have a marine surveyor inspect it. They even confiscated your screwdriver as you walked in! Before bidding your hard-earned cash on a boat, here are a few tips for pulling off an inspection in three minutes.

START WITH A WALK-AROUND Is the boat maintained? Is she clean and free of rust? Look at the hull, paying particular attention to the stem, chines, and strakes. These will suffer the brunt of any collision and show cracks best. Any unusual stress-crack patterns? All open cracks need to be repaired before she'll float again.

REMOVE THE OUTBOARD COWL Dry white "curtains," past the head gasket, are signs of seepage. The shift and throttle linkages should be greased and without

corrosion, and their springs should snap back smartly when tested..

SHAKE THE I/O If you find a lot of play, it might need gimbal bearings. Without a mechanic or a confiscated spark plug wrench, you won't learn much about the engine(s), but you can still check for leaks around the seals and gaskets. Turn the wheel and operate the trim/tilt to check for full travel.

PULL THE DIPSTICK Does the oil smell burned? Does it look milky? There's water in it. Black? It's the wrong viscosity or was never changed. All are signs of a hard life. Check the drive belt and the serpentine belt. New or worn? Tight or loose? One quarter-inch deflection is normal; more indicates improper installation or undue wear.

CHECK THE WIRING Shrink-sealed butt connectors are good. Bare wire and terminations twisted together or "sealed" with electrical tape are bad. Check for

corrosion around the motor and under the dashboard as well.

TEST THE FUEL AND OIL Today's gasoline is sold with 10 percent ethanol, which attracts moisture, which dissolves the fuel. Water sucked into an engine is bad news. Water in oil is worse—it means a cracked block.

021 BUY A USED BOAT

Given how expensive a new boat can be, it's no mystery why many buyers turn to the used market to find the boat of their dreams—or at least, the best boat they can buy for their budget. As with anything you buy used, you may get a treasure that was lovingly treated, or a lemon that was treated terribly by the previous owner. This is why a marine survey (see item 020) is particularly crucial when buying used. Here are your options for finding that lightly worn gem.

BROKERS If you're on a budget, it's not likely that a broker will be your best option. They tend to deal mainly in larger, more expensive boats and, since they work on commission, it's in the broker's best interests to get the highest price they can.

DEALERS Just like a car dealership, a boat dealer may well have quality used boats that came in as trade-ins. Often, they may still be under partial warranty, and you will likely have access to the dealer's service department. To evaluate dealerships, check out items 009–010.

PRIVATE SELLERS Should you even consider buying a boat from a private individual via eBay, Craigslist, or a flyer at your local marina? If you're cautious and they're honest, you can get a good deal, although without the post-purchase security you'd get from an established dealer. You'll want to really check the vessel out, have a good survey, and do a thorough sea test (see items 022–023). For all these reasons, "buy local" should be your mantra. You may find amazing deals online, but this is far too important a purchase to make sight unseen.

022 CHECK OUT A NEW BOAT

You wouldn't buy a car without giving it a test-drive; the same holds true for a boat. A warranty might cover manufacturer defects, but there's no insurance for poor choices. Here are a few general tips to keep in mind when water-testing a new boat.

KNOW YOUR ELECTRONICS You need everything to power up, but you also must verify installation and real-world performance. Check display visibility in bright lighting by running to and from the sun. And check your depth sounder both at speed and in the shallows of the marina.

ACT LIKE A PASSENGER Sit in various positions around the boat. Is it easy to move around? Is the ride comfortable for the conditions? On the transom, are you breathing clean air or smelling exhaust?

LOOK FOR A PROPER PROP During your trial, be sure to run the engine up to wide-open throttle and note the rpm. The higher the reading relative to the specified range, the better. If it doesn't fall within the recommended range, your boat might be outfitted with the wrong propeller.

CHECK YOUR VIEW You can't gauge the view from the helm when a boat is stationary. Look forward and aft and, especially if the boat has a hardtop or an enclosed helm, be sure you can see another boat coming up your wake and passing you close on either side. Note how close under your bow you can spot objects at cruising speed and in cruising trim.

MEASURE YOUR STABILITY Have increasing numbers of crew stand on one side of the cockpit and note, using an inclinometer or a small bubble level, how much the boat lists. This is a gauge of the boat's static stability. Generally, boats with increased static stability have a quicker, snappier motion than boats with less static stability. In short, the boat that lists less will rock shallower and quicker, rather than deeper and slower.

ENGAGE A SURVEYOR Even boaters looking for brand-new boats can enlist a marine surveyor. Services range from helping to ensure that new-boat issues are fixed before delivery (instead of under warranty after you own the boat) to receiving the serious "suitability for service" report a pro surveyor can deliver.

023 GO FOR A RIDE

If you're checking out an offshore model, you should insist upon the chance to run it in open water. Set a course directly into the seas, trim the boat, and adjust the throttle for the most comfortable speed in those conditions. In addition to "tuning in" to how you feel, note how accessories like tops and towers are reacting to the ride. Use the same procedure while running down-sea, noting the conditions and adjusting trim and throttle. On this heading, attune yourself more to handling than to ride softness. How much is the boat slowed as it enters the back of each wave? How much must you advance and let up on the throttle? Does the boat climb waves or try to go through them? Now adjust your heading so you are running a quartering course, away from the waves at 45 degrees. This is generally the sea state in which many boats are most challenged to stay on course. How vigilant must you be at the wheel in order to keep the boat on the desired heading? These are all crucial considerations that you just can't evaluate without a proper test.

024 BUY THE RIGHT BOAT TRAILER

Shopping for a boat trailer can be daunting, but we can help point out the features you need to look for when buying a trailer or assessing the value of one that comes with a new boat.

SIZE IT UP The gross vehicle weight rating (GVWR) is the maximum weight the trailer is rated to carry. Include boat and engine weight, along with gear and fuel, when considering size. For safety, add 15 percent more weight.

CHECK THE AXLES Trailers with a single axle can cost less and require less maintenance than dual-axle trailers, and they're easier to move manually in driveways, garages, or other tight spots. Trailers with two or more axles may cost more and require more maintenance. They're also harder to manually push and pivot into tight spaces, but track better on the road and are safer if a tire blows out.

FRAME IT Galvanized steel is strong and corrosion-resistant for coastal boats, but it is generally heavier and more costly than painted steel, which is fine for freshwater use. Aluminum trailers offer great corrosion resistance and are lighter in weight and have high aesthetic appeal.

LIGHT UP LEDs are durable and waterproof and tax your tow vehicle's electrical system less than incandescents (so you have brighter lights). Look for trailers with brackets that protect the light fixture versus exposed types.

HIT THE ROAD Radial tires are better than bias-ply tires. Bias-ply tires transmit sidewall flex to the tread, increasing the chances of slipping. And they present a smaller footprint, which results in less grip on the road.

HIT THE BRAKES Electric brakes offer low maintenance and let you brake the trailer prior to the tow vehicle, which is handy going downhill. They're not recommended for saltwater application; surge brakes are more complex, but are more reliable in marine service. Laws vary by state, but multiaxle trailers should have brakes installed on all axles.

SPRING INTO ACTION Torsion axles provide a smooth ride and require low maintenance, but are not readily repairable. Leaf springs absorb the load better from uneven ground or shock from a pothole, especially on multiaxle trailers. They're also readily repairable, but require more maintenance.

PICK YOUR STYLE Bunk trailers cost less and have minimal maintenance, but are harder to use at a ramp with a shallow angle or low water level. Adding glides can obviate this somewhat. Some boats with cored hulls require bunk trailers for warranty. Roller trailers cost more and need more maintenance, but are easier to use at ramps with a shallow angle or low water level. You may not be able to launch stepped-hull or pontoon boats from roller trailers.

GET WIRED Look for tinned-copper wiring, especially if you'll be in coastal waters. Heavy grommets and chafe protection are needed where wires enter and exit the trailer frame. Look for solid and accessible ground (white wire) points.

FIND YOUR BEARINGS Traditional greased bearings are relatively easy to repair on the road. Oil bearings run cooler and with less friction, but can develop condensation in the hubs if not used regularly and are not as easily repaired. Most boaters are better off with grease-packed hubs.

025 TREAT YOUR TRAILER RIGHT

Whether your trailer is new or used, here are a few basic safety and care tips to follow.

Don't confuse gross axle weight rating (GAWR), which is for each axle, with GVWR, which is for the whole vehicle. Mistaking one for the other could lead to an overloaded trailer.

If your trailer is a bunk type, and you choose to install glides, use hard plastic glides for aluminum boats. Carpeted bunks hold water, which can corrode the metal of the hull.

No matter what material was used to construct the frame of your trailer, if you use acid-base hull cleaners on your boat, be sure you cover up the trailer fenders so that you don't remove the zinc galvanized coating or paint.

If you should ever need to replace tires on your trailer, look specifically for trailer tires. Never substitute them by using auto tires, which have thinner sidewalls and can blow out much more easily if subjected to stress.

026 TAKE A TEST DRIVE

Make sure the boat, trailer, and tow vehicle are loaded as close to the weight as they will be on your trip and that you get up to cruising speed on the highway to test for any tendencies to fishtail.

027 LIGHT UP WITH LEDS

LEDs prove more reliable than incandescent bulbs. LEDs boast life cycles of 100,000 hours and use less power, putting less strain on the rest of the vehicle's electrical system. Unless you are planning to replace only one light and the system is incandescent, we recommend LEDs. Once your incandescent lights start to go, you can keep replacing them or redo the whole system with LEDs and solve the problem, probably for the life of your trailer.

Brighter is better, and light intensity levels are regulated by the Department of Transportation. LEDs give more bang for the buck and provide more illumination per unit of power over incandescent lights, which can draw up to 100 times the current by comparison.

All LEDs are electronic devices and must be protected with a watertight polymer poured and cured over the circuits to keep them functioning. Tinned wire is an essential feature for added corrosion protection, especially in salt water.

028 POWER UP

It's nice to have a little help putting the boat back on the trailer. A 12-volt winch can make the job easier, but there are critical factors to consider to ensure you get the help you need. A quick tip: Make sure the safety chain between the winch stand and the bow eye is adjusted so that it's a tight fit.

CONSIDER CAPACITY In addition to the boat's weight, remember to consider the weight of the gear and fuel aboard the boat. Underestimate and you'll fry the winch. Always err on the side of too much hauling power rather than too little.

COMPARE CABLES AND STRAPS Cables offer more length and strength but can corrode. Cables can also bind and hang up on themselves when paying out. Straps are less likely to wrap up on themselves. Some strap-equipped winches rate up to 7,500 pounds (3,402 kg); cable models start at 3,500 pounds (1,587 kg).

SEE IN THE DARK Launch or load at night? Get a winch with a light to help you see better.

FEED YOUR NEED FOR POWER In a power-in, freewheel-out system, the winch's motor pulls the boat onto the trailer and a clutch release uses gravity to launch the boat. If you want more control—or you launch at steep ramps—definitely get the power-in, power-out option.

GRAB A REMOTE A remote control unit will let you retrieve the boat when you're standing a short distance from the winch, which makes the operation safer for you in the event of a malfunction.

GET SUNBLOCK If the winch you are considering has any plastic parts, make sure the manufacturer uses an ultraviolet-protected ABS plastic. Many winch housings deteriorate rapidly with exposure to the sun.

029 HITCH A RIDE

A trailer hitch serves as a critical connection — the only thing keeping your boat and trailer attached to your vehicle. Yet, not all hitches are created equal. Weight-carrying (aka dead-weight) hitches are the type most commonly found on vehicles for towing boat trailers, and there are five classes, each based on the total combined weight of the boat and trailer. The ratings are usually labeled somewhere on the hitch. If you order a new truck, van, or sport-utility vehicle (SUV) with the factory-towing package, it will probably come with a hitch. If not, you will have to choose one to install. Here's how to decide.

CLASS	TOW WEIGHT RATING	FEATURES	NOTES
Class I	This hitch is rated for up to 2,000 pounds (907 kg) gross towed weight (GTW) and up to 200 pounds (91 kg) tongue weight (TW).	The Class I hitches are available with fixed ball mounts or receivers that accept a 1¼-inch-square (31.75-mm) removable drawbar/ball mount.	The light-duty rating limits towing to the smallest of boats.
Class II	The Class II is rated for up to 3,500 pounds (1,587 kg) GTW and up to 300 pounds (136 kg) TW.	The hitch attaches to the vehicle frame but may need extra bracing or backing plates. They are available as light-duty receiver hitches with removable 1¼-inch-square (31.75-mm) drawbars.	It is usually good enough for small aluminum boats and personal watercraft.
Class III	This hitch is rated for up to 6,000 pounds (2,721 kg) GTW and up to 600 pounds (272 kg) TW.	One of the most common hitches, it bolts to the frame of a vehicle (usually a truck, van, or full-size SUV). The receiver accepts a 2-inch-square (51-mm) drawbar.	It can also be used with a weight-distributing system, which boosts the rating to 10,000 pounds (4,536 kg) GTW and 1,000 pounds (453 kg) TW.
Class IV	In weight-carrying mode, frame-mount receiver hitches are designed for a max of 10,000 pounds (4,536 kg) GTW and up to 1,000 pounds (453 kg) TW.	The receiver accepts a 2-inch-square (51-mm) drawbar and is found almost exclusively on full-size trucks, vans, and SUVs.	In weight-distributing mode, the rating increases to 14,000 pounds (6,350 kg) GTW and 1,400 pounds (635 kg) TW.
Class V	Designed for heavy-duty trucks and vans, these receiver hitches are rated to take up to 12,000 pounds (5.443 kg) GTW and 1,200 pounds (544 kg) TW.	The matching drawbar increases in size to 2½ inches (63.5 mm) square.	The rating is increased up to 17,000 pounds (7,711 kg) GTW and 1,700 pounds (771 kg) TW with a weight-distributing system.

030 INSPECT YOUR TRAILER

Before you head off on a trailer-boating vacation adventure this summer, take some time to inspect your boat trailer to make sure it's in top condition. The time and effort you spend on this might make the difference between a wonderful trip or breaking down on a remote highway without access to parts or service. There's always some part that requires maintenance on a boat trailer, especially one used in salt water. Here are the key areas you will need to concern yourself with.

TIRES Pay particular attention to tires (making sure they are at or just below the maximum inflation). Don't forget to check the trailer spare tire(s), too. If the tires are five or more years old, replace them, no matter how the tread or sidewalls appear, as trailer tires rot unseen from the inside. In addition, look at your vehicle's factory jack to make sure it will work for the boat trailer, too. If it won't fit under or sufficiently raise the trailer in case of a flat, you'll need a separate jack. Make sure you have a lug wrench that will fit the lug nuts on the trailer wheels, in case you need to fix a flat.

WHEELS Trailer wheel bearing and seals are trouble-prone, so have these completely serviced, packed with fresh lube and capped with a bearing protector before a long trip.

BRAKES If the brakes bind, the wheel hubs will overheat, literally welding the bearings, hub, and spindle together within a few miles on the freeway. So having the trailer brakes and surge-brake actuator inspected and serviced before a trip is critical.

LIGHTS Make sure your trailer's running, brake, clearance, and turn signal lights are operating properly, regardless of whether you plan to drive at night or not.

CONNECTIONS Inspect and, if necessary, adjust the trailer coupler, trailer safety chains, trailer-lights plug, bow-winch strap, bow safety chain, and transom straps. Stop every few hours on a long haul to recheck these items. Also, make sure the outboard or stern-drive remains tilted up and well supported, and that everything inside the boat is still secure.

TOOLS Carry spare parts and a full tool kit specific to the trailer, and you're on your way.

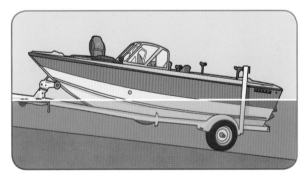

031 PROTECT TRAILER LIGHTS

The lights on your boat trailer are probably not found at the top of your list when you think of important safety gear, but, in fact, they're pretty essential. And they're particularly vulnerable, since electricity and water have a problematic relationship at best. Here's how to keep them going strong so you can worry about far more interesting things.

COOL DOWN Folks trailering a boat to a launch ramp often forget that boat-trailer lights can burn out when the hot bulbs are submerged in water. After driving even a short distance, the trailer lights need time to simmer down. To do this properly, disconnect the trailer's electrical wiring plug from the vehicle and let the bulbs cool as you load gear into the boat before launching. Hang the wiring plug over a high point so that it won't get dunked.

STAY DRY Even better, prevent shorting by rigging your trailer's wiring so that no junctions or terminals are ever submerged. You can do this by elevating the lights on upright poles bolted to the frame. Don't join the wires in a Y-formation on the trailer body. Instead, run separate wires from each taillight all the way to the vehicle plug. For extra protection, use an outdoor extension cord rather than standard electrical wire.

032 FEND 'EM OFF

A fender is the first line of defense between your hull, the dock, and other boats. Knowing the difference can help you pick the right fender for your boat.

HAVE A BALL As the name implies, this is a ball-shaped bumper, made from hollow, pressurized plastic vinyl, with a single attachment point for line. Ball fenders can be difficult to store because of their shape and size, but most have valves allowing users to inflate or deflate the ball to their specific needs.

PICK UP THE TAB Featuring durable plastic attachment points at both ends, tab-end inflatable fenders can provide a buffer between pilings and other boats or docks. Hanging them horizontally can help protect your boat from vertical dock pilings; vertical deployment can protect the hull from shifting tides or other moored boats.

FOLLOW THE CONTOURS Made of inflatable vinyl or closed-cell foam covered with a durable trilaminate skin, contour fenders are ideal for boats with low freeboard or step-down curved or slanted gunwales. Since they follow the contour of the gunwale, they offer additional protection in case the boat gets trapped under the dock.

HOLLOW OUT Molded from durable PVC vinyl, hollow-body fenders incorporate an internal rope tube, allowing the fender line to run through it. These can be deployed horizontally or vertically; several can be ganged along a line to broaden protection. Molded ribs add durability and allow the fender to roll rather than slide out of position.

BUMP UP A great option if you moor your boat on your own dock, dock bumpers, or vinyl edging, are permanently attached to the dock, providing protection from rough edges. Fender boards can also be suspended from the boat to press against pilings while fenders protect the hull.

033 LINE UP

There are myriad choices in dock lines. Just as there is no perfect boat, there is no perfect type of line for use in tying a boat to a dock. That said, the following tips reflect our preferences and are intended to help you make more informed choices when selecting dock lines for your boat.

GET YOUR NYLONS Nylon is the best choice for a dock line. It offers good resistance to fuel, chemicals, and the sun's rays. It stretches 15 percent when loaded to about 20 percent of its total breaking strength, providing shock absorbency. Dacron lines soon become too stiff, and polypropylene lines can degrade rapidly in sunlight.

SLIM DOWN Bigger isn't necessarily better. Larger-diameter line won't provide as much cushion as thinner line under equal loads. It may also be cumbersome to fit around existing cleats. As a rule of thumb, use 1/8-inch (3.1-mm) diameter for every 2 inches (50.8 mm) of boat cleat length.

GO LONG For your home slip, cut and splice the lines to a length that suits the tidal range or expected water level changes. For use at transient docks, we recommend that spring lines be as long as the boat and that bow and stern lines be half the length of the boat. You can always deal with some excess line, but a too-short line can be useless.

TRIPLE UP Less expensive than braid, tougher on the hands, and available in limited colors, three-strand nylon provides excellent shock absorbency. When used over wood pilings or poles, three-strand nylon slides down and/or around such pilings easier than other types of line. It's also easy to splice, if you want to make custom-length lines to suit your boat and slip.

DOUBLE UP TOO More expensive, double-braid line is soft on the hands and supple to coil; it also comes in a kaleidoscope of colors to match your boat. Double-braid provides less shock absorbency because it stretches less than equivalent three-strand line, and, for lines used around pilings, the fine weave may snag, making loops recalcitrant to drop or slide into position.

034 GET KNOTTY

There are three basic knots that work equally well to secure a fender to a stanchion or rail: the clove hitch, the running hitch, and the round turn/half hitch. A cleat hitch is used when securing to a deck-mounted cleat. It's not exactly a hitch, just a series of figure eights around the horn of a cleat, finished with a half hitch.

035 HANG ON

You can best protect your boat by hanging your fenders properly. Assuming you have fenders correctly sized to your boat, there are various techniques for maximum effectiveness and the best methods of securing them to a cleat, stanchion, or railing.

CUSHION THE BLOWS When rafting with other boats, use the largest-diameter fenders in your inventory (A), since different boats tied together will rock differently and have varying freeboard and hull flare. Large-diameter ball fenders are a smart choice because they can hang from the rail or cleats over the topsides, yet are wide enough to keep rub rails from knocking together as well as areas with protruding decks, such as on boats with large bow flare.

GO VERTICAL When tied to a smooth-surface pier, bulkhead, or floating dock, vertical placement is the easiest, most practical and preferred method (B). Place the fender a few inches above the surface of the water to keep it from getting gunked up. A minimum of two fenders should be used, with one being placed at the widest point of the hull and one near the stern. However, the more, the merrier—and less chance of hull damage.

HANG IT Cleats and deck-mounted specialty fittings (B) are best for hanging fenders, since they have a low profile and cannot exert much leverage on the deck or the fasteners securing them. Rail stanchions are also okay to use. Due to the extra leverage created by extra height, hanging fenders to rails may subject the rail and deck to undue stress if a fender gets pinched during the rolling from a large wake. All tie-off points should be through-bolted.

GET HORIZONTAL If tying to a dock or pier with exposed pilings or a navy-style bulkhead, horizontal placement is best (C). Some fenders have molded eyes at either end; some let you pass a line through from top to bottom. In either case, center the fender on the piling and tie it horizontally. If the location is rough, or roiled by current, or you are leaving the boat unattended for a bit, use a fender board. A pair of cylindrical fenders placed vertically behind a two-by-four is as basic as it gets. The fenders protect the hull and the two-by-four takes the beating.

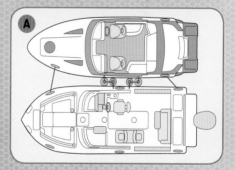

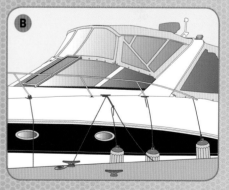

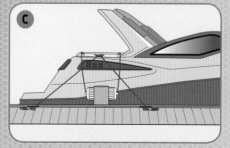

036 BE SAFE

Boating safety encompasses a broad range of disciplines, ranging from maintenance to seamanship. That said, there are four cornerstones that underlie your boating safety foundation according to the experts (including the US Coast Guard and the National Safe Boating Council). They are as follows:

1. TAKE A BOATING SAFETY COURSE

2. KNOW THE RULES OF THE ROAD

3. DON'T DRINK AND BOAT

4. WEAR A LIFE JACKET

Follow these basic tenets, and be sure your passengers do as well, to keep your head above water today . . . and every day.

037 FLOAT ON

The most recognizable piece of safety equipment is probably the throwable flotation device. There really are differences between the three basic types, and each has pros and cons, as well as variations in what enables them to float or makes them sink. The list below will help you figure out what you need and choose the right float for your boat.

	PROS	CONS
Flotation Cushion	More than a comfortable cushion to sit on during a cruise, the flotation cushion can provide valuable supplemental flotation during a man-overboard situation until help arrives.	It may not float all adults on its own, and a larger person might not be able to get his or her arms through the straps to be able to hold it in a hugging position.
Type IV Horseshoe	A more serious lifesaving device than a flotation cushion, the horseshoe is designed to be secured to a boat's rail so it can quickly be thrown to a victim in the water. The regular horseshoe form has 50 pounds (22.6 kg) of buoyancy and is made with closed-cell foam wrapped in a vinyl-coated fabric for durability.	It's the most expensive Type IV on the market, and you can't use it for anything else, such as a cushion. Also, you need to buy a mounting bracket for it.
Throwable Life Ring	An adult can probably throw this device farther than the other two because of its rigid design and circular, frisbee-like shape. The urethane foam core is wrapped in vinyl-coated nylon, and the ring has webbing straps so the person in the water has something to grasp. The grab line passes through the webbing. It provides 19 pounds (8.6 kg) of buoyancy.	It's made of hard foam, so you don't want to try using it as a cushion, and it could actually hurt if you hit a person with it when you throw it.

038 INSPECT LIFE JACKETS

We know this tip may be obvious to many of you, but we also believe safety discussions bear repeating. So take the time to regularly inspect your life jackets. Discard any with worn fabric, unraveling seams, inoperative buckles, tears, rips, or just plain old age. Anything appearing even remotely out of sorts goes directly into the garbage. Remember, your life may depend on it.

039 STOW LIFE JACKETS

Purchasing life jackets is easier now than it's ever been, with a lot of rules and regulations being simplified. However, it's still up to you to do the most important thing—wear one. And if you're not going to, at least store them in a spot where you and the crew can have immediate access when needed. So where do you store your personal flotation devices (PFDs)?

KEEP IT HANDY Let's start with the throwable PFD. In the case of a man-overboard situation, is it easy to grab? On center-console boats, on or under the leaning post, where the captain or a crew member can quickly grab it, is a great choice. On boats of all shapes and sizes, try to find a place to stow it in the cockpit on deck, and not packed underneath other gear.

DON'T GO BELOW The worst place to store a throwable, or any life jacket, is below deck. Many boat owners try to meet regulations by sticking a "Coast Guard kit" bag, stuffed with life jackets, whistle, flares, extinguisher, and other safety gear down in the salon or in the stowage under the berth in a stateroom. That means, in an emergency, someone has to go down below. Instead, put the jackets in a zipper pouch underneath a T-top or hardtop, where they can be quickly taken out when needed. On boats without a top, it's easy to designate a storage spot just for life jackets.

040 CHECK THE FIT

When buying a life jacket for a child, make sure his or her weight falls within the jacket's range and that it's not too loose or too tight.

041 DON'T GET SHOCKED

Faulty dockside wiring is a surprisingly common cause of marine fatalities. Many deaths listed as drowning were likely actually caused by electric shock drowning (ESD).

BE ESD AWARE Electric shock drowning is a catchall term that covers any in-water electrocution and drowning that results from becoming paralyzed by electricity in the water. Experts say that many such drownings go unreported, as an autopsy won't reveal evidence of ESD. Investigators have to rely on eyewitnesses hearing cries for help or accounts of others in the water who have felt a tingling sensation. Otherwise, it will be reported as a drowning. Meanwhile the real cause of death—the electricity in the water—goes undetected.

WATCH THE WATER While most ESD fatalities happen around boats at marinas, there have also been cases in water fountains, irrigation ditches, golf course ponds, and other bodies of water dating back to the mid '80s. It's not uncommon for would-be rescuers to jump in to help and end up as victims themselves. There have even been cases in which people jumped in to help their dog, which survived while the people perished.

UPDATE FOR SAFETY The American Boat and Yacht Council (ABYC) recommends that all older boats be brought up to current ABYC shore-power standards. Trained marine electrical technicians should be called upon to inspect older boats and make the necessary repairs.

DO YOUR PART There is also plenty that marina operators can do to protect against ESD. Some operators are beginning to post no-swimming signs and install dockside ground fault protection (GFP) devices, especially in areas hard hit by ESD. Some marinas also provide monitoring and require boats leaking electricity to fix the problem or leave.

042
HANDLE ENGINE FIRES

Never open the hatch if you suspect an engine fire: You will only add oxygen and feed the flames. If the motor box has been fitted with a port through which the nozzle of a fire-extinguisher is to be inserted, use a gaseous extinguisher, which is designed to quench fire by displacing oxygen. Dry chemical extinguishers are inappropriate since they need to be aimed at the base of flames to smother the fire, which you can't do aboard a boat unless you open the hatch.

043
USE A FIRE EXTINGUISHER

Never fight a fire aboard a boat unless you can do so with your back to an exit and you're sure you have a way out or off the boat. Also, fire extinguishers are meant for containing fires that have just started, not for ones that are blazing. If there's any doubt, vacate the boat immediately.

KNOW THE RATING Fires are classed as: A (combustible materials), B (combustible liquids), and C (electrical). The Coast Guard requires onboard extinguishers to handle B- and C-type fires. Extinguishers also have a number indicating their relative size; you will need a B-I or B-II, depending on the size of your vessel.

AIM LOW (A) Hold the fire extinguisher upright and point the nozzle at the base of the fire, not at the top of the flames. You may need to crouch down to get a good shot.

SWEEP (B) Sweep the base of the fire with the extinguisher. Short bursts are often best, conserving extinguishant so you don't run out before applying it to the hottest spot.

WATCH FOR REFLASH (C) Glowing embers may reignite the flames and often do. Be prepared for a reflash and be ready with your extinguisher.

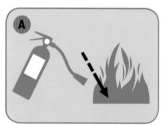
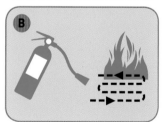

044
BE FIRE SAFE

Be sure your fire extinguishers are mounted where they will be easy to grab. The Coast Guard requires that you have a second B-I extinguisher (or the bigger B-II) if your boat length is more than 26 feet (7.9 m). Conduct fire drills with your crew and check the extinguisher gauges routinely.

045 ASSEMBLE A DITCH BAG

If your boating trips take you anywhere that rescue might take more than a few minutes, a ditch bag filled with survival aids should be part of your standard gear. Keep it stowed somewhere handy, so that if the worst happens, you'll be able to grab it and go. The bag should be brightly colored, inherently buoyant, and designed to keep your gear organized and easily accessible. Every so often, you will need to check and replenish as needed. Here's what to include.

A first-aid kit that includes Dramamine and any prescription medications you may need

Rope

Cash and a copy of your passport in a zip-seal plastic bag if you are traveling in foreign waters

Safety lights and strobes that can emit SOS or flashing lights to alert rescue personnel

A whistle

Flares

Waterproof VHF radio

Sunscreen

Signal mirrors

Drinking water along with a measuring device to make rationing easy

A personal locator beacon that activates on command to communicate your position to rescuers (see item 046)

A serrated blunt-point knife, which is less likely to puncture a life raft but can slice rope or bandages

046 DRESS FOR SAFETY SUCCESS

When running a boat offshore, supplement your ditch bag with safety gear you can keep on your person. Start by augmenting your life vest with essential gear, then add a fanny pack crammed with energy bars, packaged water, light sticks, and sunscreen. Here are safety choices for inspiration.

VHF RADIO A floating, waterproof VHF worn with a belt clip and lanyard (A) lets you make mayday calls and communicate with rescuers. Some also include a GPS display.

DYE MARKER Highly visible (B), it enables rescuers to follow the direction of your drift.

PLB (PERSONAL LOCATOR BEACON) This device (C) communicates your position directly to SAR satellites, notifying rescue agencies and helping them home in on your position. Models with integral GPS allow for more precise location. If you use one that displays GPS coordinates, you can verbally communicate your location to the SAR crew via VHF.

WHISTLE Using a whistle is louder and more reliable than yelling to alert nearby rescuers. Considering swapping your plastic whistle for a stainless steel model (D), as it is less likely to become cracked when and if you need it most.

SIGNAL MIRROR Learn how to use one correctly (E) before you need it.

STROBE LIGHT PLBs and VHFs are also available with integral strobe lights, but pin a dedicated, water-activated strobe light to your life jacket anyway (F). Redundancy and safety go hand in hand. If you hit the drink unconscious, the light flashes; if you're conscious, you can hit the "off" button to conserve the battery.

REFLECTIVE PATCH Apply SOLAS Grade 3155 patches to all of your boat's life jackets and any other relevant fabrics (G); for life rings and other hard objects, select SOLAS Grade 3150-A.

047 POP PILLS FIRST

If you do have to ditch your boat with little but your emergency supplies, experts say to take seasickness medication immediately. Save water rations, survival food, and hard candy for later if you can.

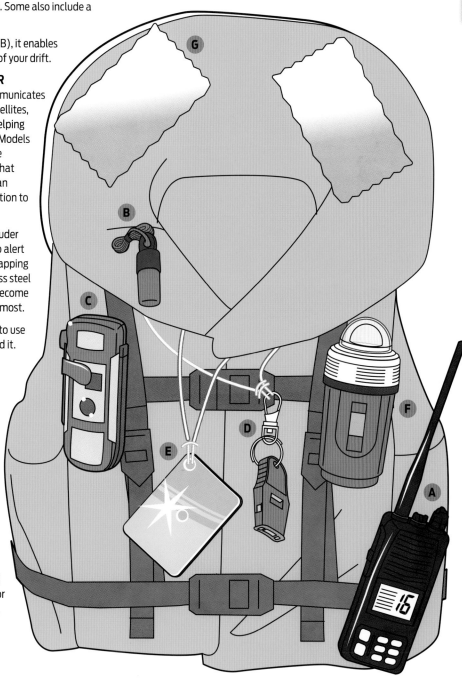

048 LIGHT UP THE NIGHT

Flares represent just one entry in a varied mix of devices, all known officially as visual distress signals (VDS). Why so much variety? All of these distress signals have their own distinct advantages and disadvantages. No single device is ideal under all conditions or suitable for all purposes; consider using more than one. Here's a sampling of types to help get the right VDS (or two) for you.

HAND-HELD PYROTECHNIC FLARES

PRO: Approved for day or night use; universally recognized

CON: Short burn duration; can burn user

TIP: Carry more than the required three

ELECTRONIC FLARES

PRO: Bright SOS signal; safe to use

CON: Approved only for nighttime use; may blend in with shoreline lights

TIP: Make sure to maintain the battery

SMOKE SIGNALS

PRO: Excellent daytime attention-getter; visible beyond horizon

CON: Approved for daytime use only

TIP: Deploy downwind of boat/raft/persons in water

AERIAL FLARES

PRO: Excellent nighttime attention-getter; visible beyond horizon

CON: Requires experience for safe use

TIP: 25 mm pistol launcher offers superior versatility

049 BE BATTERY SMART

Keep the health of your batteries as a top priority or the performance of your electronics and electric appliances will suffer. If you're lucky enough to be able to start your engines, that is!

GET THE GEAR Check your batteries routinely. Buy a multimeter and learn how to use it. This is one of the handiest instruments for finding, correcting, and preventing electricity-related problems.

CHECK EVERYTHING Be alert for any loose connections, which can, over time, result from a boat's normal impacts when underway. And keep an eye out for corrosive buildup on terminals and electrical connections.

DON'T FORGET THE LITTLE GUYS If you don't already have one, install a 12-volt cigarette lighter outlet to charge all of your handheld devices that have rechargeable batteries.

050 KNOW THE NUMBERS

There are a number measurements and ratings that you'll need to be familiar with when battery shopping. Here are some basics.

GROUPS A battery's "group" (i.e., 24, 27, 31, 34, 6D, 8D, etc.) refers to its physical size. These are standard across manufacturers, with slight variations for handles, post height, and so on. Match the group size on the label to manufacturer specifications.

OUTPUT "Cold cranking amps" (CCA) is the number of deliverable amps at 0° F (-18° C) for 30 seconds and is needed to determine starting suitability. "Marine cranking amps" (MCA) is basically the same as CCA but determined at 32° F (0° C). "Reserve capacity" (RC) is the number of minutes a fully charged battery at 80° F (27° C) will discharge 25 amps until the battery drops below 10.5 volts and "dies." "Ampere-hour" (Ah) is a rating referred to for deep-cycle or "house" batteries and is typically based on a 20-hour draw on a fully charged battery.

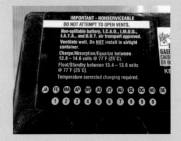

DATE CODES Battery labels indicate the date of manufacture. The month is indicated by letters and the year by numbers. For example, "D2" denotes a battery that was manufactured in April 2012. Always buy the freshest one on the shelf.

051 BUY THE RIGHT BATTERY

Many boats are set up with a dual battery system, using one purpose-built battery for starting the engine and one to meet most other power needs. These batteries are not interchangeable, and trying to use one in place of the other can lead to serious trouble of the stranded-in-open-water sort, so be sure you understand your options.

CRANK IT UP Engine cranking requires lots of power in a short burst, and cranking, or starting, batteries are designed for this sort of short, intense burst. Your engine's manual will give a recommended marine cranking amp (MCA or sometimes just CA) rating for starting batteries; the rating will be on a battery's label. Choose one with a rating equal to or greater than the recommended value.

GO DEEP Your boat's electronics, as well as trolling motors and other accessories, need steady ongoing power, and that's what deep-cycle marine batteries, also known as house batteries, are designed for. The key rating here is reserve capacity (RC)—the higher the RC number, the longer the battery can go before you will need to recharge it.

GO BOTH WAYS Dual-purpose batteries can be used for both short-burst and deep-cycle functions, although often with some trade-off in performance or life span.

052 CHOOSE A CELL

Marine batteries come in a sometimes bewildering number of flavors, especially for the new boat owner accustomed to the one-size-fits-all world of car batteries. Here's the skinny.

	WET CELL/FLOODED ELECTROLYTE	GEL CELL	ABSORBED GLASS MAT (AGM)
BATTERY TYPE			
CONSIDERATIONS	Lowest initial investment cost for cold cranking and deep-cycle use Prone to sulfation, which reduces power One deep discharge can drastically reduce the effectiveness	Ideal as pure deep-cycle batteries, but less than ideal as starting batteries Not as rugged as AGMs	Rugged and fast to recharge; kept up to snuff by a short run of the engine Offer more power in smaller footprints and more versatile installation options
MAINTENANCE	Distilled water should be added to plates monthly On an annual basis remove cables, clean posts, and clean or replace terminals	Sealed cells mean no need for monthly monitoring Annually, remove terminals and clean and lube connections	Sealed cells mean no need for monthly monitoring No need for charging during storage if isolated from current requirement Annual removal and cleaning may not be necessary
CHARGING	Simple automatic chargers are recommended; overcharging with a manual charger can cause major damage	Specific charging voltage requirements, often requiring a special charger	Requires more voltage and a special charging profile to properly recharge
THE BOTTOM LINE	Low initial investment cost is the main advantage; regular charging and more frequent maintenance add up Batteries discharge rapidly in storage; have charging power available to avoid towing or jump-starting costs	Superior cycling ability a plus for deep-cycle use; low resistance to vibration and lower cranking voltage make them less useful in all but slower moving powerboats	Good for both cold-cranking and deep-cycle power Charge can be heavily drawn down without damage Long battery life (3–5 years) and ability to recover from repeated deep discharges negate initial sticker shock

053 LIVE LARGE

Do you need to turn your boat into an on-water entertainment center? Of course not. Is it a lot of fun? You know it! For catching up on your shows while on an overnight jaunt or rocking the party at the swimming hole, there are fun options for a range of budgets.

GET THE VISUALS Just because you may not have a multi-thousand-dollar satellite HDTV antenna doesn't mean you can't have spectacular onboard TV reception. For a couple hundred bucks, you can buy a compact, 14- to 21-inch-diameter (355-mm to 533-mm), flat, saucer-like antenna that can pull in a plentiful supply of HDTV programming from local TV stations.

PLAY SOME TUNES Marine stereo systems have improved mightily in recent years, offering excellent quality for the price. You'll be able to find high-quality equipment that has a small footprint, runs cool and efficiently, and, in the case of amplifiers, is stackable. That makes the options for powerful, high-fidelity boat installations almost limitless.

STREAM YOUR MEDIA Many marine electronics multi-function displays (aka, "MFD") can play music and video streamed via Bluetooth from your iPad, tablet, or mobile device.

REPEAT COORDINATES Many boaters use the TV in the cabin as a repeater, to display the navigation information from the helm for the entire crew to see on the big screen. This also allows the skipper to see what's happening should he hand the wheel over to a guest for a few minutes to use the head or make a sandwich.

ZONE OUT It's best to get a multizoned entertainment system if you intend to cruise. This way, Dad can check the game at the helm while the kids play video games in the cabin and Mom catches the news in the cockpit. Apps to relay signals to mobile devices enhance flexibility even more.

054 BOOST YOUR SIGNAL

Not a must-have but certainly a nice-to-have, Wi-Fi and cellular range-boosters designed specifically for boaters can keep you in cyberspace at a very reasonable price when your boat has ventured beyond normal range.

055 GET SOUND INFORMATION

Do you absolutely need a fish finder, also known as a sounder, for your vessel? If you're using your boat for tow sports, day-tripping, or other recreation rather than fishing, you might not think so. The thing is, even if you're not looking for the catch of the day, it's smart to have a device onboard that gives you an accurate reading of the depth of the water that you're traversing. This is information that will enhance your safety when you are navigating and help to avoid any unwanted contact between your boat and the bottom of the not-so-deep blue.

056 PICK UP THE BASICS

Most of us love gadgets, and it's easy to fall in love with some of the latest tech that just makes your boat that much cooler than the next guy's. But sometimes the fun stuff has to be put on hold, simply because you need a better chart plotter or piece of communications gear. We could fill all the pages of this book with gadgets to buy, so here are some basic suggestions. Whatever it is you need (or want), the one reality of boating is that there will never be a shortage of things for you to buy (or want to buy!). These are the absolute basics for outfitting your boat's electronics.

VHF RADIO Your very high frequency (VHF) radio is absolutely essential for safety (A). They're monitored 24/7 by the Coast Guard on channels 16 (for emergencies, distress calls, safety alerts, and special-event broadcasts) and 13 (for vessel bridge-to-bridge communications). A handheld VHF radio is a good backup for a fixed mount, and on some small boats, the handheld might suffice as the main radio.

GPS Ubiquitous these days in cars and on phones, a Global Positioning System (GPS) is particularly crucial for mariners, letting you pinpoint exactly where you are on the water when there are no other handy points of reference. Marine-ready GPS devices are available as handheld units (B) or permanently-mounted GPS/chart plotters.

DEPTH SOUNDER Receiving its signal from a sensor (called a "transducer") mounted on either the bottom of the transom or the boat's hull, a depth sounder (C) provides the skipper with an instant reading of the depth of water. Knowledge of depth is as imperative for safe operation as it is for swimming and beaching convenience. It is also helpful for fishing or even confirming one's location on a chart, should the GPS go kerblooey.

MARINE STEREO Built to withstand moist, salty air, and with speakers rated for the same kind of duty, it's important to select a "marine" versus an automotive style stereo (D). Along with providing music for entertaining or enabling you to listen to the big game while relaxing aboard, a marine stereo radio can also receive National Weather Service reports to provide a safety backup for your VHF radio.

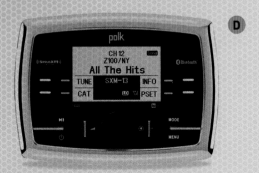

057 CUT OUT THE NOISE

Electronic interference can be a real problem on the open water. Sometimes the solution is a simple tweak, other times a trip to the electronics store may be in order to eliminate unwanted noise.

TRY TWISTING Sometimes just twisting the wires together along their entire length can suppress noise intrusion (you can also purchase pretwisted cable).

GROUND IT Connect a wire from an instrument's metal case or grounding stud to your boat's ground to squelch electrical noise.

SEPARATE CABLES Transducer cables should be run separately, not bundled together with other wiring or run close to the engine, as this can cause noise-generated marks on the sounder's screen.

TRY A CAPACITOR A 0.01-microfarad capacitor connected across the two leads of a radio's or stereo's speaker will often eliminate noise caused when transmitting on a radio. This also works for gauges that experience fluctuation when one is talking on a radio.

CHOKE UP Those snap-on "ferrite core RF chokes" that are commonly used on computer cables to minimize RF interference (available at most electronic parts stores) also reduce noise on electronics cables.

INSTALL A FILTER Power-line filters can silence noise when connected to an instrument's 12-volt power cables. Install the filter close to the offending equipment.

SHIELD WIRES If all else fails, you can often screen out noise being picked up on equipment wiring like a stereo set by replacing the affected wires or cables with shielded wiring.

058 CHECK GEAR DOCKSIDE

Being out on the water is the wrong time to discover you have an issue with a critical piece of electronic gear. Follow this simple checklist as part of your dock-side routine every time to verify that your electronics are working properly before you leave port.

BE RECEPTIVE Perform a radio check to confirm that you are transmitting and receiving properly.

CHECK YOUR REFERENCES Confirm your position dockside with your GPS. Make a range and bearing check with a known point of reference. Become familiar with how many satellites you normally receive and their relative strengths. This will let you know if your GPS is operating normally.

AUTOMATE IT When leaving port, make sure your autopilot has no difficulty holding a course and responding to commands.

VIEW THE BLIPS Check your radar by viewing familiar targets on long and short ranges to make sure they appear normal.

059 RECOGNIZE A RIP-OFF

An improper installation of electronics on your boat can lead to all manner of problems, including not being heard over the radio, a buoy or rock not being visible on your radar screen, experiencing navigational inaccuracy, or nearby fish not detected by the finder. Unfortunately, poor electronics installations are commonplace, and they can even happen with professional setups on dealer- or factory-equipped boats.

Protect yourself, your family, and your investment from an improper installation by asking these questions and looking for these problems.

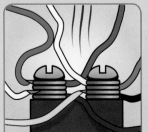

THE OCTOPUS Multiple tentaclelike wire terminations forced onto a single point.

THE SPIDER Lots of weblike dangling, suspended, and unsecured wires and cables.

THE RAT Sloppy, haphazard, unorganized wiring that tends to resemble a rat's nest.

THE SNAKE Wiring that lies loose and unbundled on deck or at the bottom of the bilge.

060 RESET, RESTORE, OR REBOOT

Your marine electronics are basically small computers and, like any computer, the may freeze up unexpectedly at the worst possible moment. While you may well have some stand-alone devices, it's likely that you largely rely on multifunction displays (MFDs) that act as a chart plotter and GPS positioning device, maybe with radar overlay and a separate screen with fish finder/depth-reading capability. It may even have trip and fuel-log data and perhaps engine data displays selectable. So, what to do when these crucial devices get buggy?

UNPLUG AND RESTART When a GPS/chart plotter, fish finder, radar, or other gear locks up or fails to respond to the controls, sometimes disconnecting the power cable or switching off the set's circuit breaker and reapplying power can restore normal operation, just like with your home computer.

FACTORY RESET When all else fails, you can perform a master reset of an individual device. Follow the instructions in the owner's manual for the unit. Be advised that this is a last-resort procedure, as it can also delete all your waypoints, routes, and custom settings.

HOT REBOOT AN MFD When your boat's information runs through an MFD, a freeze or crash is serious business. If a strange error message pops up or the screen freezes, you may need to do what is called a "hot reboot." Most boats have a main switch on the power distribution panel labeled "electronics." With the device turned on (at the unit), turn off the master power feed labeled

"electronics" and wait a minute, then repower it, and let the unit come back online. The odds are your problem will go away, at least for a while.

UPDATE EVERYTHING Do a firmware/software check of your equipment with the manufacturer and install updates as needed. Often, a firmware update will correct any glitches for good.

061 DON'T LOSE YOUR DATA

Regularly back up your waypoints and other data to a blank data card or to your home computer or a mobile app (see item 053), using the manufacturer's guidelines.

062 KNOW YOUR INSTALLER

The most qualified technicians are certified by the National Marine Electronics Association (NMEA). These technicians follow strict NMEA installation standards and guidelines which parallel the American Boat and Yacht Council (ABYC) and the U.S. Coast Guard electrical wiring standards for safety and equipment performance. No matter who does the installation, you should know the answers to a few basic question.

PROFESSIONALITY Is the installer a trained professional, or is it the boat seller's yard boy who also installed the batteries, painted the bottom, and washed down the boat?

SERVICE Does the installation include setup, adjustment, and calibration of the equipment?

TESTING Was the autopilot and navigation gear sea-trialed and adjusted under way?

CONNECTIVITY Have the electronics been properly interfaced to share information?

TRAINING Will you receive training on how to use all of your new electronics on your boat?

063 UNDERSTAND VHF RADIO

A VHF (very high frequency) radio is your most basic piece of electronic equipment. Every boat is required to carry at least one VHF radio, and it's a good idea to have both a console model and a handset one in case one fails in an emergency.

LINE YOUR SIGHT Marine VHF radios work on a line-of-sight basis. That is, they can transmit and receive to and from another antenna as long as that antenna is above the horizon. How far is that? Standing in the cockpit of a boat, the distance to the horizon for most adults is about 3 miles (4.8 km). If you mount an 8-foot (2.4-m) antenna 12 feet (3.6 m) above sea level, the distance to the horizon increases to about 4.5 miles (7.2 km).

AIM FOR HEIGHT You might be able to communicate over longer distances if the person on the other end has a taller antenna. If your buddy has an antenna mounted atop his large cruiser at 18 feet (5.4 m) above sea level, you could converse while about 6.7 miles (10.7 km) apart. If the Coast Guard's

antenna is 100 feet (30 m) tall, you can expect a reliable range of about 13 miles (20.9 km). Your buddy's 18-foot (5.4-m) antenna would net him a range of about 13.3 miles (21.4 km). Any atmospheric refraction means that the real-life distances are probably a little farther, but you shouldn't count on that.

BACK-UP YOUR DEVICE VHF's limited range means that anyone cruising open waters would do well to supplement the VHF with a satellite phone, EPIRBs (emergency position indicating radio beacon), and/or PLBs (personal locator beacon).

UNDERSTAND POWER It's a common misconception that more power means longer range, but in fact, it's all about antenna height. Higher-powered units will do a better job of punching through static and other radio traffic, but only within the range dictated by antenna height.

064 CHECK YOUR CONNECTIONS

Your VHF radio is connected to the antenna with coaxial cables, often by using a PL-259 connector. Any connection is a potential weak spot and an opportunity for increased noise, so it makes sense to minimize connectors and maximize efficiency with these options.

JOIN CABLES Most VHF antennas come with 20 feet (6.1 m) of coax cable. When that's insufficient to reach your radio, you can avoid soldering in new connections by using antenna cables that come from the manufacturer with preassembled male PL-259 connectors on both ends. Then just use a PL-258 double-end female adapter to join the antenna and extension cables together without any soldering or complicated assembly.

PASS THEM THROUGH If you need to pass cables with connectors already installed through decks, bulkheads, and instrument dashes, it will be a tight fit, and one solution is to cut the cables, pass them through, and then reinstall the connectors. A better choice is special fittings that allow you to pass a cable with a connector attached to it through a deck or dash. These fittings are available in various sizes to fit a wide range of connector and cable diameters, and ensure a water-tight seal around the cable when installed.

065 CONFIRM YOUR RECEPTION

One of the best ways to test your radio, antenna, cable, or connectors is to measure the actual power the radio delivers to your antenna by investing in a consumer version of the tools used by professional installers. As a bonus, you get a confirmed radio check every time you press the transmit button on your microphone.

A much simpler test is to use a familiar but distant marine weather channel to confirm that your radio's reception is normal. Consistent two-way radio contact with distant sources indicates that your radio and antenna are operating properly.

If you're unsure, seek help from an experienced marine electrician. Your life may indeed depend upon this equipment, so you need to be absolutely certain that everything's working as it should.

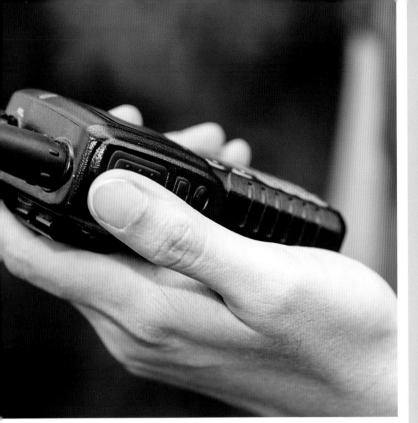

066 DON'T BE THAT GUY

VHF etiquette is a matter of both safety and courtesy. Here are four newbie (or not-so-newbie) errors to avoid when communicating over the radio.

MAKING A GENERAL CALL "Calling any vessel" is not only the incorrect radio procedure, it can actually land you a citation and even a big fine from the Federal Communications Commission (FCC). You must always call a specific vessel or shore station. And whatever you do, never dial up the Coast Guard for a radio check. The Coast Guard is in the business of saving lives and property, not providing a service to check your radio. Instead, monitor one of the ship-to-ship channels and listen for radio traffic. After two parties conclude a conversation, call one of them by name and request a radio check. Most captains will gladly help you out.

NOT IDENTIFYING YOURSELF FCC regulations require each party to identify themselves by either radio call sign or boat name at the beginning and at the end of a radio communication. A pleasure craft is only required to have its own radio station license and call sign if the boat is 65 feet (19.8 m) or longer, is engaged in transporting six or more paying passengers, has a single sideband radio aboard, or visits a foreign port (including Canada, Mexico, and the Bahamas). So, unless any of that describes you, you'll probably be using your boat's name as ID.

MISUSE OF CHANNEL 16 VHF Channel 16 is reserved primarily for emergency and boating safety communications, and using it just for conversation is strictly prohibited. Every channel has a purpose and the fact that your radio might have more than 50 channels doesn't mean you are allowed to use them all.

Remember that you're sharing a few VHF channels with thousands of other boating radio users. Aimless, long-winded chitchatting ties up the frequency you're on and forces others who might need to get a message through to stand by and wait until you're finished. Keep your on-air conversations short.

067 SPEAK THE LINGO

If you want to sound like a pro on the radio, learn to talk like one. Over the years, radio users have developed a verbal shorthand to abbreviate communications and make their meaning crystal clear. Here are the basics.

OVER I have completed my message and am asking the other party to reply.

OUT I have finished my message and expect no further reply.

AFFIRMATIVE OR NEGATIVE Yes or No. (When speaking on a radio, the words yes and no can be easily misunderstood.)

ROGER I have received and understood your entire message.

WILCO I understood your last transmission and will comply. (This is a contraction of the two words "will comply.")

FIGURES I am about to say numbers. For example, if you wanted to tell a boat with a deep draft approaching your location that it's entering shallow waters of only 15 feet (4.5 m), you might say, "My depth here is figures one-five feet (or, four-point-five meters)."

I SPELL I will now be using the phonetic alphabet to spell out something that might be difficult to understand. "I'm anchored at Bogg Harbor. I spell, Bravo, Oscar, Gulf, Gulf." A complete listing of the phonetic alphabet (Alpha, Bravo, Charlie, Delta, and so on) can likely be found in your owner's manual. Post a copy of it next to your radio.

068 TRY CHANNEL 9

Unless you've prearranged to call someone on a specific ship-to-ship channel (such as 68, 69, 71, 72, or 78A), use Channel 9 as your calling channel to contact another vessel or station. Once you've made contact, arrange together to switch to a ship-to-ship channel that's not in use.

069 USE RADAR RIGHT

Mention the word radar, and most boaters naturally think of using it for collision avoidance, and rightly so. Beyond a certain distance, human eyes will not detect even large objects that are peeking above the horizon. We rely on radar to identify the location, course, and speed of potential threats so that we can make collision-avoidance decisions well in advance.

Radar is essential, even in clear weather and bright sunshine, because it enhances your situational awareness. You don't want to be constantly looking over your shoulder for potential danger, and with radar you don't have to. But it can do even more.

HEADING UPDATES A heading sensor is an electronic compass that updates a boat's heading information faster than most GPS devices can, enhancing radar's performance as well as that of autopilots and other marine electronics.

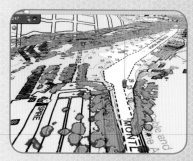

VISION ASSISTANCE Visibility is compromised by darkness, fog (even a faint haze), and precipitation. Some boaters mistakenly think they'll be safe so long as they follow their GPS or chart plotter route from waypoint to waypoint. The problem is that it isn't the known, charted land that will probably kill you—it's the uncharted objects such as other boats or floating debris.

WEATHER PREDICTION Radar sensitivity can be adjusted to indicate rain squalls in the distance, so you can decide whether you'll need to batten down the hatches, take evasive action, or initiate other heavy-weather tactics.

COLLISION WARNING Your radar's guard zone is an invisible barrier that can be placed around your boat to alert you audibly and graphically on-screen to a possible navigation hazard. A guard zone can be configured as a 360-degree circle around your boat or as a pie-shaped wedge of any size.

070 MARK THE SPOT

Radar has two very useful controls that allow you to determine how far away an object is and where it's heading. The EBL (electronic bearing line) function tells you a selected target's direction relative to your boat, while VRM (variable range marker) lets you see just how far away it is, for a number of purposes.

COLLISION AVOIDANCE Position your EBL on any vessel that appears to be headed toward your location. Should it continue to maintain a course down along that EBL, you'll know that it is headed for a collision with your boat. In navigation, this is known as a CBDR (constant bearing decreasing range) scenario. Change course, speed, or both to avoid a collision. If the target veers off your EBL, you'll know you're safe (for now) from contact with that vessel.

SAFE NAVIGATION You can also use VRM and EBL to grab a waypoint for any object that shows up on the radar screen. So, if you spot a dead whale, floating debris, or other hazard to navigation, you can chart its exact location and radio that information in to the Coast Guard.

SECRET FISHING GROUNDS You can also use this technology in a slightly more nefarious way to get the jump on your fishing buddies. Most successful anglers keep their favorite spots secret, but radar can give you a secret weapon. Use VRM and EBL to determine the exact direction and distance from your coordinates to a successful fishing boat. Then, chart the coordinates of that prime fishing ground for future reference.

071
GO ON GUARD

Set your radar's guard zone out 1 to 2 miles (1.6 to 3.2 km) to provide adequate warnings. If you have a watch or sleep mode on your radar, it can be set to periodically check your surroundings. While you are at anchor and asleep, a guard zone or sleep-mode alarm will warn you of approaching objects. A remote radar alarm module can be mounted below to deliver warnings while you're snoozing.

072
PLOT A COURSE

As technology improves, so do the tools available to boaters. Radar tracking devices have gotten more sophisticated and more readily available to the average person, with great results for safety and ease of navigation. Here are a few terms you may hear and what they mean for you.

MARPA (MINI AUTOMATIC RADAR PLOTTING AID)

This tool that lets you track several nearby targets and determine their speed, bearing, and their CPA (closest point of approach) to your boat, as well as the TCPA (time to closest point of approach) on the screen of a MARPA-enabled radar.

AIS (AUTOMATIC IDENTIFICATION SYSTEM)

Linking AIS reception to your radar adds additional information, letting you track AIS-broadcasting vessels (generally, larger commercial boats and ships) as they relate their positions and any other navigation data via VHF. You can then "see" the vessel on your radar screen, even if it's behind an island, ship, point of land, or other obstacle that obscures it from radar's line of sight.

073
SPLIT THE SCREEN

Most modern chart plotters let you overlay radar returns on the chart screen, giving you enhanced information about conditions. If you have the option of a split-screen, run one screen showing the chart plotter/radar overlay and the other with radar only. This will give you a clearer understanding of your surroundings and help you to improve your radar-interpretation skills. For example, if a radar target corresponds to a buoy symbol on the plotter overlay, it's probably a stationary marker, not a boat. On the other hand, if you see a target on the overlay but the plotter indicates nothing, it is probably a boat.

074 FIND A KEEPER

Electronic fish finders, or sounders, use sonar to give a picture of the bottom beneath the boat, as well as other items, notably schools of fish. As the technology advances, fish finders are keeping pace and getting more sophisticated. Here are some developments that avid anglers will want to check out.

NOISE CONTROL When shopping for a new fish finder, look for one with digital signal processing (DSP), a digital noise filter that identifies and enhances desirable signals, such as fish, bait schools, and bottom features, while eliminating interference.

CHIRP Compressed high-intensity radar pulse (CHIRP) is most likely the most significant advance in recent years. Conventional fish finders use a single sonar frequency signal; CHIRP transmits across a wide spectrum of frequencies, allowing it to detect fish at far greater distances and better discriminate between closely spaced targets. It also filters out "noise" masking fish targets and

structures. CHIRP is available on an increasing number of devices, and it will no doubt dominate many fishing electronics until the next big breakthrough.

DOWN-IMAGING Concentrated high-resolution scans create lifelike depictions of bottom contours, marine life, and vegetation down to about 600 feet (183 m).

SIDE IMAGING High-resolution, detailed imaging is designed to capture targets in a wider area, giving you readings for waters up to 180 degrees to both sides of the boat.

075 STICK TO IT

Automatic positioning systems use propulsion to hold a boat on station at the push of button, using either a trolling motor or a multiengine system. Each has its pluses and minuses.

ELECTRONICALLY ANCHOR This system uses a single bow-mounted electric trolling motor, which can swivel 360 degrees and employ variable speeds to keep the boat "anchored," typically silently and with remarkable precision. As with a conventional anchor, the bow tends to point into the current or wind, whichever is strongest. Unlike with an anchor, there is little swing. The boat holds tight to the position you set. If you wish, you can jog side to side or back and forth to fish new areas—a valuable function when, for example, you're fishing wrecks or the edges of a river channel.

The downside is that the motor's short shaft limits its use to freshwater fishing boats and bay boats with low-profile bows. Also, to adequately control a boat larger than 20 feet (6 m), you

need a 36-volt system, which means three, heavy, 31-series deep-cycle batteries dedicated to the trolling motor.

MULTIPLY YOUR ENGINE This system uses one or more GPS receivers and multiple engines to a hold the boat in position. It is particularly useful along a crowded waterway, when waiting for a drawbridge to open, or while waiting for a spot at the fuel dock. If there's a strong current, this system will save the helmsman a lot of work in holding steady. Plus, if you're running the boat single-handedly, you can let the system take over temporarily while you rig fenders and lines before docking.

GO OLD-SCHOOL With any automatic positioning system, resist the temptation to set and forget. Engines stall. Fuses blow. Electronics blank out. If your head's not in the game, you'll quickly be at the mercy of wind and current if your system fails. Need to relax? Drop the old-fashioned anchor in a quiet cove. Better yet, find a dock and tie up. That's a positioning system you can trust.

076 GET STRAIGHT ON YOUR TRANSDUCERS

A transducer serves as an antenna for a boat's sonar system. Transducers operate on the same frequency as the sonar unit and can pick up very sensitive echo signals at various depths. Here are the most common types.

TRANSOM MOUNTS

ABOUT: Well-proven option, with power that goes up to 1 kW

PRO: Easy screw-on installation, maximum transmit-and-receive sensitivity, allows use of echo sounder even when underway

CON: Not for inboard boats, as turbulence generated by rudders, shafts, and props disrupts the signal

THROUGH-HULLS

ABOUT: Installation requires cutting a hole in the hull; add angled fairing blocks inside and outside the hull to account for the deadrise angle and ensure the transducer points straight down

PRO: Works well on inboard craft

CON: Susceptible to collision damage, may make trailering somewhat difficult

GLUE-IN PUCKS

ABOUT: Installation requires a flat spot in the aft bilge near the keel; puck is installed in a bubble-free puddle of epoxy resin

PRO: Small, easy to install, and effective; usually gives a solid bottom reading at any speed

CON: Does not work in cored or foam-filled hulls, lower sensitivity in solid fiberglass hulls

SEA-CHEST

ABOUT: A sealed plastic box filled with mineral oil that is epoxied into the hull

PRO: Higher-power outputs than the puck, multiple frequencies

CON: Since transducer face is not in the water, you lose some sensitivity for depth limits and ability to read thermoclines

077 PEAK YOUR TRANSDUCER

To get a crisp image on your fish finder that shows the fish you're after as well as the contours of the bottom, you have to do two things. One, position the boat over a school of fish! Second, adjust the power output to match the depth and bottom composition you are fishing over.

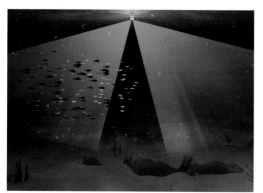

STEP 1 Set the gain and range to manual, in that order.

STEP 2 Adjust the range to three times the water's depth.

STEP 3 Punch up the gain until a "second echo " of the bottom appears on the screen.

STEP 4 Adjust the range to a setting appropriate to the actual depth.

If you move to a new spot, repeat these steps to match the new location.

078 COVER UP

Whether custom-made or off the shelf, boat covers are a better-looking, better-fitting option than simple tarps for protecting your investment, whether for winter storage or keeping leaves and clutter off the deck between outings. Unlike shrink-wrap, they're also reusable time and again. But all boat covers are not created equal.

CHECK THE SEAMS Double-stitched seams rate most durable. Flat-felled seams eliminate raw edges, reducing wear. Demand weather-resistant threads like UVR-treated Dacron or Tenara, from the makers of Gore-Tex.

PICK YOUR MATERIAL 300-denier nylon and similar fabrics can better resist the elements. Also try polyester duck for durability or acrylic fiber silicone for water resistance.

TIE IT DOWN An elastic draw cord sewn around the hemline provides a snug fit. Combined with tie-downs that fit over the cover, these prevent the cover from blowing off when trailering or in high winds during storage.

CONSIDER THE OPTIONS Your choice could be as simple as a console cover, a cockpit cover attached to the gunwales and windscreen, or a full cover protecting the interior cockpit and topsides from exposure to the sun and other elements.

CHOOSE GOOD HARDWARE Look for metal or Delrin grommets and rings, which see few ill effects from the constant beating inflicted by sunlight. Loops of heavy-duty nylon webbing stitched to the cover are another good choice.

079 KEEP IT CLEAN

You can clean canvas by hand with warm soap and water or a commercial canvas cleaner, like Star Brite Sail and Canvas Cleaner. You can also put it in your washing machine with a small amount of laundry detergent and clean it on the gentle cycle, then hang it out to dry. If your Sunbrella cover has stains and you know what caused them, their website has a helpful table with hints on treating stains caused by everything from ketchup to nail polish to red wine.

080 CHOOSE THE RIGHT BIMINI TOP

Folding open cockpit tops, known as Bimini tops, rank as one of the most popular marine accessories. These covers can block out the sun without obstructing airflow and can be folded up and stored when not needed. A Bimini top can scrub up to 2 mph (3.2 kph) off your boat's speed, but the added comfort outweighs the drawback for most boaters. Of course, there are multiple considerations to look for when buying a boat with a Bimini top or fitting your current ride with a replacement shade.

FRAME Look for stainless steel, the strongest, most durable choice for the frame, bows, and fittings. Period. Aluminum frames cost less, but don't hold up as well.

BOW COUNT Demand one bow—the frame cross-member—for every 2 feet (0.6 m) of Bimini length. Continuous bows will provide better long-term service than those built in sections to ease shipping.

DECK FITTINGS Quick-release hinges that swivel and allow the frame to pop in and out are great, but pricey. Simple hinges with pull pins—either those with toggles or the captive-ball type—serve much the same purpose at a lower cost.

MATERIAL Canvas is the traditional material for a Bimini top, but you have some other options, too. Here are the top alternative options, and their pros and cons.

BRAND	FABRIC	PROS	CONS
SUNBRELLA	Solution-dyed acrylic	Holds color well, resists shrinking and stretching, easy to clean	Not 100 percent waterproof, less abrasion resistant
STAMOID	Vinyl-coated polyester	Waterproof, resists abrasion, very easy to clean and keep clean, highly resistant to ultraviolet light	Less colorfast
SEAMARK	Vinyl-coated acrylic	Waterproof, excellent abrasion resistance, very easy to clean and keep clean	50 percent heavier than the other options

081 INSTALL A BIMINI TOP

A Bimini top creates shade and folds back to let you catch some rays. Tops can be mounted in various ways; the simplest are anchored at the gunwales, with adjustable web straps fore and aft keeping the canvas taut and the structure secure. See item 080 for advice on the best materials and accessories to look for when shopping for a quality top. They're pretty easy to install. Here's how.

STEP 1 Measure between the points where the two deck hinges attach to determine the top's width. Length and height can vary to suit your needs: Off-the-shelf models are usually 4 to 8 feet (1.2 to 2.4 m) long. If you want to stand underneath, make sure you have sufficient headroom.

STEP 2 Decide where the deck hinges should be placed; these will mark the midpoint of the top. Set the deck hinges exactly opposite each other, or the top will bind when folded. You can use special hinges for mounting on vertical surfaces, such as cabin bulwarks if gunwale mounting won't work. Ensure the folded top stows with minimal interference in the cockpit.

STEP 3 Place masking tape on the mounting surfaces and use the deck hinges to mark the mounting holes. Before drilling, clear the underside of any obstructions. Chamfer the holes with a countersink to eliminate gelcoat cracking. Remove the masking tape, bed the surface with a marine polysulfide sealant, and screw each deck hinge into place (use nuts and bolts where possible). Clean up excess sealant with a rag dampened with solvent.

STEP 4 Bolt the main bow to the deck hinges and erect the top. Extend the fore and aft web straps in line with the bows to form an M-shape, to find where to mount the eye straps. Mark, drill, chamfer, bed, and mount each pair with self-tapping screws. The eye straps work best when mounted horizontally. Attach the snap-hooks to the eye straps and use the buckles to evenly tighten the top.

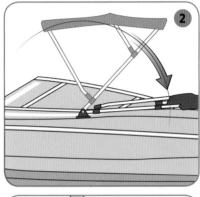

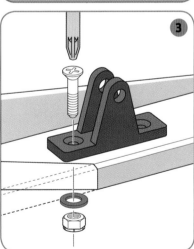

082

STOP STRAP BUZZ

Bimini top straps can make an annoying buzz at certain speeds. At the right speed, air flows over the strap and causes it to vibrate at a frequency that registers with the human ear. The specifics depend on wind speed, strap length, strap width, and more. The bottom line: "strap buzz" is annoying!

A simple fix? Put a twist in the strap. Simply unhook it from the boat or the Bimini top, and put a twist or two in the strap, then reconnect it. Twisting the strap disrupts the airflow, eliminating vibration that causes the noise.

Of course, you could replace those straps with support poles. It's nice to have options, isn't it?

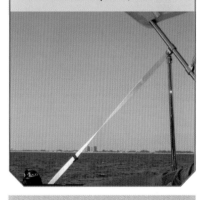

083

MAKE IT LAST

To keep your Bimini top nice, make sure it's dry, retract it at the end of the day, and store it in the zippered boot. Use the same protectants as you do for your cockpit and bow covers on the Bimini top. Finally, upgrade to quick-release "grenade" pins in the deck hinges to do away with thumbscrews and make removal easier.

084 BOOT UP

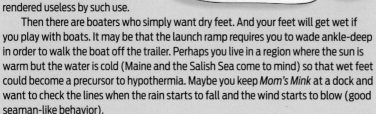

Every serious boater owns a pair of deck boots. Why you'd wear them depends on your particular notion of what constitutes boating fun. For instance, fisherman wear them when decks are bloody and the slime is flying: footwear made from absorbent material is rendered useless by such use.

Then there are boaters who simply want dry feet. And your feet will get wet if you play with boats. It may be that the launch ramp requires you to wade ankle-deep in order to walk the boat off the trailer. Perhaps you live in a region where the sun is warm but the water is cold (Maine and the Salish Sea come to mind) so that wet feet could become a precursor to hypothermia. Maybe you keep *Mom's Mink* at a dock and want to check the lines when the rain starts to fall and the wind starts to blow (good seaman-like behavior).

Many boaters also don deck boots for dashing out of the office for a cappuccino when it's drizzling; boaters rarely miss an opportunity to show off their superior resistance to wind, weather, and curbside puddles.

085 BAG YOUR BOOTS

Keep a few LDPE shopping bags—the kind many grocery stores use for produce and bulk foods—on hand. They come in handy for donning foul weather gear. These bags are as slippery as a landlubber's knot, and if you cover your shoe- or boot-shod foot with one, you can step into your raingear pants without having to remove your footwear because your foot jammed in the leg.

086 DRESS FOR SUCCESS

Your outfit varies with the activity and your personal preference. But we have your best interests at heart, whether you're on a cruise up the Inside Passage to Alaska or simply headed to the nearest sandbar or cove to relax.

PUT ON A HAT You need to keep the sun off to prevent skin cancer, avoid fatigue, and cut the glare so you can spot navigation aids such as buoys—not to mention ID'ing celebs on passing yachts. The Tilley Hat checks all the boxes and has become the official headgear of sailing kooks and snobs around the world. In addition, it floats, comes with a chinstrap, doesn't shrink after getting wet, and it looks great. Did we mention it comes with a chinstrap?

KEEP YOUR FOOTING

The classic boat shoe—a brown, lace-up leather moccasin with a siped sole—became a classic for good reason. They drain water and dry fast; provided you aren't wearing socks, your feet can get wet but won't stay that way. The slits in the sole drain water and grip wet decks like a barnacle on a piling. They can be kicked off easily for walking a beach or a "no shoes" teak boat deck. Tie your laces in a perfect bow and soak the knot in glue to create slip-ons that fit snugly and retain the classic look.

BLOCK THE SUN The sun is one of the main reasons to go boating, but it's also one of the main hazards. Fret not; modern textiles have sun protection built right in. Sunblocking shirts range from athletic, fitted rashguards that dry quickly, to super-functional "technical" shirts with built-in ventilation, loads of pockets, and features such as Velcro straps to support a fishing rod while you tie on a new lure. All are made from UPF-rated fabric to protect you from the sun while you're out enjoying it.

GRAB YOUR SHORTS Even if you have no intention of swimming or waterskiing, the chance to wade ashore and beachcomb or walk hand-in-hand with your first mate may be too much to resist. Shorts that can get wet, dry fast, and offer a secure pocket or two are perfect—even better if they go from boat to dockside bistro as the need arises.

087 WEAR THE RIGHT OUTFIT

Your location on the waters, the season, and the prevailing weather conditions all influence how you should dress for the best comfort and protection. Here's a quick reference to guide your sartorial choices.

WARM AIR, CLEAR; COLD WATER

INNER LAYER Wool/hi-tech base layer

MAIN LAYER Wool/blend long pants; wool/blend long-sleeve shirt

OUTER LAYER Rain top on; rain pants on hand

HEADGEAR Wool cap (worn or on hand)

EYEWEAR Polarized sunglasses, gray or blue lens

FOOTGEAR Deck boots

MISC Lip balm

WARM AIR, CLEAR; WARM WATER

INNER LAYER n/a

MAIN LAYER Nylon or blend shorts; UPF shirt

OUTER LAYER None

HEADGEAR Ball cap; brimmed cap with drawstring

EYEWEAR Polarized sunglasses, gray or blue lens

FOOTGEAR Boat shoes

MISC Tropics: sun-protective balaclava face mask and gloves

WARM AIR, CLEAR AND WINDY

INNER LAYER n/a

MAIN LAYER Nylon or blend shorts; UPF shirt

OUTER LAYER Windshirt; windbreaker

HEADGEAR Brimmed cap with drawstring; ball cap worn backwards

EYEWEAR Polarized sunglasses, gray or blue lens

FOOTGEAR Boat shoes

MISC Don't forget " keeper" strings for any eyewear

WARM AIR, RAINING

INNER LAYER n/a

MAIN LAYER Nylon or blend shorts; UPF shirt

OUTER LAYER Lightweight, breathable raingear

HEADGEAR Brimmed cap with drawstring; ball cap

EYEWEAR Polarized sunglasses, yellow or amber lens

FOOTGEAR Deck boots

MISC Ball cap may be worn backwards on hi-speed craft

COLD AIR, CLEAR SKIES

INNER LAYER Wool/hi-tech base layer

MAIN LAYER Wool/blend long pants; wool/blend long-sleeve shirt

OUTER LAYER Rain top on; rain pants on hand; heavy sweater or winter coat

HEADGEAR Wool watch

EYEWEAR Polarized sunglasses, blue or gray lens

FOOTGEAR Deck boots; wool socks

MISC Warm gloves and rain pants to keep wind off and keep you warmer

COLD AIR, RAIN OR SNOW

INNER LAYER Wool/hi-tech base layer

MAIN LAYER Wool/blend long pants; wool/blend long-sleeve shirt

OUTER LAYER Rain top on; rain pants on; heavy sweater or winter coat

HEADGEAR Wool watch cap; Sou'wester rain hat over

EYEWEAR Polarized sunglasses, yellow or amber lens

FOOTGEAR Deck boots; sock liners; wool socks

MISC Warm gloves

088 SEE IN COLOR

Sunglasses are an essential bit of boating kit. A polarized pair cuts the glare and lets you see rocks, obstructions, and shallow water in scenarios wherein the naked eye is blind. Shades come in a kaleidoscope of colors. How to choose? We tested three of the most popular lens colors, all in the same pair of Costa Del Mar frames just for your information.

BLUE

PRO: Cuts glare; helps with visual acuity and contrast to spot fish or hazards; reduces eyestrain

CON: Too dark in any shaded or unlit areas

BEST FOR: Offshore or blue water

AMBER

PRO: Best visibility in fog and dawn/dusk, especially to see beneath surface glare

CON: Too bright in full sunlight

BEST FOR: Flat light

SILVER

PRO: Reduces glare and eyestrain offshore; good for perceiving depths inshore

CON: Second to blue in very bright light; second to amber in low light

BEST FOR: Best all-around

089 GET A GOOD LOOK

The ability to see what the naked eye cannot is of immeasurably valuable when operating a boat. Spotting a buoy, inlet, or other landmark sooner helps keep the boat on course—not to mention saving fuel. Fishermen use "binocs" to find flocks of diving birds, often a sure sign of feeding fish. But since the differences between binoculars can be hard to see, we created this handy chart to help you pick the best pair of marine binoculars.

MAGNIFICATION	PRISM
BEST 7X	**BEST** Porro
GOOD 6X	**GOOD** Roof
DON'T BOTHER 10X	**DON'T BOTHER** n/a

OBJECTIVE LENS	CONSTRUCTION
BEST 50	**BEST** Mil-spec
GOOD 30	**GOOD** "Water-resistant"
DON'T BOTHER 20	**DON'T BOTHER** "Weatherproof"

090 STAY COOL

Keeping your food fresh and your drinks cold goes a long way toward ensuring a long day afloat is a long day of fun. Here are three cool tips for your cooler.

FOIL THE HEAT Make your cooler more efficient by cutting a piece of foil-backed insulation from a home-store for a snug fit just inside the lid. This extra insulation makes ice last almost twice as long.

THROW IN THE TOWEL Tie-downs are safest, but if you soak a towel, wring it out, fold it in half and place your cooler on it, the cooler will not slide unless the seas are very rough or your maneuvers very fast and aggressive.

CHILL OUT For longer trips, you can make more of the available space in your cooler by freezing some bottles of water and drinking them last. In so doing, they act as (and actually are) ice until you drink them.

091 SQUELCH MAL DE MER

If seasickness happens, press the thumb of one hand into the lower center of the palm of your hand—hard. You will know you have hit the right spot when you find it. Doing so can provide instant relief from nausea.

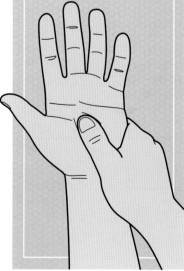

092
BUG OUT

Ahh . . . sunset on the water! What could be better? Well, if you are anchored out, enjoy the tapestry in the sky. But, if you find yourself just getting back to the dock at dusk, you will find that bugs come out when the sun goes away. To make washing down your boat and snapping on the covers less miserable, be sure you have bug spray on hand.

093
RAID THE CUPBOARDS

It's been a joke among boaters since the first papyrus raft voyaged down the Nile: If there's an anchor or a seagull on the bottle and the label includes the word "marine," you pay double for it. But are those specialty products worth it? Many are, in our experience, but there are also many chores for which ordinary household products can do a great job. Here are some of the maybe unexpected items *Boating* editors use aboard our own boats.

OIL UP
Extra-virgin olive oil is a good, nonacidic lubricant for the water pump.

DO THE DISHES
Dishwashing soap cleans up oil and fuel spills great— plus it kills odors.

BUG OFF
Avon Skin So Soft is an excellent bug repellant.

SCRUB AWAY
Gentle abrasive cleansers such as Soft Scrub are great for cleaning nonskid decks.

USE YOUR NOODLE
Pool noodles make great hook and lure hangers.

LUBE IT
Lip balm makes a great lubricant for the snaps and zippers on your boat's canvas.

ON THE WATER

If out in bad weather, and given the choice between being aboard the best boat with a mediocre captain or the mediocre boat with experienced captain, I'd choose the latter all the time. So would most experienced boaters. The very definition of seaworthiness, after all, is a sound vessel *in capable hands*.

Mariners cannot buy seaworthiness nor rely solely on boat design and naval architecture to save their asses if the gull guano hits the bilge blower while out at sea. The captain of the vessel; for our purposes here, the skipper, the boat owner—you and me—must make a practice of seamanship. It is the only way we can assure ourselves of operating a seaworthy vessel.

Seamanship is as much as set of skills as it is the use of judgment. Skills and judgment are honed on the stone of experience. Experience is something this book cannot deliver.

Instead, the *Total Boating Manual*'s promise is to engage and enlighten the boater with a desire to practice good seamanship. The subject matter presented in this chapter will provide a framework, or construct, within which curiosity can be piqued, and because of which learning can be accelerated. Whether the topic is docking a boat, operating in fog, or running a breaking inlet, or any one of dozens of other areas of seamanship, the information presented in this chapter will allow you to pursue the experience you require with greater confidence and knowledge.

094 BACK UP SAFELY

Having to twist around every time you back your boat down a launch ramp can become a real pain in the neck, and with larger boats, the view over the seat doesn't take in the entire picture. The solution is to learn to use the mirrors as your primary reference when backing. Practice these simple tips in a parking lot or on a day when the ramp isn't crowded, and before long, you'll be backing up like a pro.

GET READY Your mirrors only show little sections of the landscape—and in reverse. It's a lot easier to understand the reverse image if you first have a nonreverse image of the staging area and launch ramp. After prepping the boat for launch, take a few moments to walk the ramp area, visualizing your path to the water, and note any landmarks that can serve as reference points on your path.

STEER STRAIGHT Place a hand on the bottom of the steering wheel. Watching your boat in the rearview mirror, move your hand in the direction you want the boat and trailer to go. Move your hand to the right, and the boat goes right in your mirror. The goal is to keep the boat straight between your mirrors.

ORIENT YOURSELF If at all possible, try aligning your rig for a straight shot backward onto the loading ramp. Then, before you put your vehicle into reverse, take a moment to look in one or both of your mirrors and identify any fixed reference points. This will help to keep you on the straight and narrow once you begin backing up.

TURN SAFELY On ramps that have shorter lead-ins, you might have to back around a turn in order to reach the water. The key to a smooth turn is in the setup. Ideally, you will want to make a smooth, medium-radius turn that will leave the tow vehicle and trailer aligned and facing the ramp a bit before the trailer hits the water.

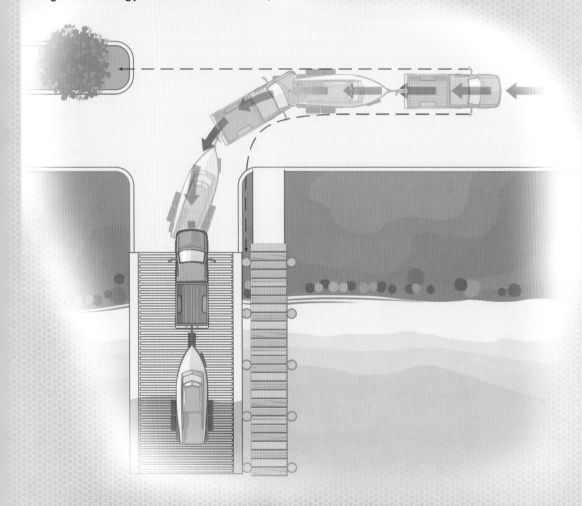

095 COOL DOWN

You've driven all the way to the lake and you can't wait to get that boat off the trailer and start having fun! Fair enough, but it'll do your trailer a world of good if you take just a moment to cool off. After any reasonable amount of driving, the trailer's wheel bearings, brakes, and other components are probably hot, and should be allowed to cool down before you plunge them into cold water. Otherwise, you're giving those components a shock that can weaken the metal and seals, leading to damage and corrosion.

You can combat this by parking a little way from the ramp and letting the trailer cool down while you load up the boat and take time to make sure everything's ready for launch. Your local ramp may have a "staging area" for just this sort of thing, or you can make your own safely out of your fellow boaters' way.

While you wait for the trailer workings to cool, you can load up, take the tie-down straps off the back of the boat, and double-check the drain plug. Now you're ready for launch!

096 LAUNCH YOUR BOAT

When backing down the ramp, be sure to leave your bow strap attached, in case the ramp is steeper than you think. You don't want to dump your boat prematurely! Now back your trailer into the water until the tops of the fenders are just above the waterline, which is usually the right position for floating your boat off the bunks. Some trailers are set up a little differently and might need to be a bit farther into the water or farther up the ramp, but this is a good place to start. Remove the bow strap, put the boat in reverse, and gently back it off the trailer. Go park the trailer in a designated area, and have a fantastic day on the water!

097 LOAD UP

At the end of the day (or the fishing trip, or the season), it's time to load up and go home. Here's how to get your boat on the trailer without mishaps.

STEP 1 Pull up to the end of the dock and drop your driver off so he or she can go get the trailer. If there's room, go ahead and tie up now. If not, don't be a jerk. Back up a bit and idle until you see your ride approaching.

STEP 2 Once it's time to load up, get everyone but the operator off the boat (don't worry about taking gear with you at this stage). Hold the lines to keep the boat steady just beyond where the trailer will back up to.

STEP 3 Have the trailer driver back down the ramp slowly and carefully; signal when they're at the mark that indicates where the boat will float.

STEP 4 With a smaller boat, you can just walk alongside it, towing the boat with a bowline, and then tossing that line to the driver

standing at the trailer winch. With a larger boat, you might want to drive it very slowly onto the trailer, with the engine just in forward.

STEP 5 Standing on the trailer tongue, attach the winch cable to the boat's bow eye and crank it onto the trailer.

STEP 6 Once your boat is snug against the winch post, attach the safety chain.

STEP 7 Have the driver proceed slowly up the ramp, stopping so that you can raise the sterndrive if necessary. Make sure that you get out of the way as quickly as possible, as other folks are likely waiting to load up as well.

STEP 8 Pull the drain plug right away, so the boat can drain while you're loading up your gear.

STEP 9 Strap down Bimini top, lower antennas, plug in trailer lights, and stow anything else you need to so as to make the whole package road-ready.

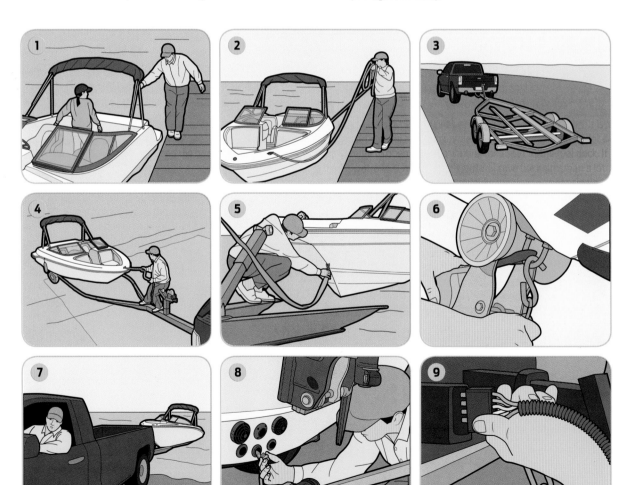

098 KEEP IT SLICK

The draw bar, the long piece of steel channel to which the hitch ball is mounted, is designed to slide in and out of the hitch receiver. While it might be tempting to just leave it in place all of the time, the draw bar can rust into place if you don't periodically remove it, wire-brush the rust off, and apply a light coat of lubricant.

099 DON'T YANK YOUR CHAIN

Don't let your safety chain go slack. Should the winch cable fail on the road, the chain would undergo shock loading (a sudden and drastic increase in load). You can prevent this by shortening the chain so that it's just long enough to reach the bow eye when the boat is winched tight. To do so, undo the fastener and then refasten it through a different link. Other trailers have a keyhole-shape slot through which the chain passes before being bolted to the winch stand. To shorten chains for these, pass the chain through the wide part of the slot and then pull the link that marks the final length into the slot's narrow section.

100 AVOID MOORING MAYHEM

Approaching the dock, especially in front of a crowded marina, can be one of the most nerve-wracking experiences facing any boat captain. But it really shouldn't be. Here are 10 simple rules that, if followed to the letter, will not only make you better at close-quarters maneuvering and docking, but will also make you a better all-around boater.

RULE 1 Never approach the dock faster than you are willing to hit it.

RULE 2 There is room for only one captain on your vessel.

RULES 3–10 See rules 1 and 2; when in doubt, refer to rule 2.

101 SLOW DOWN

And now, a visit from our main sponsor: Rule 1. Less damage occurs at a slower speed, and it'll usually give you plenty of time to make corrections and salvage your approach.

Whether you are operating a single-engine or multiengine boat, slow, deliberate moves with the throttle work best. Make small, slow adjustments by bumping the boat in and out of gear, in either forward or reverse. With your helm amidships, this push/pull of countering thrust is highly effective, allowing you to steer the boat within its own length and without touching the wheel.

You will also want to avoid short bursts of high power; boats don't have brakes, and once you get a head of steam on, it will be a lot more difficult to slow down. Once again, both the wind and current play an important role here, because an application of additional forward or reverse thrust might be needed to slow or speed up your advance.

Not comfortable with how your approach is going? Then just wave it off. Anybody who tries to tell you they have never had to go around is lying.

102 TAKE COMMAND

More problems are caused when you're trying to dock alongside "that guy"—yeah, the one over there on the dock offering you advice and distracting you from the task at hand. He thinks he's helping, but he's really not. There is only one person solely responsible for your vessel and crew safety: you.

Even the most experienced captains and crews have a little pre-docking briefing. Managing the crew and its assigned tasks

prior to and during docking is one of the most important (and simplest) things to get a handle on. Go over each of the crew member's responsibility precisely—well in advance of docking maneuvers. Also, decide who should remain seated and out of the way until all of the lines are secure.

Make sure that everyone aboard is aware of your expectations through every stage of docking. For example, determine who you want handling the bow, stern, and spring lines, as well as who is responsible for deploying fenders or fending off from the dock, piling or seawall. It's also important to let them know in what order you want the boat secured.

Lastly, be sure to always stress safety first: no hands between bulkheads, seawalls, and pilings, and make sure that no mooring lines are wrapped around hands, legs, or feet.

Remember what you just learned—the part about how there's only room for one captain on your vessel, regardless of size. That rule will help to resolve a lot of conversations that you don't need to be having!

Now go boating, and look forward to coming back to the dock instead of dreading it!

103 PERFECT YOUR APPROACH

To paraphrase an old military-based adage: proper prior planning prevents poor performance. This saying can definitely apply to docking, regardless of whether the vessel is a dinghy, a 150-foot (45.7-m) motoryacht, or the *USS Enterprise*.

KNOW YOUR BOAT First and foremost, you must be very aware of how your boat handles, particularly at bare steerageway. The more comfortable you become, the more confident you'll be when trying to slip it into a tight space in a jammed marina.

REHEARSE IT The more time that you spend at the helm, the better feel you will develop. You will be able to anticipate any issues before they reach a critical mass. Some captains have even made virtual slips via polyballs and mushroom anchors in open water. It's easy to re-create your slip with exact dimensions in this manner, thus allowing you to duplicate a wide variety of docking scenarios with regard to current and wind and to see how your boat responds.

ANTICIPATE Wind and current are often big obstacles, but by thinking out your approach ahead of time and factoring them into the equation, you'll be amazed at what

an effective ally Mother Nature can be. Try to set your approach so that the wind and current help you into the dock.

BE RESPONSIVE Other considerations are the entry and exit areas to the marina. It's important not just to know where you are going but also to know where other boats might be coming from, so you can anticipate any interfering traffic in your response. The more alert and aware you are of your surroundings, the fewer problems you'll have.

104 FIND YOUR DOCKING ZEN

Most docking articles detail techniques for manipulating wheel and throttle, or focus on wind and current. Some discuss the use of lines to "warp" or "spring" yourself into a berth. Get in touch with your boat, learn some of its intimate secrets, and operate on a higher plane. Osmosis can be a great teaching tool for your inner captain.

COME FULL CIRCLE A turning circle is how much space your boat requires to complete a turn. Knowing the turning circle is helpful whether you "dead-end" in a marina fairway or encounter a strong current at the fuel dock. Boats with props aft of the transom turn wider than those with props forward. Watch how sharply your boat turns at various speeds. Note the distance between your boat and objects such as pilings, bow pulpits, and raised outboards, especially when you have the procedure down cold. With enough repetitions, you'll know the turning circle at all speeds intuitively.

DON'T GET CARRIED AWAY Once shifted into neutral, carry is how far your boat drifts and with how much force. Familiarity with carry is part of using current, wind, and throttle, as it varies with underwater form, propeller diameter, and windage. A deeper or taller boat, or one with bigger wheels generally carries farther. Carry varies with the speed of the boat, current, and wind; pay attention to all three while docking. I suggest monitoring engine rpm rather than boat speed for this purpose. Do so, and hopefully you'll avoid having to open up the engines wide in reverse just to prevent a collision.

GIVE IT A KICK A turning propeller induces torque, a sideways force. The effect of prop torque on a boat is kick—the direction and amount of sideways movement imparted to the stern when shifting into gear. Stopping is a primary component of docking, so ignoring kick results in problems when reverse thrust is applied. Kick varies with rpm applied and the direction of the prop's rotation. Rudder or gear case position can enhance or diminish kick's effect. While docking, focus on the rudder/drive/gear case position and the engine's rpm before shifting. Shift into neutral before making a change to the rudder. Practice keeping the rudder/drive/engine centered, and soak in the effect that changes in gear and rpm have upon your vessel.

106 TALK THE TORQUE

Prop torque allows you to fine-tune the boat's position while staying within the boundaries of your slip, basically maneuvering at a standstill before reaching for the lines. You can make your boat cant, slide, and shift without moving forward or back much. The effect is subtle; you have to wait a beat for the boat to react. It's not a critical seamanship skill, but it engenders pride in the doer and admiration from the onlooker.

STEP 1 Take your boat out and, with a straight helm, shift into reverse at idle speed. The stern will kick to port. Greater throttle increases the motion. This effect is heightened when the drive is trimmed under. Practice to determine the extent to which prop torque makes your boat's stern "kick" in reverse and then try it at various throttle and trim settings. Whichever direction the stern swings, the bow moves in the opposite direction.

STEP 2 Now, put it into play. Say you tie up bow-to. Just before your bow gets between the poles, aim for a point at the head of the slip on the port side. This will have you canted toward the orientation of the slip, the bow facing the left forward corner and the stern facing right aft corner. Remember what you learned in your practice sessions: When reverse power is applied, the stern kicks to port, the bow to starboard, and you'll come to a stop perfectly parallel. Stopping becomes a vector; instead of just changing speed, you change direction as well. If you come in parallel and hit reverse, you'll kick the stern into the dock and the bow away—possibly into the neighboring boat.

STEP 3 Prop torque can be used to equal advantage backing into your slip. You might see a fellow boater halfway into his slip trying to use the wheel to steer a boat "around a corner" in reverse. Boats steer from the back, so that causes the boat to get sideways to the intended direction. Positioned slightly off-center of the target, keep the helm centered and apply reverse. Your prop torque will move the stern to port. When the transom is lined up, shift into neutral, wait a beat, then shift into forward, using prop torque to induce a starboard slide, just enough to straighten out the bow. Reverse again. You're home.

105 GET PITCH PERFECT

As the plane of a prop's rotation increases beyond 90 degrees to the direction of water flow, the pitch of the propeller is effectively increased. Since pitch (minus slip) is a measure of how far the boat will move with each prop rotation, drive or engine trim affects how much "kick" is induced by a burst of throttle.

107 BEAM-TO WITH ONE ENGINE

Probably the most common problem posed for boaters is approaching the dock beam-to with a single engine. Despite lacking the maneuverability of a twin-engine vessel, this really is one of the simplest docking maneuvers around.

STEP 1 Approach the dock at a 45-degree angle.

STEP 2 As you near the dock (by about a boat length), turn to become parallel with the structure. This would be the point at which you'd want a crew to prepare to fend off.

STEP 3 As you turn, the bow will approach the dock, while the stern will remain outboard. Apply reverse thrust toward the dock, bringing the entire vessel parallel with the structure.

STEP 4 To arrest motion, apply forward thrust with the rudder amidships. Now get off the boat and go have some fun!

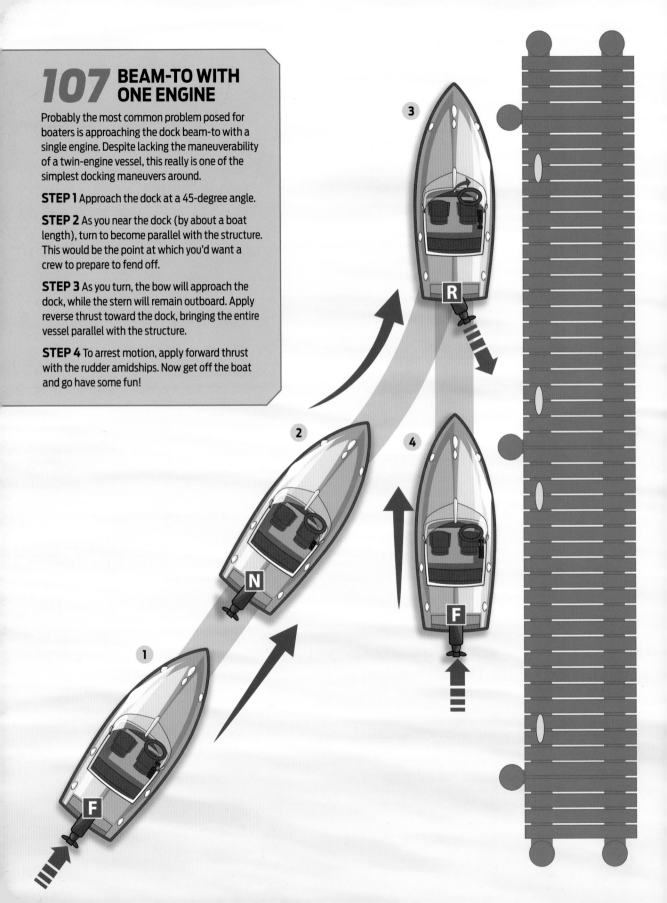

108 DOUBLE UP

This scenario is common when fueling up or when using a transient slip at a strange marina on a multiday trip. By utilizing a spring line cleated off amidships, you'll be able to counter any negative effects of wind and tide, which can blow you off the dock in a maddening counter-thrust. With the wind and tide on your side, it's as simple as bringing your boat parallel and allowing Mother Nature to help your vessel gently kiss the dock.

STEP 1 Approach the dock at a near-perpendicular angle with boat engines in forward.

STEP 2 Begin your turn to port with the help of countering thrust, and have a crew member ready with the spring line.

STEP 3 Make your turn harder by increasing your outside counterthrust, and then deploy your crew member onto the dock to make fast with the spring line.

STEP 4 Slide your engines out of gear and allow the spring line to arrest your momentum and bring your boat to the dock; make adjustments and bring the boat to rest by sliding the outside engine into reverse.

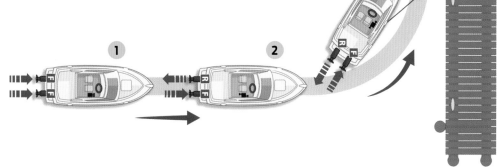

109 TRY TWIN-ENGINE STERN DOCKING

One of the most common docking scenarios for larger, dual-inboard boats is the classic stern-to docking arrangement— better known as backing into a slip. It's one of those signs of an assured captain, but with a little prior planning, it also turns out to be a fairly straightforward (or backward) move.

Dual inboards or sterndrives offer boaters a great deal of control. By utilizing counterthrust (forward on one engine and reverse on the other), boaters can literally spin their boat 360 degrees in a little more than a boat length. The rudders or lower units (in the case of sterndrives or articulating drives like Volvo's IPS) should always be amidships. The process works with dual outboards, though pivot maneuvers are more problematic due to their narrow set.

STEP 1 When nearing your slip, try to plan your approach so that wind and current will work with you, bringing the boat to the dock. Pull a little past your slip and then begin backing with both engines (always with your rudder amidships).

STEP 2 As you near the point that you need to pivot, pull the starboard engine in reverse and slide the port engine into forward.

STEP 3 As you move parallel to the slip, enter with both of your engines running in reverse, adjusting position by countering thrust and bumping in and out of gear when needed. When ready to tie up, put both engines in forward to arrest the movement and bring the boat to dock.

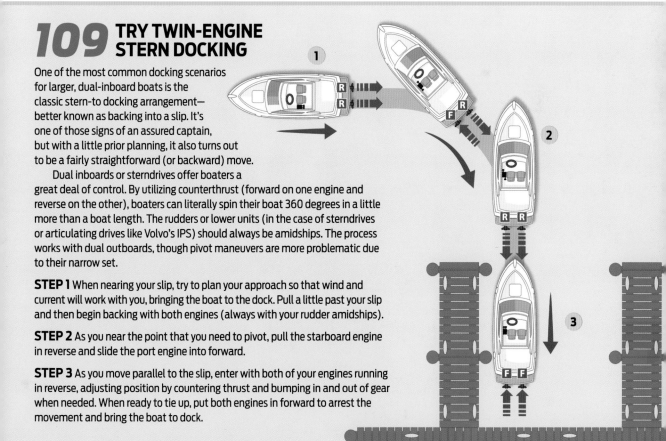

110 MAKE ALLIES WITH THE ELEMENTS

Docking's double-edged sword of wind and current causes fits with skippers lacking know-how. Those who've mastered some simple principles take wind and current in stride, often counting on an assisting push or a shove from the breeze or the water.

LOOSEN UP Fenders provide cushioning but can damage hull striping and graphics. If prevailing winds are blowing the right way, you can tie loosely to a dock in the short term, giving a few feet of slack and providing better protection against wakes. If the wind shifts, you can always retie.

GO AGAINST THE FLOW Let's say you're docking in a space that gives you barely any room between two other boats and you have no crew to help deploy a spring line. On approach, put the bow into the current and the engines in gear, giving just enough rpm to stay in place. Gently nudge the throttle a little at a time, ease up parallel to the open space, and jockey the wheel; you'll zigzag gently into the spot. Any boat has better steerage when at speed because of the increased flow of water across its rudder. By using the current you can control a "dead" boat as though it were still moving.

SLIP AND SLIDE When docking in a tough spot, wind and current (coupled with knowledge of how they affect your boat), plus situational awareness, can be better than an army of deckhands. If the current or wind runs at right angles to the slip, don't wait until the bow is even with the pilings before turning. Begin your turn earlier instead, allowing the boat to drift sideways; when you're lined up with the slip, scoot right in.

111 HEAVE A DOCK LINE

Thanks to joystick controls, almost anyone can dock a modern motoryacht like a pro. But if you're on the deck crew, there's still some skill to smart line-handling. One skill that's fairly easy to master—and sure to impress—is the art of tossing a coiled line.

STEP 1 Run the entire line through your hands to remove kinks or tangles. Let it fall loosely at your feet. Secure the tail or "bitter end" of the line by attaching it to a cleat, creating a loop and securing it to your wrist, or simply holding it under your foot.

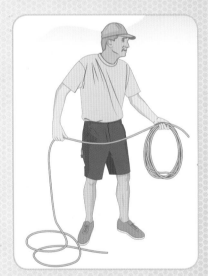

STEP 2 To ensure uniform coils, drop your left hand toward the thigh, lay the line over the open palm, and stretch the line out the full length of your right arm. Lay this length back into your left palm to create the first coil. You'll probably notice that the line likes to twist in a certain direction. Go with it, giving the rope a half-turn in this direction to allow subsequent coils to fall neatly into place.

STEP 3 Hook your left thumb over the existing coils once you've coiled about half the line; finish coiling the remaining length over your still outstretched fingers. This will naturally separate the coils into two halves. Keep one half in your left hand and transfer the other to your right. Keep at least three or four coils in your right hand to ensure enough weight for a proper toss.

STEP 4 With a coil in each hand, step into a sidearm throwing motion, releasing when the coils are about shoulder high. Let the weight of the thrown coil pull the loops from your opposite hand as well. If you're tossing to someone on the dock, aim a bit overhead so the line can drop across the body or outstretched arms. Aim low and you might clout the person in the face or cause a fumble on the catch.

112 BUILD A MOORING

Moorings are often a less costly alternative to docks. Just be sure local authorities say that it's OK to set a mooring in your area. Old engine blocks are not dependable; mushroom anchors will provide more security. A light boat up to 22 feet (6.7 m) long can get by with a 125-pound (56.7-kg) mushroom, but local regulation often dictates the size and type of anchor.

STEP 1 Connect the anchor to a ⅝-inch (1.6-cm) chain using a ⅝-inch (1.6-cm) shackle.

STEP 2 Attach the swivel shackle to the other end of the ⅝-inch (1.6-cm) chain and to one end of the 5/16-inch (8-mm) light chain.

STEP 3 Connect the other end of the 5/16-inch (8-mm) chain to the bottom of the buoy with the 5/16-inch (8-mm) shackle.

STEP 4 Wrap the shackle pins with seizing wire so the pins will not unscrew.

STEP 5 Eye-splice a thimble to one end of the ¾-inch (1.9-cm) line and make a 2-foot (61-cm) long eye splice in the other end to put over the boat's cleat.

STEP 6 Shackle this line to the top of the mooring buoy and secure the pin with wire.

STEP 7 For the pickup buoy, attach a thimble to the ¼-inch (6.3-mm) line and shackle it to the mooring buoy.

STEP 8 Splice or tie the other end to the ¾-inch (1.9-cm) mooring line.

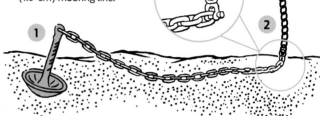

113 TAKE COMMAND

The outhaul technique, or clothesline moor, lets you get off a boat in water shallow enough to wade ashore, but also secure it so that a drop in water level won't leave it high and dry. As with any technique, the first time may be rough, but you'll nail it and adapt it to your circumstances.

The clothesline needs two anchors: one on the beach and one in the water. The shore anchor can be in situ, like a boulder or tree. The second anchor is your boat anchor; you'll also need line, and a pair of galvanized rings or pulleys (blocks) or some shackles attached to each anchor. (In weedy waters, a ring is less likely to become jammed, although it is a bit harder to heave the boat in than it is with a line rove through blocks.)

STEP 1 Wade ashore, secure the anchor, and return to your boat.

STEP 2 Head out deep enough to drop the seaward anchor in a spot that will carry your boat's draft at low tide. Reeve the line to its midpoint through the block or ring shackled to this anchor. Pay out the doubled line off the stern until the anchor is set, and cleat it off with one leg of the loop.

STEP 3 Motor to shore, paying out the other leg of the line as you go. On the beach, reeve the line through the block or ring of this anchor, bring it back to the boat, and cleat it off at the bow.

STEP 4 Heave on one end of the line to pull the boat out to the seaward anchor; heave on the other leg to bring it back in to the beach. Now dine ashore, hike in the woods, or camp for the night without fear of returning to the boat and finding it high and dry.

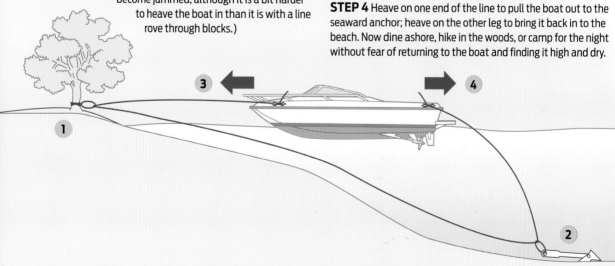

114 RIG A SLIP

Tying up in your berth is easy if you've got a floating dock. It's easier still if you're not on tidal waters, where the water level changes throughout the day. So while these tips apply in general to all, we picked the scenario wherein a tidewater boater uses a slip without a float. Tie one on with us.

HANG UP Your boat can't just be tied tight. You have to allow for the rise and fall of the water (A) lest the boat be left hanging by its lines at low tide or pulled under by its lines at high tide.

DOUBLE-CROSS IT Crossed stern lines (b) keep the boat from moving sideways. They also provide more length than uncrossed lines, helping to allow for changing water levels. But you can't just cross the lines and walk away.

FIND THE MAGIC SPOT The height at which the lines are secured on the pilings (C) is critical to ensure that there is enough slack for the boat to rise and fall. Check the boat through a few tides to nail this height down. Get a head start by tying off level with the cleat at half-tide.

GET SPRUNG Spring lines' length and height must also be factored from trial and error (D). Too long and your boat will bang the dock when current or wind is astern; too short and you'll have to make a leap to board during high tide. Experiment through several tides.

AVOID LOOPS Lines looped over cleats can become too tight to loosen during astronomically low and high tides (E). Use cleat hitches and you'll always be able to untie. Leave a length of tag end so that you can adjust for extremes in water level caused by weather events.

> **LINE UP** Bow and stern lines should be as long as the boat, spring lines 1.25 times the length. This will accommodate even the most extreme tidal ranges.

A

115 FLY THE FLAG

Whenever you enter foreign waters, you should always fly the quarantine flag—also known as the "Yellow Jack"—upon entering port, as a signal to authorities that you are requesting entry, and also upon returning to the United States after traveling from a foreign port. Once you've cleared customs and taken down the quarantine flag, the accepted practice is to fly a foreign courtesy flag, which is the accepted nautical flag for that particular country. Fly the flag off the bow or a starboard antenna if it's strong enough.

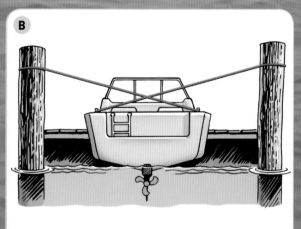

B

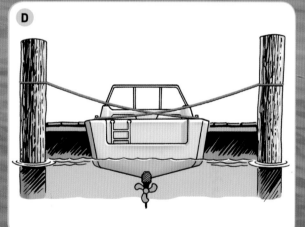

D

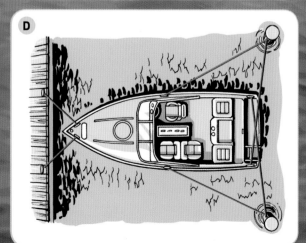

D

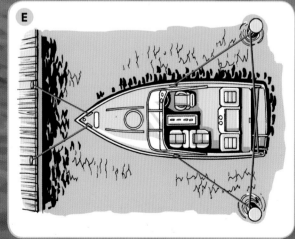

E

116 PRACTICE GOOD MANNERS

Boating traditions run deep and nowhere will you run afoul of more traditions than when at harbor. Good manners, while they may seem antiquated, are a must. Here are some things to remember the next time you're in a harbor, even if you're an Old Salt.

GO FENDERLESS As soon as you clear the dock, get your fenders in. Not only do you look more competent, you also minimize the risks of snagging a line on a prop or other obstacle.

FLY THE FLAG There are rules about how to fly the American flag. If your boat has a gaff, display it at the peak of the gaff (the outer end of the spar extending aft from the mast of your boat). If your boat does not, fly it from the flagstaff form the stern of your boat. An overhanging boom or an outboard motor obstructing your flag means you can offset the flagstaff to starboard (preferably) from your boat's centerline.

ASK PERMISSION It's common courtesy and custom to "request permission to come aboard" before you set foot on another person's boat.

POLICE YOUR BUTTS It's illegal to litter, no matter where you are on the water. Throwing things overboard in a harbor, especially cigarette butts, is disrespectful and harmful to the entire ecosystem.

STAY CLASSY We probably don't think much about hanging our clothes out to dry when we're at home. But harbor etiquette might consider it gauche. Be mindful, and dry them on shore, hang them to dry in the head or other part of the boat, or air 'em out once you're underway, just not at anchorage.

MIND YOUR PETS It's hard to predict how and where a dog is going to do its duty. Do your best to head straight to the pet-relief area of any marina and avoid any unnecessary "territory marking" along the way.

KEEP IT DOWN Especially across the water, sound carries. Be mindful and respectful. That also means silencing cell phones and turning off generators. If you need to charge your batteries overnight, go to an empty anchorage.

117 FOLLOW THE LEADER

One point of etiquette is absolute: The first boat into any harbor gets its choice of location. Later arrivals must not infringe upon the first boat by anchoring too close. In fact, this is the only rule of etiquette that actually has legal precedence; maritime courts have decided that an earlier arrival has the right-of-way even though it's at anchor. Boats that arrive later must stay clear and, if they don't, they will have to bear responsibility for any damage.

The "first-come, first-served" rule also applies to the anchoring style. If the first boat is lying to a single anchor, then all later boats should do the same. If the first boat has bow-and-stern hooks out, others must follow suit.

118

BE A GOOD NEIGHBOR

Once you're settled at anchor, don't stop being a good neighbor. If you plan to use your barbecue, don't go sending clouds of smoke into the boats downwind. If you need to run your engine to charge the batteries, pick a time when it isn't going to foul the anchorage with noise and fumes. And please don't impose your cellphone conversations on the entire anchorage, either.

MINIMIZE NOISE Whether your musical preference is Jimmy Buffett or Snoop Dogg, don't assume the rest of the anchorage is dying to listen. Remember that noise carries far on the water.

BE FRIENDLY One of the greatest pleasures of an anchorage is getting to cruise around in a dinghy, visiting with those aboard other boats. If you see people out on deck or in the cockpit, proper etiquette is that you approach on their starboard side to strike up a conversation.

TAKE YOUR TURN There are marina manners to heed as well. When you're stopping at the fuel dock, remember that other boats may be waiting for their turn—so ask before cutting in front of boats idling nearby. After you're fueled up, move out of the way if you need to shop for groceries or stretch your legs ashore, so others can get to the fuel pumps.

BE HANDS ON In the absence of a dockmaster or line handlers, it's always thoughtful to help out other boats approaching or departing the marina with their lines. Keep your area tidy, too. Coil up your docklines and hose, don't block the dock with barbecues or gear, and make sure that your shorepower cord isn't going to trip anyone.

119

DON'T BE A DRAG

If your anchor drags, you're the burdened vessel in the eyes of the law and you must keep clear of all other boats. Everyone drags anchor at some point; it's how you handle the situation that makes the difference. If letting out more scope doesn't stop the dragging, up anchor as soon as possible and move to a spot with a better bottom for the anchor to bite so you don't bang into other boats. This situation is better resolved sooner rather than later because the burdened vessel is the one responsible for any damages.

120

GO IN SLOW

It's common in an anchorage to be anxious to get to shore, talk with your friends, or get to the bar. However, don't let the excitement get to you. Don't go full throttle on your dinghy because there might be people (especially kids) swimming near the boats and plenty of other hidden obstacles in the way. Be cautious on your way to and from your boat.

121 ANCHOR POLITELY

Most boaters know not to anchor in the middle of a navigable channel or fairway. But not every anchoring scenario is so cut and dried. How's your anchoring etiquette? Here are a few basics.

FOLLOW THE LEADER Let's say you motor to a cozy cove for a picnic. Rounding the headland, you see another boat already anchored, swinging by a single hook. Etiquette dictates that you follow suit (A), deploying a single anchor off the bow at a location that will keep both boats clear of each other should wind or tide change direction.

PREPARE TO SHARE Now, let's invert the scenario. Instead of a remote cove, you pull up to the local "hot spot" sandbar on a summer Saturday. In such places, it's almost always the rule to deploy two anchors—one off the bow and one off the stern—which allows more boats to enjoy the anchorage (B). If you are first in, take the trouble to deploy the two anchors. Your protests of being "first in" are sure to be shouted down once the fleet arrives.

HOLD OFF Once the hook is set, don't just hop overboard and head off seeking fun (or clams, or picnic baskets). That risks dragging into other boats. Ensure your anchor is holding by taking shore ranges. You need at least two landmarks to get a "transit range." A house in the foreground and a steeple behind it are good examples (C). As long as they stay lined up, your boat is securely anchored. If two shores are within sight, take a range on structures on either side of your boat. If your boat remains between them, you're set. Grab that clam bucket and go wild!

122 CALCULATE SWING RATIO

Once you've anchored, your boat will almost certainly swing in a circle around the anchor point. Take the time to calculate a safe size for that circle, to determine the correct length for your anchor rode. You'll hear different rules of thumb (see item 123), but the basic starting point is usually assumed to be 7:1 where 1 is the corrected water depth. What does that mean? Read on, it gets a little mathy.

STEP 1 Determine the charted depth in the spot you're planning to anchor, using navigational charts or your GPS.

STEP 2 Next, look up how far the tide will rise to high tide.

STEP 3 Estimate your bow freeboard (the distance from your boat's bow to the water surface), then add all three of these numbers together to get your corrected water depth.

STEP 4 This number is the "1" in your 7:1 ratio. Do the math to determine how much anchor rode to pay out. Here's an example:

Let's say your charts and tables give you 12 feet (3.7 m) of charted depth and a 5-foot (1.5-m) rise at high tide, and your bow freeboard measures 3 feet (0.9 m). Those add up to 20 feet (6.1 m) of corrected water depth.

Remember your high-school algebra? A 7:1 ratio equals 140:20. You will want to use 140 feet (42.7 m) of anchor rode. The maximum swing circle will be 280 feet (85.3 m) in diameter (we just switched from algebra to geometry there).

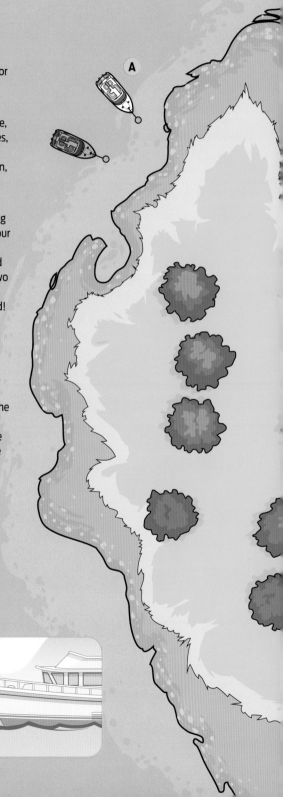

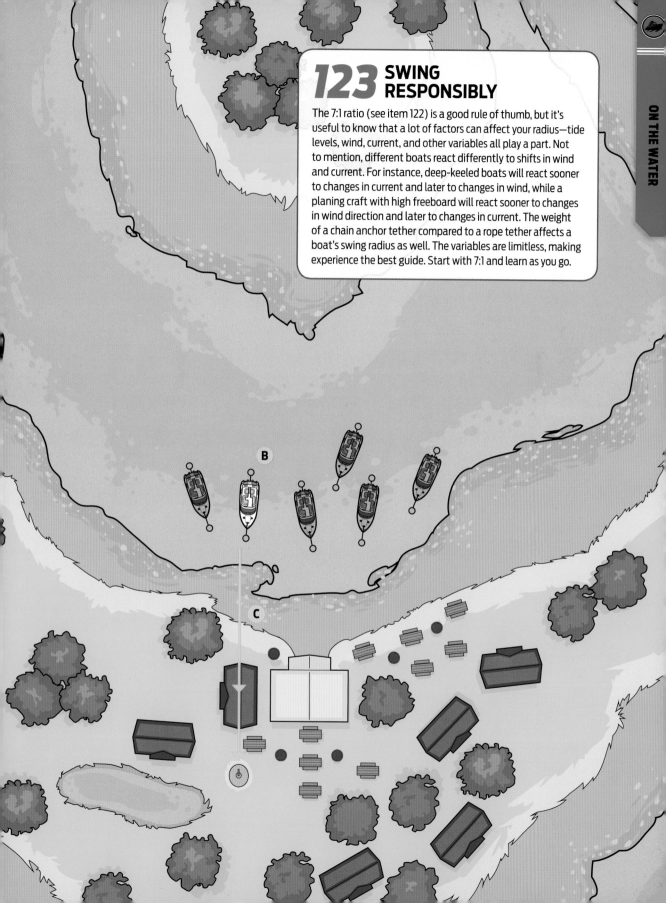

123 SWING RESPONSIBLY

The 7:1 ratio (see item 122) is a good rule of thumb, but it's useful to know that a lot of factors can affect your radius—tide levels, wind, current, and other variables all play a part. Not to mention, different boats react differently to shifts in wind and current. For instance, deep-keeled boats will react sooner to changes in current and later to changes in wind, while a planing craft with high freeboard will react sooner to changes in wind direction and later to changes in current. The weight of a chain anchor tether compared to a rope tether affects a boat's swing radius as well. The variables are limitless, making experience the best guide. Start with 7:1 and learn as you go.

124 ANCHOR FROM THE COCKPIT

I see a lot of boatmen anchoring from astern. Not good. Even boat wakes can swamp a stern-anchored boat. Here's one way to anchor safely from the cockpit when traveling solo. You'll need an anchor roller and a hollow-base cleat or set of chocks to the bow, so install these as indicated.

To use, starting with the anchor in the roller, bring the rode back to the cockpit, passing it through the chock or cleat base on the bow. With the rode in the cockpit and the anchor in the bow roller, cleat the anchor line to a spring cleat. This keeps the pull on the boat from the bow, so your vessel will still lie bow to the wind and waves. Use another cleat or chock as a "fair-lead" in running the rode aft, so that it doesn't bear upon your windshield or cabin side.

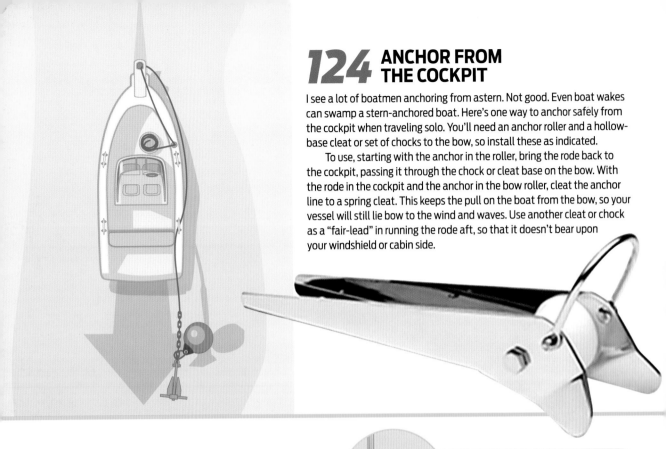

125 RIG A REMOTE ANCHOR

Dealing with mooring when you're sailing solo can be a challenge sometimes, but not an insurmountable one by any means. Let's say that you're by yourself out on the water and you need to get off your mooring. The wind is blowing, or the current's running, and the mooring field is crowded. You're alone. If you go forward and drop the painter, by the time you scramble back to the helm, you likely will have drifted into a neighboring boat. A neat solution is to "cat the painter"—that is, to rig a quick release that allows you to drop the painter from the helm. Here's how.

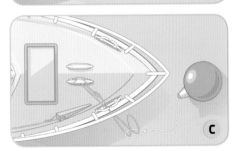

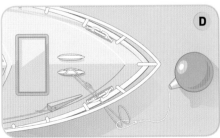

CUT A WEDGE Make a simple wooden wedge out of scrap (A), about 8 inches (20 cm) long, an inch (2.5 cm) thick, and tapering in width from 3 inches (7.6 cm) to 1 inch (2.5 cm). Drill a hole in the wide end and attach a length of stout cord long enough to reach from your bow to your helm.

TIE IT OFF Next, double a length of line and cleat it off at the bow (see item 126). Run the loop through a chock or the base of another cleat (B).

LOOP IT UP Remove the painter from your bow eye or cleat and take it over to the cleat with the loop rove through. Pass the loop through the thimbled eye of your painter, back through the cleat or chock and over the wedge (C).

Note: If the painter's eye fits through a cleat base, you don't need the doubled line. Just insert the loop through the cleat and then insert your wedge through the painter's eye.

HEAD ON OUT Wedge-secured, return to the helm with the "leash" for the wedge in hand. Start the engine. Tug on the leash to drop the painter (D), then maneuver away with all due care.

126 TIE A CLEAT HITCH

This basic boating knot is the best way to secure a line to a cleat on your boat or on the dock. As such, you'll use it almost constantly. In fact, in no time at all you'll tie it almost without thinking, and forget you ever even had to learn.

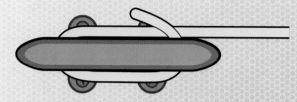

STEP 1 Begin by passing the working end of the rope in a full turn around the cleat. Continue under one horn, over the cleat, and under the other horn in a figure-eight.

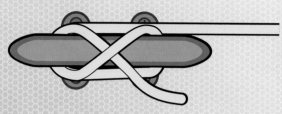

STEP 2 Bring the working end around the horns again in another figure-eight.

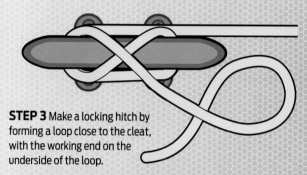

STEP 3 Make a locking hitch by forming a loop close to the cleat, with the working end on the underside of the loop.

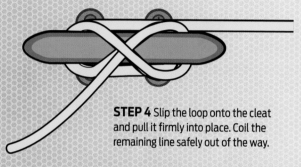

STEP 4 Slip the loop onto the cleat and pull it firmly into place. Coil the remaining line safely out of the way.

127 AVOID HANG-UPS

A hung anchor is one of those annoyances that can really put a crimp in your day. If you sometimes head into sketchy territory in pursuit of fish, or should you find yourself needing to anchor over "sticky" bottom while cruising, trip-wiring your anchor can help get you out of trouble. Here's how to rig it.

Many anchors have a hole in the forward part of the shank for this very purpose, but you can drill a hole in the crown if there isn't one. Next, shackle the bitter end of the chain to the hole, and then run it back along the shank, wiring a link to the normal shackle point. A length of thick, solid copper wire, like stripped residential wire, works well for this; nylon tie-wraps can also do the job. If you should foul the anchor, the wire or wraps will then break under enough pressure, thus allowing you to pull the anchor out by the crown rather than the tail of the shank. Always keep some extra wire aboard to rerig the anchor if needed.

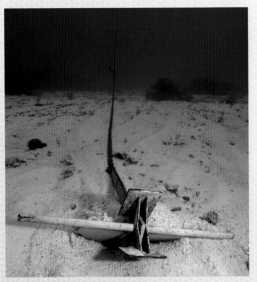

128 BREAK FREE

In that dreaded moment when the windlass groans under strain as the rode stretches taut, you realize that your anchor is hung. There's no one guaranteed way to deal with a fouled anchor, so be prepared to be both patient and resourceful.

GET A NEW ANGLE Whether or not you've rigged a tripwire, you may well need to try a few different angles before you hit on the right one for retrieving your anchor. For example, if you're scoped out with the bow at 180 degrees, try pulling the anchor out backward by pulling on the rode from 0 degrees. Be careful not to foul the anchor line in a prop as you reposition, and be cautious not to swamp the cockpit if you are backing into seas.

TUG ON IT Don a pair of gloves and prepare to tug—making sure to avoid wrapping the line around your hands. Pull the fouled line up by hand, stretching it as tightly as possible, and then let go. The recoil from this often causes the anchor to shoot away from the snag. It might take a few tries!

CUT YOUR LOSSES If you foul the anchor in rough conditions, your best bet is almost certainly to cut your losses—literally—and head back to the harbor. Things can go wrong very quickly out in heavy seas, especially if you are in a small boat. Always keep a sharp knife handy so that you can immediately cut free if needed. New ground tackle is relatively inexpensive, especially when the cost is compared with your crew's safety.

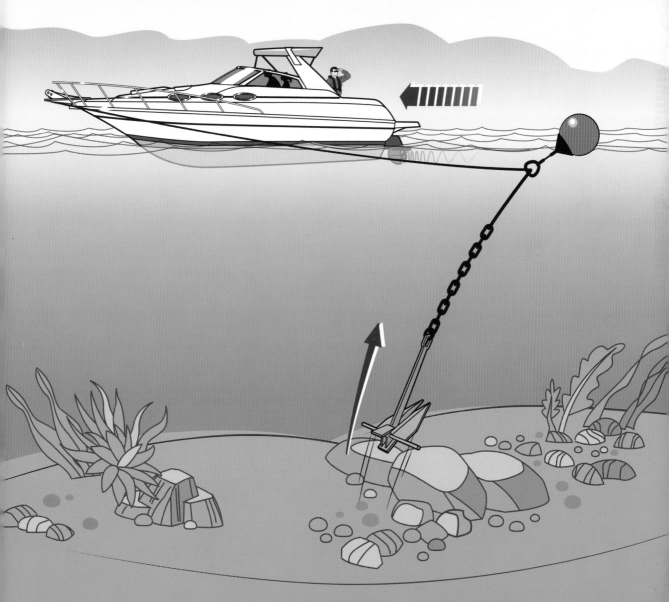

129 THINK ABOUT COMPASSES

The compass is an easily overlooked but vital piece of boating equipment. Out on the water, it's taken for granted—that is, until it's needed. If one did not come standard on your new ride, you would be wise to install one because even electronic equipment can fail and, if it does, you want to be prepared.

READABILITY Find the most readable compass for your helmsman and their positioning. Flat cards often have a lip like a saucer that is read easiest from above. Front reading compasses are domed and best read at about eye level. Dual-reading cards combine elements of both the flat card and the front reading card. If you're quite mobile (standing and sitting), a dual reading compass is probably the best for you as it offers the most variable viewing angles.

SIZING If you're traveling long distances, you'll want a larger compass because you'll be checking it constantly. So you'll want it as easy to read as possible.

MOUNTING Space is likely to be your biggest concern when mounting your compass. Compasses should be mounted as far away as possible from iron and any magnetic sources such as speakers. Flush mounting is the most integrated looking, but does require a level surface, a fair amount of space, and a hole cut in to your boat. Bulkhead mounting is the same as flush mounting except that it is vertical instead of horizontal. Limited console space means bracket mounting is best, since it requires the least amount of real estate and can be easily swiveled to suit your needs. Conversely, binnacle mounts take up the most room and are mounted on top of the console or dashboard.

GIMBALING While gimbaled compasses are more expensive, they're worth it because they are more stable, easier to read, and remain level over a wider range of angles compared to nongimbaled compasses.

130 GET YOUR BEARINGS

How far are we from shore? With GPS, that's easy to answer. But long before electronics, experienced mariners had a bag full of tricks to help estimate their distance and position relative to a given shoreline. With just a chart and a compass, you can get a pretty good fix on your position.

Using the center of the compass (your heading) as the first reference point, find a conspicuous landmark on shore as the second (A). With one eye, follow the sight line from compass center to the landmark, making note of the numeric bearing it intersects on the outer edge of the compass. Repeat the process with a second landmark (B). At this point, you'll have two sets of bearings—say 270 degrees to the old lighthouse and 330 to the water tower. Now figure reciprocal bearing (the number on the opposite side of the compass) for each of these. For bearings more than 180 degrees, subtract 180; for less, add 180. (You'd be 90 degrees off of the old lighthouse and 150 from the water tower.) Get out your chart and parallel rules, and using the compass rose, draw bearing lines outward from the landmarks. Your estimated position is where these lines intersect (C).

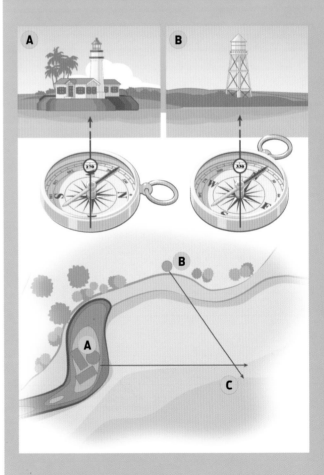

131 GIVE YOURSELF A HAND

There may come a time when you need to estimate distance and position without the aid of electronics. Fortunately, this requires nothing more complex than your upraised hand.

First, pick a landmark on shore and extend your arm with one finger raised. Close one eye and cover the landmark with your finger. Now switch eyes, and note that the finger jumps to another point on the horizon.

It just so happens that the distance between your eyes and your outstretched finger is ten times the distance between your two eyes. Without going into all of the geometry behind this fact, suffice it to say that the distance between two objects measured using the "eye blink" method will be about one-tenth that of your distance from those objects. Multiply that eye-blink distance by ten and you'll know just how far from shore you are.

132 AVOID A COLLISION

The cardinal rule of navigation: Two boats should never occupy the same coordinates. Even if you're an experienced skipper, the other guy may not be. Fortunately, there are a number of useful safety tools at your disposal; you might already own one or two.

RADAR A marine radar lets you put an invisible guard zone around your boat at a set distance. Any object picked up inside it will trigger an alert. The radar's electronic bearing line (ELB) and variable range marker (VRM) can help you keep tabs on a nearby vessel. ELB provides relative bearing to a target; VRM determines its exact distance. (Tip: Line up the ELB on a target that is headed toward you. Should it keep crawling down the ELB line toward the center of the screen, you need to take evasive action.)

AIS Automatic Identification System (AIS) places a triangular icon on a dedicated screen, or right on most current chart-plotter displays, when an AIS-equipped vessel is in your area. This reveals the exact position, speed, heading, and more. This is a great tool for understanding commercial traffic, and for staying out of harm's way when boating near large commercial vessels that might not see you and can't stop in time.

HAILERS Essentially a bullhorn/speaker unit, hailers are often overlooked as anticollision devices, and they are also essential for communicating with a nearby vessel. A hailer's foghorn function broadcasts your presence to all vessels in the vicinity. The listen feature helps you hear nearby craft and buoys, and warn you of waves breaking on shore to keep you from running aground at night. Look for a hail or public address feature on your VHF. Usually all you will need to do is to mount a hailer or PA speaker on deck.

NIGHT VISION There are basically two types of night-vision technologies: scopes that take a small amount of background light—even starlight—and night-vision cameras, which depict very slight temperature differences in objects and then display them as a detailed picture.

133 LEAVE A TOUGH BERTH

There are no hard and fast steps for close-quarters maneuvering. Every boat handles differently, and the number of scenarios is unlimited. But there are some principles and practices that, if understood for one situation, can be applied with other techniques to get you out of a tough spot with grace.

One common predicament finds you tied to a fuel deck with an onshore breeze pressing your boat against the bulkhead. Leave this berth using forward gear, and you'll bump the dock with your stern. You might never get off, as each transom bump straightens the boat's heading, negating your efforts at the wheel. Remember that boats steer from the back. Put the helm hard over, away from the dock, then put the engine in reverse. Don't be shy with the throttle. The stern will move away from the dock, and the bow will follow. You will have made a U-turn going backward that will get you clear without a bump.

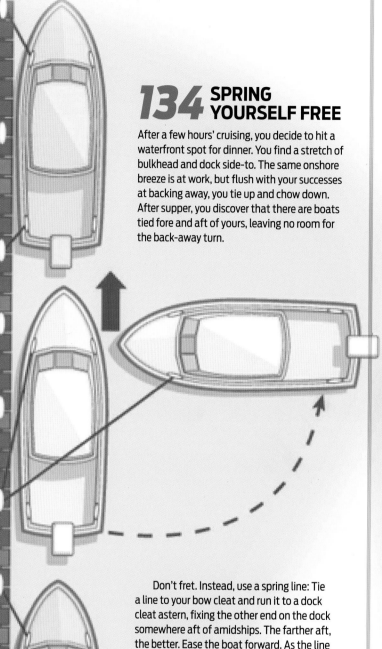

134 SPRING YOURSELF FREE

After a few hours' cruising, you decide to hit a waterfront spot for dinner. You find a stretch of bulkhead and dock side-to. The same onshore breeze is at work, but flush with your successes at backing away, you tie up and chow down. After supper, you discover that there are boats tied fore and aft of yours, leaving no room for the back-away turn.

Don't fret. Instead, use a spring line: Tie a line to your bow cleat and run it to a dock cleat astern, fixing the other end on the dock somewhere aft of amidships. The farther aft, the better. Ease the boat forward. As the line comes tight, the stern will swing seaward—turning the wheel toward the dock helps this along. Do this until you are bow-on to the dock. Release the line and back away. This may require some scurrying if you're alone. With crew aboard, assign someone to "tail" the spring line. So, instead of hitching the line to the cleat, have someone maintain pressure until you give the signal to release it.

135 LOOK LEEWARD

Let's say you decide to visit a friend's marina so you can regale him with your tales of dock-leaving mastery. When it's time to go, the wind is again on your beam, but even stronger now. You're tied bow-on in a slip, your stern lines fixed to pilings aft. You don't even want to think about bumping your boat or someone else's. Help yourself out by remembering that a slack line does no work. Remove the lines on the downward side first, since only the lines to weather are holding your boat in position. After releasing the windward lines, back out without hesitation. Had the windward lines been released first, you'd have banged that woody before you even put the boat in gear.

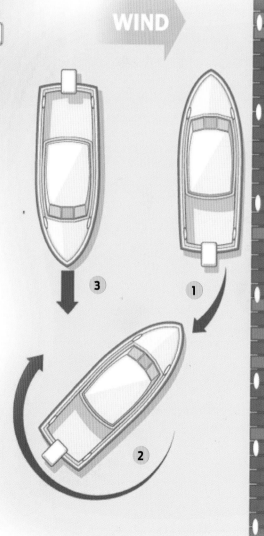

136 TAKE THE ELEVATOR

A lock is how a waterborne vessel traverses differences in elevation. It's essentially a gated channel that a boat enters; the lock is then filled with water to raise the boat up, or drained of water to let the boat down so that the boat can continue its journey.

When you're using a lock, shut your engines off, even if you're just locking-through for a few minutes. Toxic exhaust fumes can be dumped on boats lower in the lock, it's loud enough to the point that your engine noise can cause ear damage, and it's just plain all-around annoying.

Many locks are also equipped with traffic lights. Red means stop and stay back a prudent distance; yellow means approach the lock, but do not enter; green means enter the lock. A yellow light does not mean proceed into the lock with caution; it actually signals boaters to position themselves to see inside the lock, making sure no boats from the opposite direction have yet to exit, and to anticipate the final approach to tying up against the lock sides.

137 WATCH THE TRAFFIC

A beautiful summer day on the boat should be relaxing. But when boaters without basic knowledge of commercial shipping play in traffic, that nice day can quickly turn tragic. The basic truth is that in a collision between a 28-foot (8.5-m) boat and a 1,000-foot (305-m) tanker, there will only ever be one outcome for the small boat.

CLEAR THE CHANNEL If you should see a ship approaching a channel from a few miles (around 5 km) out, clear the area and then stay away until it has passed through. Moving to the side is not enough. If a ship loses its steering or breaks a rudder, it can take a shear (unexpectedly turning to one side).

DON'T DROP ANCHOR In an active channel? Say the anchor gets stuck or you can't restart the engines; a large commercial vessel won't be able to stop in time or take evasive action. Any accident will be your fault. You are not allowed to impede a vessel transiting a narrow channel or fairway that's constrained by its draft or ability to maneuver.

DON'T DISAPPEAR From the helm of big tankers, the pilot can lose sight of you from as far as five football fields (500 m) away. If he doesn't know where you are, all he can do is keep going straight.

DON'T CUT IN FRONT If you cut too closely in front of a ship and the engine quits or you get stuck, there's no way it can stop in time to avoid you. If you have to cross a commercial vessel's path, cross on the stern.

COMMUNICATE AIS is a great tool for understanding local commercial traffic. Barring that, monitor Channel 13 to hear wheelhouse-to-wheelhouse communication. If you've broken down in the shipping lane and don't have a VHF or AIS, wave something orange such as a life jacket. If the pilot knows you're in trouble, he'll call the Coast Guard for you.

138 LEARN THE LIGHTS

The U.S. Coast Guard has long-established a set of light-display standards for nighttime navigation, and these rules apply to both vessels and navaids, such as channel markers. If you know the navigation light patterns, you can identify any type of vessel and its activity, as well as determine where to safely enter and exit a harbor at night.

If you do much night boating, knowing the meaning of lights is essential and might save your boat and your life. For example, you see two vessels in the distance and they're a few hundred yards apart. So to save time, you think about cutting between the two. However, if one of those vessels is displaying three-stacked white lights on the masthead, going between them could be fatal, because the vessel is a tug towing a barge (the second vessel) with a massive hawser. Cut between them, and at best the hawser will rip out your running gear; at worst it will saw across your deck and everything on it.

139 BE POLITE AT BRIDGES

When transiting bridges, it's not uncommon for a kind of slow-speed race to develop. The boats begin without leaving wakes. Then, apparently some deep psychological trigger fires up the competitive instinct. A skipper realizes that the other boat is going to "beat" him. At this point, some otherwise civilized folks begin increasing throttle in an attempt to pass, as everyone tries to squeeze through the opening. Calls for reason are usually futile.

While 5 knots might be "wake free," this kind of 5 knots that creates a roiling wave as the transom is pulled down by increased propeller torque. Upset by such a wake, an idling boat can lose control or be carried aside into the bridge or another boat. So hang back, slow down and let the other guy go. Once one boat starts acting squirrelly in close quarters, a domino effect occurs. Better to be clear of that fray.

140 RIDE SMOOTH IN HEAD SEAS

A head sea refers to waves coming from directly ahead. Running in head seas is a rough experience. Ease that experience by trying these tips the next time you're headed directly into the waves.

SLOW DOWN Pounding occurs because the boat stops short. The faster you come down off the previous wave, the faster your boat will slow down when it hits the next, and the harder you will pound. Back off the throttle to mitigate the pounding.

RIDE IT OUT Riding the chine (the point of the boat where the two sides converge) presents a sharp, narrow corner to the waves. It's wetter and a bit awkward, but it softens blows. This is all relative to hull design, since a sharp, narrow hull sinks deeper into the water than a wider, flatter one before coming up short, and thus slow down slower instead of fetching up abruptly. If your boat has minimal deadrise (the vertical distance between the keel and its chine), heel it over using trim tabs, or by shifting weight or crew.

KEEP IT LEVEL Get a deep-V boat's deadrise working for you by keeping it level for the softest ride (A). If your boat leans in to the wind, instead of riding a sharp-V section, you're riding on the flatter panel between keel and chine. You can also change course so that the wind is no longer abeam, but it's more realistic to shift weight or use tabs to keep your boat on its lines (B).

GET TACKING In large swells, you can achieve a smoother ride by bearing off a few points instead of hitting the crests head-on. Crossing on a diagonal keeps more of your hull supported as you go over the crest, letting the boat ride rather than fall. This costs time, but rough water is likely to slow you down anyway.

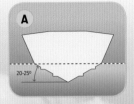

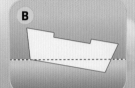

141

BE SAFE IN LOW VISIBILITY

Low visibility afloat typically comes from fog, rain, or snow; darkness itself doesn't necessarily mean low visibility. You can see at night if it's not otherwise "weathering" out. But you can't see a thing in pea-soup fog, torrential downpour, or squalling snow. Here's what to do when nature draws the drapes.

STAY SLOW Make enough speed to maintain steerage, but definitely stay off plane. If the current or wind is setting you off course, compensate with the wheel, not the throttle, steering a tad upwind. Engage the autopilot if you have it. You need to be able to avoid what appears in front of you, and you won't be able to do that if you are zooming around.

GET RADAR Most of us do. And we use it in fair weather and in foul. We can't list all the times we've come upon a boat idling beside the buoy clearly noted on screen. Many boaters find security in hanging near a buoy in the fog. Your radar may not resolve the two as separate targets. Additionally, radar may not see logs and other debris. Use the technology—but not as a crutch to go fast.

SET A WATCH A crew member on the bow has a completely unobstructed view. Plus, they're closer to any boat, marker, or flotsam you might encounter, so they'll see it first. And it goes without saying, with a loved one forward, you'll be keeping your speed moderate.

LISTEN UP Lighthouses, boats, and buoys all make noise; you'll hear them before you see them. Crash surf or general life noise can help you hear where land might be. Some boaters are unfamiliar with the various fog signals, so here's a quick update: A prolonged blast of a horn every two minutes is a powerboat under way; two prolonged blasts every two minutes means a powerboat under way but not making way; a ringing bell means a powerboat at anchor. Of course, you can't hear any of this with the motor roaring, so (once again) slow down.

142 LIGHT THE MOOD

Onboard lighting is a tricky thing when navigating at night. You need backlighting to see your instruments and electronics, and an overhead light to read a chart. Yet once your eyes have acclimated to the dark, too much light can destroy your night vision. Once this happens, your eyes need to readjust, which can take as long as 40 minutes. Most marine electronics allow you to adjust the brightness of the backlighting, and many units also have a "night mode" with a darker background to keep illumination levels to a minimum.

143 HAVE AN ILLUMINATING EXPERIENCE

When it comes to instrument panel illumination, red is the best color since it doesn't desensitize the rods of your eyes. Most newer instruments are equipped with dimmers to adjust the intensity of backlighting and help preserve night vision. If yours isn't, a dimmer switch can be wired in for control. Most dimmers handle only one type of lighting, such as incandescent, halogen, or LED. However, some can handle any or all of these lights at the same time. Overhead and chart lights are also available in red—including low-draw LED versions—should you need to read something at the helm. Keep the lighting dim to preserve your night vision.

144 LIGHT UP THE NIGHT

Boats don't have headlights, and with good reason. In open water, light reflecting off waves and mist is often more blinding than beneficial at night. Shine a light ahead of the boat at night while under way when there's nothing to see but water and sky, and you'll agree. However, there are occasions when a searchlight or spotlight is handy, particularly if you are trying to locate or identify a nearby object such as an unlit boat, buoy, shoreline, or jetty.

There are three basic types of spotlights: fixed-mount, remote-control searchlights, and rechargeable battery-operated handhelds. Fixed-mounts are nice on bigger boats, while handhelds lend themselves better to smaller boats. Whichever you choose, try to use the light sparingly and briefly, particularly if there are other boaters in the immediate vicinity. The harsh glare of a spotlight is not only annoying to others, but also can ruin the night vision of nearby skippers.

Docking lights are another option, usually flush-mounted just below the rub rail on both sides of the bow. They are designed for use only in close-quarters situations such as when pulling into a slip at night. They don't cast their beam far enough to be of much use even though they resemble auto headlights.

145 TAKE IT SLOW

The first rule of night boating is to slow down, no matter what high-tech navigation equipment you have on board. Even on a moonlit evening, you just can't see as well as during the day. Objects won't come into view until they are fairly close. If you are going too fast, you might not be able to maneuver quickly enough to avoid a collision with an unlit object such as a crab-pot buoy or floating timber.

The best speed on any given night depends on visibility. During a full moon, you might feel comfortable running the boat a bit faster than you would on a night when everything fades to black. Are you out in open isolated water, or are you bound by the confines of a narrow channel? The locale plays into how fast is safe as well. The important thing is not to rush. Just like on a romantic date, take it easy, cowboy.

146 GET SOME RADAR LOVE

Seeing everything that's around you at night makes you feel more confident while cruising, and that's just what radar (radio detection and ranging) really is meant to be: your sight when your eyes are blind. It shows you what's out there and tells you how far away it is. Ask a group of experienced boaters what they rely on when they're out at night—besides their own eyes—and most will say radar.

BANG ON While a chart plotter shows fixed objects, radar can show you just about everything above the water's surface, including other boats. Older radars lose effectiveness at very close range due to a phenomenon called "main bang," which results in a blob in the middle of the screen that obscures targets close to the boat. However, newer radars don't have the main bang, so they can read an object very close to the boat. While such units are not very effective at ranges beyond a few miles (around 5 km), the close-in target detection feature can be useful when cruising crowded waters in the dark.

LAY OUT A CHART Most multifunction displays also can be configured to "overlay" the radar readings on an electronic chart display. This provides an enhanced view of the surroundings at night, and also allows you to more readily interpret the radar images, relating them immediately to objects on the chart. Plus, you know any radar target that is not on the chart is most likely another boat or barge, though it could also be an off-station buoy.

GUARD YOURSELF You can also set the radar guard zone, but in crowded waters with lots of fixed objects, the guard zone alarm tends to sound too frequently. This feature is most helpful when cruising open water far from the clutter of the harbor.

147 SCOPE THINGS OUT

Night vision technology amplifies dim light to increase night visibility. This amplification lets you see as if it were daytime, though everything's cast in green. For tricky harbor entrances or foreboding shorelines, night vision is tough to beat.

An affordable night-vision device will cost about $300. These scopes are small and compact, but they make a huge difference even for experienced captains. Quality rechargeable scopes do not only amplify available light, but also beam infrared light.

Though it's invisible to unaided human eyes, the reflected infrared light is picked up by the scope and illuminates objects up to 200 feet (61 m) away. Especially at night, with the risk of other boaters nearby and any number of other objects, that added visibility could be the difference between returning safely and a catastrophe.

35° 30' 16" N – 12° 36' 35" E

148 CHOOSE THE RIGHT FISHING BOAT

Fishing boats tend more toward the rugged end of the scale as far as amenities go. That's not to say that "fish boats" are without amenity. Many of today's models rival cruisers and runabouts while retaining seakeeping and high levels of fishability. While you can fish from a wide range of boat types, if fishing is your main activity on the water, take this into account when shopping for and setting up your vessel. Here are some things to keep in mind.

WATER The waters you want to fish in should be a consideration when choosing a boat. Fishing in the ocean means you need a higher-grade steel to resist corrosion than you would need for a freshwater boat. Size matters if you're running offshore. So if the choice boils down to two or three extra feet in length, opt for the bigger boat if you plan on serious blue-water fishing. You'll truly appreciate the upgrade when battling mean, green, foaming seas miles offshore or running a windswept inlet on an outgoing tide.

HULL If shallow-water trips are part of your fishing, check the draft of the hull. Manufacturers' specs reflect the draft at rest with the outboard motor tilted up, and no fuel, gear, or people in the boat. That changes once the outboard is down and the boat is loaded. Ask for a measurement with the outboard down; remember that draft will increase when accelerating from a standing start but decrease when on plane.

POWER Most big sport-fishers come equipped with twin diesels, but center-consoles and walkarounds often have outboard motors. Still, there are variations. With inboards, you can order different horsepower or brands, as well as different drives—straightshafts, pods, and sometimes sterndrives. With outboards, you can vary the number of engines and horsepower.

LAYOUT Will you need access to the bow for cast-netting? Consider a center-console with plenty of walk-around space. Do you fish on anchor, working baits from the cockpit? If so, does the transom design allow you to fight a fish around the stern?

STORAGE If you want a boat for wakeboarding, you want room for people. If you're buying a boat mainly for fishing, look for room for tackle, rods, and catch. Be sure you have enough cold storage, with compartments that are insulated and drain or pump overboard.

COMFORT Fishing is but a fraction of the time spent aboard your boat. Much is spent running or trolling; no one wants to stand up all the time. Have places for crew to sit—cushioned ice chests, flip-down aft bench seats, jump seats in aft corners, or seating near the helm.

149 SLEEP ON IT

Some anglers return to port at the end of each day, and others like the idea of spending the night at distant anchorages on multiday trips. Center-consoles are great, but a cabin with berths, galley, and a head compartment makes sense for overnighting. This also is convenient for crew to catch some winks on long runs or for the occasional family outing. Keep in mind, also, that many buyers envision overnighting, but actual sleepovers usually are rare.

150 GET HIGH

Elevation can offer an important angling advantage in various situations, such as sight-fishing for cobia off the beach, tailing marlin offshore, or chasing down schools of redfish on the flats. Marine fabricators can build towers for anything from sport-fishing yachts to Texas-style sleds. Also, consider a second station in the tower so you can drive the boat from aloft, as well as from the helm. For trailer boats, make sure the tower folds down for towing and storage.

151 ADD ROD HOLDERS

If your fishing boat doesn't have enough rod holders, there are a number of ways to add some in, such as a second-tier rocket launcher on the leaning post, holders clamped along the aft rail of the flybridge, or a rack bolted to the bait tank.

152 GO IT ALONE

If you sometimes like to—or have to—go out solo to fish, take that into account. After all, just departing the dock or launching the boat can be difficult all by yourself, let alone fighting in a big fish while keeping your boat under control. With a center-console or bay boat, solo trips are very doable. With an express or flybridge type boat, however, you might need crew to go fishing.

153 GET THE RIGHT BOAT FOR TOWING

Because water skiing has mutated into so many different tow sports, from boarding to skating to surfing, one boat doesn't fit all needs. Today, each sport has its own preferred wake size and shape, and boatbuilders have devised a host of ways to respond. It all starts with the power and how it's delivered.

BE DIRECT Installed amidships, direct-drive inboards provide the quick planing, minimal wake, and precision tracking required by tournament skiers. It helps the hull to plane quickly for easy starts. The engine's location, along with a relatively flat hull, means little deadrise, and thus creates the small wakes and straight tracking desired by water-skiers. A low wake table and less turbulence also means a good ride for barefooters.

DRIVE ON V-Drive boats are excellent for big wakes and increased space, meaning they're perfect for wakeboarding! V-drive engines are installed aft and backwards, turning the shaft through V-shaped gears and weighting the stern for bigger wakes. The V-drive also opens up the cockpit for increased space, passenger movement, seating, and stowage.

CROSS OVER Maybe you have found yourself wanting the perks of both direct drive and V-drive. Dual-purpose models exist for the water-sports enthusiasts who do it all and the people who can't decide. The crossover is either a direct-drive or V-drive model that shares wake and tow characteristics with the other style.

BE STERN Sterndrives provide a more affordable, mainstream power option for a family that's looking for a more versatile boat. Their layout spells great ride and plenty of storage (sometimes even a changing room), and the deadrise boosts wake height, which can be further adjusted with trim: down for barefooting, up for skiing, and even higher for wakeboarding.

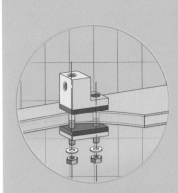

154 BACK IT UP

Before installing a towing tower on your boat, make sure it'll be placed sturdily and accurately. A backing block in the area where you'll put your tower will help beef things up. As with any other aftermarket installations, apply masking tape and mark the area to ensure accuracy and prevent chipping your gelcoat.

155 DECK OUT YOUR TOW BOAT

You don't need to hit up a showroom for the latest and greatest specialized ski boat. There are plenty of ways to accessorize your own vessel and enhance your time with tow sports on the water. Here are the important ones.

TOWER OVER THE REST You can use transom eyes as tow points, since most boats don't have tow pylons, but higher is better. Installing a tower means easier towing since it's several feet above the deck. Family boats can easily accommodate this add-on, there are plenty of factory and aftermarket versions, and they're even removable.

CONTROL YOURSELF Precise speed is important for every skier and wake-boarder, from beginner to expert. Speed controls, available in GPS- or rpm- based versions, make it easy to get the skier up and navigate without giving them a rough ride behind the boat.

LOWER THE BOOM Essentially a long bar attached to the tower or pylon and extending about 11 feet (3.3 cm) to the side of the boat, a boom lets a skier stay in sight of the boat crew, easing communication and coaching. It's even better for barefooters since they learn more quickly on a boom than the traditional tow line behind the boat.

LOOK IN THE MIRROR A pilot needs to see ahead to navigate properly, but also must keep an eye on the action behind them to keep things safe and precise for a rider. Looking back and forth interferes with both of these tasks, but a good rearview mirror (the wider the angle, the better) allows for a smooth, straight track.

GAIN SOME WEIGHT Whether wakesurfing, catching air on a board, or just needing a balanced wake to ride on skis, wake is an essential consideration for riders. Instead of solid weights, add ballast bladders to your boat. These come in a variety of shapes, hold up to 1,000 pounds (454 kg) of water weight, and can create whatever wake you need, from balanced to mega-surf.

156 CHOOSE YOUR WEAPON

Getting out with a boat fitted for towing means you have a range of choices in how you want to enjoy your time on the water.

TRY TUBING There are a vast array of floating towables, from simple one- or two-person tubes (hence the name of the game) or other shapes, all the way up to party rafts capable of carrying several people at once.

GRAB SKIS The old standard for water-based sports, this is just what it says on the label: a pair of skis, with fittings to sock your feet into.

GET ON BOARD Wakeboarding, essentially the aquatic answer to snowboarding, has become much more prevalent over the last couple of decades, and its options have expanded as rapidly as its popularity. Make sure you've got a good fitted pair of boots to go with the board.

GO BAREFOOT With a bit of practice, and maybe a boom (see item 155), you don't even necessarily need to use an inflatable, skis, or wakeboard to be on the water. Your own feet can provide all the equipment you need, aside from a towline or boom, to skid merrily across the surface of the water.

157 BE SMART ABOUT SAFETY

Accidents at sea or on remote waters can be catastrophic. The good news is, if you are aware of likely risks and plan accordingly, you can prevent or avoid many common problems. Here are some absolute basics everyone should know.

GET THE GEAR Boaters often depart without the proper number and sizes of life jackets, working flares, properly functioning running lights or horn, or alternative propulsion such as a canoe paddle. An anchor also is the first line of defense in a breakdown or storm, keeping your boat safely in place should the engine fail.

PLAN AHEAD Run out of gas in the middle of the Gulf Stream or at the headwaters of Niagara Falls, and the situation can fast become dire. So, before you leave the dock, take stock of your planned itinerary, and how much fuel you need to complete it safely. Then bring 0 to 20 percent more than that.

WEAR PROTECTION Life jackets save lives. In fact, according to Coast Guard statistics, about half of the drowning fatalities in boating involve boaters without life jackets. You might think having one nearby is good enough; you can always grab it as you need it. But it's unlikely you'll ever get it on once in the water.

CHECK ALL SYSTEMS A faulty battery means a boat won't start; if it happens at night, the light won't work either. Your boat will be stranded, helpless, and practically invisible. To prevent fires, always sniff the bilge for stray fuel fumes before departing. Look for leakage like obvious fuel on the bottom or a rainbow slick on bilge water. Never start the engine without running the bilge blower at least five minutes.

WATCH THE WEATHER Keeping an eye on the weather is as important as maintaining a lookout while piloting a vessel. Don't leave port on the news of questionable weather, and don't leave port without even checking for that news.

KEEP A LOOKOUT In boating collisions, the reason tendered by the victims is usually, "I didn't see them coming." Well, it's your job to see them coming. Whether at anchor or on the fly, maintaining a lookout is mandatory for safe boating.

SLOW DOWN One chief cause of boating accidents is failing to maintain a safe speed. At night, you can't always trust your senses to tell if the way is clear. For example, another boat's lights may have failed, creating a navigation hazard. Don't speed.

158 BRING A BUNG

The most likely cause of sinking is laughably simple: a hole in the boat. But how does a boat that's never hit anything spring a leak? Usually, as a result of the through-hull fittings, which are designed to bring water in or out through the hull but are vulnerable to damage. Bronze through-hulls are the most reliable, but stray electrical current in the water from other boats or from pier wiring can dissolve them. Keep available a handful of wooden bungs on hand—these tapered pegs can be pounded into a broken through-hull to stop the water until you can get to land and have repairs done.

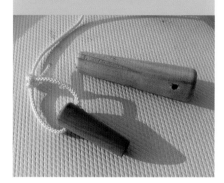

159

CHECK FOR CRACKS

Usually, grounding your boat is only an embarrassment—but not always. Too many boaters are eager to yank their craft off the rocks and end the humiliating saga as quickly as possible. Remember, it's not the grounding that will hurt you—it's the sudden stop. That wracking experience can crack your hull as well as bruise your ego. Before you shove off, go below and make sure that the bilge isn't filling with water through such a crack.

160 AVOID SOME COMMON ERRORS

As we've emphasized throughout this book (don't worry, we'll keep it up for the rest!), boating can be dangerous. The more you know about common errors and how to avoid them, the safer you and your passengers and crew will be. Here's a handy list of three common situations that can go badly fast, and the dumb things you should avoid doing. Don't you feel smarter already?

DANGEROUS SITUATION	MOST COMMON ERRORS	QUICK TIP
Fire in the Engine Room	Rushing to open the hatch.	Remember, oxygen feeds a fire. Feel the hatch for heat, and look for signs of flames.
	Forgetting about "reflash."	The fire may reignite; have a crewmember stand by with a second fire extinguish.
	Forgetting to turn off the fuel line valve to the engine.	Remember the phrase "like fuel to the fire?". Yeah, that.
Boat Is Taking on Water	Relying on too-small bilge pumps.	Be sure your boat is outfitted with pumps that can handle a true emergency.
	Running too many electronics	If you drain the batteries, you can't run the pumps at all.
	Clogging or covering your cockpit scuppers.	Just don't
You've Run Aground	Starting off uninformed.	The Coast Guard posts notices of any changes to sandbars, channels, etc. online. Check the news before you cruise.
	Ignoring the tides	Be sure you know the tidal range in your area, or anything else that could affect water level.
	Gunning the engines in reverse.	Your props are no longer protected by the skeg and thus exposed to repeated damage

161 LOOK OUT FOR LIGHTNING

Lightning always takes the most direct path to earth by striking the highest object in the area. Unfortunately, on the water, the highest and most attractive object to a lightning bolt just might be your boat. While there is no absolute protection against lightning aboard a boat, there are steps you can take to avoid or minimize damage.

CHOOSE THE PATH By grounding any likely targets such as antennas, fishing rods, towers, T-tops, or any elevated electrically conductive surface, you can create a safe path for lightning to travel. To conduct a strike safely to "ground" (on a boat this means to the water), create a low-resistance path from the highest point on your boat to a metal grounding plate in contact with the water.

AIM HIGH Start with a solid half-inch- (1.27-cm) diameter steel or bronze rod elevated about 6–12 inches (15–30 cm) above every other object on the boat. The tip should be pointed, not blunt. Run a conductor made of at least a No. 8 gauge wire from the rod in as straight a path as possible to the water-grounding point. The recommended ground is a metal plate that's mounted outside of the hull. It can be copper, monel, naval bronze, or other noncorrosive metal, and should be solid—not the porous type used for radio antenna grounds—and it should be at least 1 square foot (929 sq cm) in area. Keep in mind as well, that factory-installed lightning rods and grounding conductors are sometimes unwisely removed or disconnected by boat dealers or unknowing buyers.

GET GROUNDED Ground all electronics and large metal objects on board, including metal cases or grounding studs on electronics, and electrical equipment. Not to be overlooked are the engine(s), stove, sink, tanks, refrigerator, air-conditioner, metal railings, tower, arch, and Bimini top. When running grounding conductors, don't attempt to neatly bundle grounding cables together with the rest of the electrical wiring. Keep them separate from all other conductors, including antenna wires. Also, do not run the ground conductors in close proximity to or parallel to existing wire runs to prevent arcing.

162 AVOID A STRIKE

You don't even have to be in the lightning storm to be at risk. Lightning has been proven to strike as far as 10 miles (16 km) from any rainfall, so don't ignore those gathering clouds in the distance. If you do get caught in the middle of a thunder boomer, take these actions to avoid becoming a human lightning rod.

DON'T ATTRACT Among the more obvious actions should be taking off any metal jewelry, getting swimmers out of the water, reeling in and stowing fishing rods, and lowering antennae, outriggers, and flagpoles.

AVOID ELECTRONICS Stay away from the electronics. Don't use the radio unless it's an emergency.

STOW AWAY If the boat has a cabin, go belowdecks. Otherwise, move toward the middle of the boat and under a hardtop or Bimini (without touching it).

MIND THE GAP Avoid touching metal objects, and in particular bridging gaps — such as having one hand on the throttle and the other resting on the metal leg of a hardtop.

BALL UP If lightning strikes are coming down all around, crouch low in a balled-up position (on nonconductive cushions, if possible) to make the smallest possible target; cover your ears to prevent hearing damage, and keep some distance from other crew members in order to maintain smaller targets.

163 BOAT SAFELY IN COLD WEATHER

Early-season boating can be a rewarding experience: Trees are just beginning to bud and early flowers bloom, and the lack of other boaters on the water means more chances of wildlife sightings. But with that beauty comes added responsibility and the need to be prepared for unexpected hazards. Here are some things to be sure that you remember to do.

FIX IT NOW Check that all your spring commissioning work, and make the first run a short one close to the dock or launch ramp.

FILE A FLOAT PLAN Leave as detailed a plan as possible with a relative or friend and tell them you will check in when you get back to land. If they don't hear from you, they'll know to call for help and where to send the rescuers.

BE PREPARED Bring supplies to prepare for any emergencies, such as blankets, food, water, warm clothes and communication and location devices, including a VHF radio, GPS and emergency position-indicating radio beacon (EPIRB) or personal locator beacon (PLB). Don't rely on a cell phone, but if you bring it, keep it dry, and preprogram rescue numbers. Dialing 911 sends you to a land-based emergency system and could delay your rescue.

DO A DRILL Where's the ladder, the throwable life preserver, the ditch bag, the VHF radio? Go over the exact location of all key safety gear before you leave the dock. If you're boating with a friend, discuss who's going to do what if someone falls overboard, and how to make emergency calls.

PAY ATTENTION Monitor the weather at all times. At the first hint of bad conditions, start evaluating whether it's time to return to the dock. Know your boat's capabilities and what types of sea conditions it can handle.

HANG ON When boating in cold weather, one thing you should keep tabs on is a loss of dexterity. When walking around on deck or along the rails, always have one hand on a grab rail for support.

CLIP ON A KILL SWITCH For boaters heading out alone, clipping on the kill switch is critical. Even when boating with a crew, the driver should always wear the kill switch so the boat stops instantly if anything happens to him.

164 DRESS FOR SUCCESS

Being prepared means being properly outfitted. One of the biggest mistakes people make is dressing for the air temperature rather than the water. Water can sap your body heat 25 times faster than air can, so protect yourself from possible immersion, no matter how warm it feels outside. Avoid cotton clothing, too, as it absorbs water and reduces body temperature much more quickly than other materials. Wear water-resistant fabrics and layers that wick away moisture, and a waterproof outer layer.

For greater safety, take inspiration from the Coast Guard, which requires that everyone serving duty on a small boat wear a full drysuit if the water temperature dips below 50° F (10° C). No matter the weather, every Coastie on small-boat duty wears a search-and-rescue (SAR) vest, a life vest that holds a personal EPIRB, plus handheld pyrotechnics (flares), a signal mirror, a whistle, a strobe light and a survival knife—all tethered to the vest. Whether you have all that gear or not, the No. 1 way to prevent disaster on the water is to wear a life jacket.

165 RADIO FOR HELP

When lives are on the line—your boat is on fire or sinking rapidly with people on board, for example, or someone is in imminent danger of dying without immediate medical assistance—you will want every available resource dispatched to your position. A mayday call will almost certainly bring that kind of help.

A "mayday"—the term is derived from the French *venez m'aider*, meaning, "Come and help me"—should be transmitted if possible via marine-band VHF-FM radio Channel 16 or 2182 kHz MF/SSB. Emergencies can go from bad to worse in seconds, so try to get as much information across in as little time as possible.

International Maritime Organization protocols call for beginning with "mayday" repeated three times, followed by the name and number of your vessel and its position. If you have a marine GPS, relate your coordinates. If not, state your distance and magnetic or true bearing from the closest navigational landmark. If time allows, also relay your departure point, departure time, and the speed at which you were traveling. All of these can help rescuers locate you.

Once you've made contact, Coast Guard Search and Rescue planners will keep you advised of their actions and give you an estimate of when rescue units will arrive on the scene. If you have a medical emergency, assign someone to monitor the radio from the time you make the call until the rescuers are on the scene. The Coast Guard will direct you to the nearest safe haven and advise you on what actions you should take in the interim.

166 BEAT THE CLOCK

The instant you fall into cold water, the clock is ticking on your survival. Here's what happens to a person in 50° F (10° C) water.

0–5 seconds	Gasp reflex occurs: person immediately sucks in air or, if head is submerged, 2–3 quarts (1.9–2.8 l) of water.
3–5 minutes	Hyperventilation sets in and heart rate accelerates. Panic attacks set in.
3–30 minutes	Loss of feeling and dexterity in extremities, hampering ability to swim.
10–30 minutes	Blood pressure rises; kidneys purge fluids; urination promotes dehydration.
15–20 minutes	Core temperature starts to cool.
30 minutes	True hypothermia sets in; person becomes disoriented and starts to hallucinate.

167 RECOGNIZE DROWNING

People drown fast, often in the close company of their companions. As boat owners, it makes good sense for us to recognize the signs of drowning. So, what does drowning really look like?

FORGET HOLLYWOOD The IDR (Instinctive Drowning Response) was identified by American Red Cross member Frank Pia and describes what a person's basic response to drowning looks like. That is, lack of verbal communication, a vertical orientation in the water, and arms/legs pushing straight down. The IDR blows away the Hollywood stereotype of a flailing, screaming victim. Such behavior describes aquatic distress, and distressed persons can help themselves to a degree. Unlike people in aquatic distress, people who are drowning can't speak because their brain is too concerned about getting air, even if their head is above water.

KNOW SURVIVAL MODE A drowning person's brain automatically instructs the arms to push down on the water, in an effort to get the mouth and nose above the surface. In survival mode, body and mind don't allow for grabbing a rope or life jacket thrown nearby. With the IDR embedded deep in the reptilian part of our brain, these autonomic responses can't be overcome. The bottom line for us boatmen is that drowning crew member can't tell us that they are drowning, and they can't assist in their own rescue.

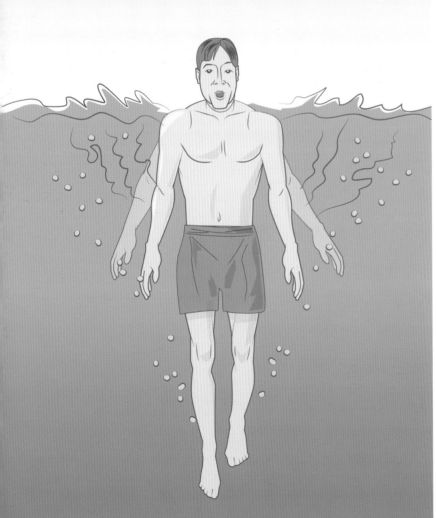

168 PREVENT DROWNING

Here are five key steps to helping to prevent drowning, besides the first and most crucial one, making sure everyone uses proper safety gear.

STAY ALERT Keep a sharp eye on anyone who's in the water. Alcohol, exposure to the elements, and unexpected bottom-structure drop-offs can cause even strong adult swimmers to suddenly drown.

KNOW THE SIGNS Learn to recognize the physical cues that someone is in trouble (see item 167).

AIM WELL When tossing a lifeline or PFD, or extending a broom handle, aim so that the apparatus lands beside the flapping arms. The arms will touch it without reaching and allow nature's clutching instinct to take over.

STAY PUT Avoid a swimming rescue as your first response unless you are a trained lifesaver—double drownings occur this way.

ANGLE IN If you absolutely must swim to save a crew member, wear a life jacket and then perform a "wading rescue," in which you angle your body toward the boat or shore at arm's length from the victim, grab the wrist, and then side-stroke to safety. Let go if the person tries to hug you.

169 RESCUE A MAN OVERBOARD

Initial reactions to an emergency can often set the stage for its outcome. At some point, you may experience a passenger over the side, a potentially dangerous situation for both you and the person in the water. Prepare ahead of time and practice rescue procedures so, if this should happen, you'll know how to get the person back aboard safely. Here is what to keep in mind.

YELL Remain calm when a person goes over the side, but do not remain quiet. You want your crew and the subject to know you see them. You should point to the individual and shout "Man Overboard!" followed by "Port Side!" or "Starboard Side." It is essential to point until the person is rescued because it's easy to lose track of a person in open water. If your GPS has a MOB button, activate it but keep pointing as the GPS won't account for the effects of the current.

REACH Swing the stern and propeller away from the person in the water. Then, if the person is conscious, alert, and within arm's length, reach for the victim and pull them toward the boat. Be sure you're wearing a life jacket. Make sure you are holding on to something stable with your other arm and lowering your center of gravity so you don't topple in to the water. If the person is farther out, you can extend your reach by using something like a shirt, towel, pole, or paddle to pull them to safety.

THROW Toss the victim something buoyant such as a boat cushion, life ring, life jacket, or even an empty cooler. It will also act as a reference point should you lose sight of the person in the water; if a search becomes necessary, emergency responders will have an immediate visual reference on the direction of drift, which can benefit the search operation.

ROW If the person is too far out for a thrown buoyant object, maneuver the vessel over to the person. Always approach them from the boat operator's side so that the person in the water is in view at all times. When you begin to get close, turn off the engine to avoid a propeller strike. Now, throw them a buoyant object and help them back aboard.

170 AVOID THAT SINKING FEELING

While knowing what to do when disaster strikes is important, so is being prepared for disaster. Being sure that you and your crew know how to activate and utilize emergency technology can be the few seconds that make a crucial difference. Here are a few things you should have prepared before you even leave your dock.

HIT THE PANIC BUTTON The red button marked DSC (digital selective calling) can instantly broadcast a distress signal and report your exact location and more to rescue agencies. To activate it, you need to obtain a marine ID called an MMSI number and program it into the radio. Also, connect your VHF and GPS.

READY YOUR BEACONS Mid-disaster is no time to pull out a manual to learn to activate an EPIRB or PLB. Review the manual now so there is no hesitation when you need to use them. They typically involve removing the safety collar before activating.

CHECK YOUR GPS Keep your boat's GPS powered up so that your coordinates are in view to report your location quickly.

CHARGE YOUR RADIO A fully charged handheld VHF can save your life should the main radio fail or if you need to abandon ship.

BACK UP YOUR BATTERIES Buy an optional backup AA battery case for the radio and keep a supply of fresh alkaline batteries handy.

STUDY MAYDAY PROTOCOL Make a copy of how to call a mayday (normally found in the radio owner's manual) and post it near the radio.

KEEP EMERGENCY NUMBERS Program the emergency telephone numbers into your cell phone for the U.S. Coast Guard Rescue Coordination Center in your area, the local harbor patrol, and other nearby agencies that can respond in an emergency.

BRIEF YOUR CREW Explain to all on board where your EPIRB or PLB is located and how to activate it if you're unavailable.

171 EVADE A ROCKY FATE

If your engine dies, your prop fouls, or your shift cable freezes and you start drifting toward a jetty, boulder field, or rocky shore, do you know what to do? Most boats can take a gentle bump without being holed. But with wave action or even a large wake, you could come down hard—and with disastrous results. Here's the best course of action.

LIFE JACKETS Have everyone aboard don their PFDs.

DROP ANCHOR Even if it doesn't grab, it will slow your drift. Add more drag by deploying a sea anchor off the side of the boat that's away from the rocks—a bucket tied to a line is a good makeshift one.

MAKE NOISE Don't be shy. Signal and shout to nearby boats for a tow. Crossing arms waved overhead is a universal signal for help.

WATCH YOURSELF Take care fending off. Manually pushing off a rock while lazily drifting across a pond is one thing, but for wave-whipped lee shores, think twice. A boat isn't worth a limb, or a life.

172 RADIO FOR HELP

One of the most crucial things to do when you hit serious trouble is to let someone know that you're going down or in real danger. You need to get to your radio, if you can, and mayday the Coast Guard or other appropriate entity.

WHO Identify yourself by boat name and radio call sign, if you have one.

WHERE Report your boat's location as precisely as possible, preferably by GPS latitude and longitude, followed by general location.

WHAT Explain the type of distress or difficulty present.

HOW MANY Give the total number of people on board and their condition, if anyone is injured.

SEAWORTHINESS State your boat's condition—dead in the water, one or more engine disabled, listing to port, or whatever else is wrong.

DESCRIPTION Describe your boat in detail (type, manufacturer, color, superstructure, striping and any other distinguishing features).

REPETITION Let go of the mike button. Wait 10 seconds and repeat, starting with "Mayday-Mayday-Mayday." Once in contact, you'll need to provide the information noted above.

173 SURVIVE A CAPSIZED BOAT

The weather report predicted nothing but good things offshore when you headed outside the inlet. Unfortunately, Mother Nature doesn't like predictions. As the swells kick up to uncomfortable levels, a following sea suddenly causes your boat to stuff and roll, and in a flash you and your passengers find yourselves in the drink with the boat's keel pointed to the sky. What now?

BE A BIG TARGET The most important thing you can do is stay with the boat. This exponentially increases your chances of being rescued. "If someone's looking just for you from a C-130 or a helicopter, it's like looking for a basketball floating in the water," says Christopher Todd, public affairs officer for the U.S. Coast Guard Auxiliary. The inverted hull makes a much larger target.

SALVAGE SUPPLIES Retrieve as many supplies as possible, such as flares, distress signals, and extra flotation devices. Find anything that floats and tether it to the boat to create a bigger target, or release it into the water to create a debris field, which also helps spotters.

KEEP WARM Try to climb on top of the hull to reduce exposure. Water steals body heat 25 times faster than air does. Also, huddle together to pool warmth and stave off hypothermia.

HAVE AN EMERGENCY BAG Keeping an easily accessed ditch bag on board with a registered emergency position-indicating radio beacon (EPIRB) can be a lifesaver (see item 045). So can a positive attitude.

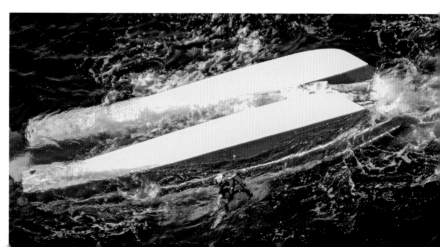

174 SOUND THE ALARM

Carbon monoxide detectors can save your life. You can't smell carbon monoxide, you can't see it, and you can't taste it, but it can kill you—or at the very least make you really sick. It's present whenever you fire up the engine, genset, stove, or barbecue. It can creep into your living space from the guy docked in the next slip, so you need one even if you don't have a generator.

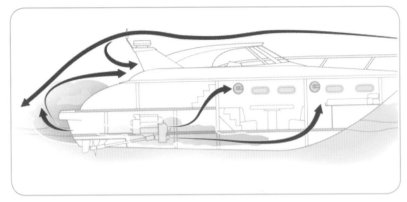

PROTECT YOURSELF The best way to alert yourself to the presence of CO is to install one or more carbon monoxide alarms in any enclosed or semi-enclosed area, wherever people congregate or sleep. This would include an enclosed flying bridge. But how do you know what a good alarm is?

BUY MARINE First, avoid residential alarms. While marine units may be more expensive, they are built to withstand the rigors of a marine environment. Plus, price should not be an issue when your life is at stake. Look for units that are UL listed for marine use.

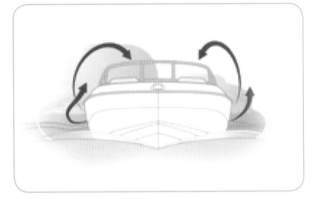

CHOOSE EXTRA POWER Most boaters opt for a hard-wired 12-volt DC unit. There's rarely a time when the ship's electric system will not be available. A better choice might be a combination hard-wired/battery-backup unit, in case boat power fails. Pure battery-operated alarms are not recommended since battery life is unpredictable and they are easy to disable by removing the batteries.

WEIGHT IT OUT It's important to know that CO can spike momentarily on board whenever an engine or genset starts or a stove or oven is lit. Time-weighted averaging takes the spike and averages it over a preprogrammed length of time, and the unit typically will trip only when the average over time reaches 70 parts per million or higher. Time-weighting reduces nuisance false alarms from momentary spikes.

REPLACE Finally, keep in mind that the sensors in CO alarms do have a specific life cycle. The entire unit should be replaced at least every five years if you want optimal protection.

175 CAP IT OFF

Rainwater can seep into the fuel fill, through the fill line, and into the tank. The rainwater can then damage the hoses, filters, and tank. What makes a boat prone to this problem? It's the fill cap. Water enters when the mounting screws protrude high enough to keep the cap from sealing. The guilty screws are typically oval or pan head. Rain can also enter through a cracked or missing O-ring on the cap. And if you have a plastic fill beware that it can crack from sun exposure or from overtightening. The bottom line? Inspect your cap, seals, and screws.

176 BE FUEL SAFE

It's important to protect the environment, but even more so to protect human life. The most common of boating tasks, fueling up, can also be deadly. The vapor from just one cup of gasoline packs the explosive power of five pounds (2.3 kg) of dynamite. Gasoline can ignite in a fireball with a temperature of 15,000°F (8,300 °C); a fiberglass boat will explode and burn to the waterline in minutes. Keep these facts in mind and review this fueling-up refresher.

GET EVERYONE ASHORE Insist that your crew stretch their legs while you fuel up.

BATTEN DOWN Close all hatches, doors and ports. Fumes are heavier than air and will sink to the lowest parts of the boat, lying in wait for a spark, or just a rush of fresh air, to induce combustion.

KNOW THY BOAT Look at the fuel gauge prior to filling. This observation, coupled with knowledge of the tank's capacity, allows you to stop the flow when full or nearly so by monitoring the rate on the pump. Can't see the pump? Ask a dockhand to stop the pump at a set number of gallons or assign a crew member to call out to you. Clicking on the ignition to check the gauge during fueling is a no-no.

SAY NO TO STATIC It's imperative to make and maintain full and firm metal-to-metal contact between the pump nozzle and your boat's fuel deck pipe. This grounds the nozzle and prevents a spark created by static electricity. FYI: Newer fiberglass docks create an inordinate amount of static. Forewarned is forearmed.

TAKE A WHIFF Fueling complete, open the hatches, and sniff for gas fumes in the bilge and engine compartment. If all smells well, run the blower for five minutes before starting the engines. This doesn't apply to outboard-powered boats for obvious reasons.

177 WATCH THAT FLARE

When you sight a flare, help rescuers narrow down the search area by noting the following.

Your heading and position
The time
Flare color
The interval between flares
The duration of burn
Flare trajectory (rising, falling, steady)

178 KNOW YOUR COLORS

A flare's color will tell you how concerned to be when you sight it.

RED OR ORANGE
These are fired as distress signals
WHITE
"Practice" flares, use for testing a flare gun
GREEN
Dropped by search and rescue (SAR) aircraft looking for victims.

179 STOP THE CLOCK

Another way to get your bearings as regards the direction from which you saw a flare is the clock method. Note your current heading and position and, using the bow of your boat as 12:00, report the direction in which you sighted the flare as a time of day. Of course, if you can take actual bearing over your compass card, or with a handheld compass, so much the better.

180 PROTECT YOUR EYES

Pack a pair of safety glasses along with your safety equipment. When using aerial flares, whether the handheld type or those fired from a pistol launcher, wearing eye protection makes good sense. You should wear goggles whenever the situation permits.

181 MAKE A HANDY ESTIMATE

If you sight a flare, get on the VHF and hail the Coast Guard. The more information you can give them about flare you saw, the better. Knowing the angle from your position to the flare's height of trajectory allows people on the coast to triangulate the estimated distance to the boat in distress. Your fist can be used as a poor man's sextant. Here's how.

Make a fist and extend your arm. Place your pinky on the horizon and note how many fingers above the horizon the flare is at the height of its trajectory. Each finger represents approximately 2 degrees of arc. For you math nuts, range = 1.856 x elevation/angle. But all most of us need to do is to tell the authorities the finger count, or "percentage of fist," as it's known. Oftentimes, such as with handheld flares, the signal will appear below the horizon. In that case, align your index finger with the horizon and provide the percentage of fist below the line.

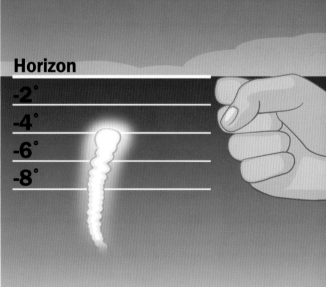

182 RECRUIT A KID OR TWO

Kids usually want to run amok, but you can involve them with specific tasks and jobs related to your excursion—and teach them to be safe, responsible boaters. Here are some ideas for deck-hand duties.

FLOAT-PLAN COORDINATOR Give a youngster a clipboard—maybe even a personalized one—and have them fill out the plan (you check it, of course). Let them help file a copy with a friend, relative, or neighbor, and then alert the contact once you've returned safely.

SAFETY INSPECTOR Do we have emergency flares, life jackets, a fire extinguisher, a first-aid kit, and a paddle? Are the lights OK? Do we have enough docklines? This job might even remind adults of the safety checklist.

HAZARD SPOTTER With a kid's favorite gadget (binoculars), the spotter scans the water and the shoreline to pick out marker numbers, buoys, boat traffic, debris, beacons, and more.

WEATHER WATCHER Deputize a child to help check current and expected weather conditions via the NOAA broadcast on the VHF radio. Consider having them print a forecast before the trip, and then to watch the sky for danger signs.

KEY PATROL This role is critical when you stop for a swim, regardless of age. Keep the key out of the ignition while swimmers are in the water, and hang it on a hook near the transom. When the driver is ready to start the motor, they'll be prompted to check the water for swimmers first.

RADIO OPERATOR School a kid in radio language and proper channels so they'll understand how to communicate with authorities over the airwaves should they ever need to. They can also help you check the radio before each excursion.

GEAR CAPTAIN Once kids see the boat being uncovered, they'll be all over it like sugar ants. Stowing gear is a great way to keep them in one place while you get situated. It'll also give them a greater understanding of supply versus space.

HOSER What kid doesn't like to spray things (like the deck) with a hose?

DOCK MASTER As you approach the dock, one child prepares a bow line, another a stern line. With all crew members on the boat, each specialist sets up the looped end on the boat cleats and holds the lines with both hands until the vessel is where you want it at the dock.

183 FIT A CHILD'S JACKET

You may not be able to protect your child from every hazard, but fitting them with a life jacket and setting a good example by wearing one of your own are a good place start.

A U.S. Coast Guard approval label on the inside of the life jacket tells you the jacket has passed stringent safety and durability tests. Type I, II, and III differentiate between minimum buoyancy requirements and vest shape. Most children should wear a Type II life jacket.

Always take your child along for a life jacket fitting to be sure the jacket fits properly. Don't buy one that they will "grow into." A child's life jacket should fit snugly from day one. To check for a good fit, put the life jacket on your child and then lift them up by the shoulders of the jacket. If fitted correctly, it won't ride up and their chin and ears won't slip through. A properly sized life jacket will stay in place even when a child is lifted into the air. Recheck the fit at the start of every boating season. If your child has outgrown the jacket, get a new one. Don't make-do by putting an adult life jacket on a child.

Test the life jacket's effectiveness in the water before going boating. With the jacket on your child, conduct a "float test" in a secure place, such as a swimming pool, and teach your child how to float in a relaxed, face-up position.

Can't afford life jackets? Or need them just for the day? Many state and local boating organizations also have life jackets available on loan that you can check out for a day or a weekend.

184 TRAIN PETS BEFORE BOATING

Before you ever bring your pet aboard, there's some serious work that needs to be done. Start by introducing your pet to the sights, sounds, and peculiarities of the marine environment. If you can, start training early.

If your boat is on a trailer, take the pets on board there, away from any motion or noises. Spend a bit of time below decks, and let them feel comfortable. Teach pets how to get on and off the boat using a single point of entry. Otherwise, don't be surprised when your pet makes a jump from the rail to the dock, only to end up in the water.

Be certain your pet understands the concept of water. It might sound silly, but a calm surface can look like a shiny floor from a pet's perspective. Just as you'd practice rescue drills with your crew, do the same for your pets. Teach them to swim around to a location that's easy for you to retrieve them should they fall overboard. Pet-overboard drills should also include what to do when underway. As for cats, a piece of carpet affixed to the corners of your boat will help a feline friend gain purchase and get back on board should they end up in the water.

If all else fails, make sure you have a long dip net handy.

185 CHOOSE A PFD FOR YOUR DOG

Just like swimmers, dogs have varying levels of swimming mastery. A skill set affected by things such as choppy water, weather conditions, the dog's age (stamina), and the dog's weight (susceptibility to exposure). While there aren't any regulations for pet life jackets, consider these guidelines when picking one out.

Check the fit in the store before you leave. Like a child's life jacket, it should fit snugly around the whole body and not ride up.

It's easier to pick up your pet by the handle. When trying on the life jacket, make sure you try lifting the dog, too. Pay particular attention to snaps, buckles, and straps, and where they're placed. Choose a bright color to make it easier to spot your dog in the water.

Before going on the boat, let your pet get used to the jacket by wearing it around the house or in the back yard. And remember, unlike human flotation devices, pet life jackets are designed to keep animals in the swimming position.

186 PREPARE FOR ANIMAL PASSENGERS

Before embarking with your pets, make sure you've got all the items you'll need in order to keep them safe and comfortable. They'll be relying on you to make sure they have a pleasurable experience on the boat.

ID An ID tag should have your address, phone number, permanent marina location, and slip number. (You might need two tags.) Always use the phone number where you can be reached afloat. Including your landline or a close relative's number is a good idea as well. Also, consider having your pet microchipped before heading out.

PFD Your pet should have a PFD (personal flotation device) just like any other member of your crew. Choose a bright color for easy visibility and get one with a handle on top. Teaching commands

like "on boat" or "off boat" could help not only when docking your boat, but also in emergency situations.

SEASICKNESS Talk to your vet before you go. The same prescriptions that help humans feel better also work on animals, but dosages will vary. Set up a pet area in the part of the boat least prone to motion. The V-berth is a bad idea, while the center of the boat is usually the best.

HYDRATION Keeping your pet hydrated is as important as keeping yourself hydrated. Bring a water bowl and plenty of fluid.

HARNESS A harness, as opposed to a leash or collar, provides a means to grab and lift the dog, even using a boat hook.

FIRST AID Make sure you have a stocked pet first-aid kit aboard. The Humane Society of the United States recommends pet-specific supplies and useful items to include in a boating dog's kit. Dogs can take Dramamine and other remedies for seasickness. Check with your vet.

NATURE'S CALL While many housebroken pets will be reluctant to "go" aboard your boat, pets can be trained to use carpet scraps, wee-wee pads, or litter boxes placed in the cockpit.

SUN PROTECTION Pets get sunburn just like people. Apply sunscreen on the dog's belly and inside the hind legs at least. Spray-on varieties are easy to apply.

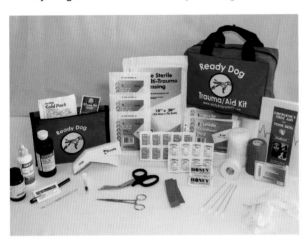

187 KEEP YOUR PET SAFE ONBOARD

Here are some considerations for getting your animal pal on board and keeping those critters safe.

HIT THE DECK Make sure your pet has plenty of traction. A bathroom throw rug with a nonslip backing makes for an easy option. Don't forget the dinghy! Indoor/outdoor carpeting tacked to the deck makes rough trips easier to handle.

MAKE WAY For those bringing a cat on board, there's not much to worry about. They can navigate just about anything. But dogs need an easy way on and off your boat. Make sure there are ramps or steps for those who can't navigate a companionway ladder.

COOL OFF It's hard for pets to regulate body temperature, so make sure there's plenty of shade. And just because the air temperatures are cool, remember the paws that are on the hot deck. Again, cooling water or a nonskid carpet does the trick.

GET EXERCISE Before getting on board, take your dog for a walk. Cats don't need much help, as they're pretty self-exercising

climbing on top of you. But you'll be thankful that your dog has had a chance to expend some of his energy.

GO SWIMMING Most dogs love water, and they're eager to jump in. But they can't tell you if they're tired, so keep a close eye on them. Before hitting the drink, give them one. Ensure they're well hydrated, and don't let them get too far from your watchful eye.

188 GO CAMPING

Don't think an overnight cruise requires a boat with a cabin. Some truly memorable overnighters can be had aboard an open boat. It just takes a little planning ahead of time to work things in your favor.

LOCATION While it's possible to sleep aboard an open boat, especially with some of today's larger models, tenting ashore can make for a great adventure. Plug "waterfront camping areas" into a search engine, along with your destination, to see what's available. Choices range from mainstream campgrounds to intimate little islands. Look for level ground, in the lee, for the best conditions. While sleeping under the stars exudes a certain romance, overnighting in a small, freestanding tent is most practical. Worried about critters? Some areas, like the Everglades Wilderness Waterway, offer raised platforms (chickees) removed from shore.

ANCHORAGE You may be able to beach, but in tidal water it's best to double-anchor. Set an anchor on shore to avoid any middle-of-the-night surprises. If you're dealing with tide changes or rocky shoreline, anchor offshore. Experienced campers use an "outhaul," a conventional anchor attached to a simple wooden float, with a loop of tubing secured to the top. Tether your boat to a line passed through the loop and to the shore anchor so that you can pull your boat onto and off of the shore clothesline-style. Fashion the float in a cross to prevent the lines from twisting.

PACKING Space will be at a premium, so repackage food into smaller, reusable containers. Avoid most refrigerated items; they require a cooler and ice, which often aren't practical. Canned goods can be heated with a simple camp stove. Use a biodegradable soap for cleanup. For clothing and other essentials, use dry bags. They stow easier and keep things from getting damp. If you really want to go all out, invest in a vacuum sealer to store everything from food to clothing.

REPAIR & MAINTENANCE

It's often said in these circles that boating is the only sport that provides its practitioners with such a wealth of opportunities—to become a carpenter, a mechanic, an electrician, and a plumber. For the DIY-inclined, owning a boat may rank as a bonanza. But what if your life's goal isn't to become a salt-encrusted handyman?

Certainly, many boat owners possess the means to pay others to fix and maintain their vessels. These same folks also invariably number among the most time-pressed in society; thee affluence of these boaters often stems from long hours " on the job"—whether we reference professionals, entrepreneurs or wage earners racking –up overtime. And it's just because of that sledgehammer known as time, that I suggest such boaters sharpen their maintenance skills and knowledge.

If you're willing to invest the time in gaining a basic understanding of a variety of systems—electrical, mechanical, plumbing, structural—small problems that would keep those who's tool kit consists of a telephone and a credit card tied to the dock or stuck at the launch ramp, are an easy match for the DIY boater who's often powering across the waves after the expenditure of a just little applied knowledge and elbow grease.

Furthermore, there is the safety aspect. Do you want to cut a long-awaited overnight cruise short because the navigation lights wont turn on, or the bilge pump stopped running? What if the engine stalls in rough water? (Believe me, if it's going to stall, rough water is exactly where it will stall.) Wouldn't you want to get it going as quickly as possible? Better yet, how about if you were able to see a problem before it developed? More than just convenience, safety is enhanced when the skipper is knowledgeable about maintenance and repair.

189 START THE SEASON RIGHT

At last! Winter is over and it's time to hit the water. But first, take the time to give your vessel a good once-over to make sure all systems are go. You may not have a lot of technical expertise, and you may not even be very handy. That's okay. Check the list in item 190 to ensure that your boat is ready for launch—it is easy for anyone to follow, and even old salts might appreciate a reminder. These simple checks don't quite use all of your senses (no licking the battery terminals!), but they do draw on your ability to see, hear, and feel what's going on with your boat.

190 LOOK FOR TROUBLE SPOTS

Not everything that looks bad is a real problem (for example, some corrosion is normal). Develop your diagnostic vision with these checks.

PAINT Check for loose, flaking antifouling paint and scrape it off before applying a new coat.

PROPELLER SHAFT Shafts should be centered in their bearings. Remember to check the stuffing box as well as at the struts. Keep in mind that a minor misalignment at the bearings is multiplied by the length of the shaft.

ANODES Replace any and all sacrificial anodes that look like they've lost half their weight—not just size. A full-size anode that looks like Swiss cheese has got to go. Don't paint them, and make sure they are fastened tightly.

SEALS All gasketed surfaces are suspect. Eyeball your engine's mating surfaces for signs of drips, salt stains, weepage, and ridges of crud. Exhaust risers and head gaskets are especially important.

PROP BLADES Your prop turns thousands of rpm. Even small dings damage gears and hurt performance. You might (carefully) apply two opposing pairs of pliers to straighten a bent blade or file off burrs along the edges. Or send the wheel out for reconditioning.

RUSTY FITTINGS Even stainless fasteners corrode in a wet, oxygen-starved environment. It's called crevice corrosion. If you see streaks of rust emanating from fasteners or fittings, remove, replace, and rebed with sealant. And find the cause of the wet core.

GEL COAT Look for any dings or chips in the gelcoat—especially along leading edges like the stem, keel, and chines. Repair the damage using epoxy filler.

INSPECTION BOWLS The bowls for filters and sea strainers can turn cloudy, making them useless. Clean them with soap and water. If clarity doesn't return, order replacements.

ENGINE MOUNT NUTS Make sure there is enough thread above and below the nuts on engine-mount studs to allow for future adjustment. Vibration and settling can cause misalignment.

MOTOR-MOUNT STUDS These should be centered between the mount base's fasteners. Mounts should not be cocked or leaning to one side. Perform these checks in the water, where the boat is best supported, for accuracy.

ENGINE ROOM To ensure the engine room is sealing out water and spray, climb inside on a sunny day and close the hatch. You should see no light sneaking in around the perimeter. If you do, repair or replace the gaskets and latch.

PLASTIC Fogged, crazed, and scratched plastic windshields and clear curtains hinder visibility, and thus safety. A fine compound can often restore clarity. Canvas shops replace clear sections, for retaining an existing top.

191 SOUND OUT PROBLEMS

Listen analytically. Pick out the individual noises that make up your engine's clatter. If you know what they sound like when all is well, you'll hear a problem early on. A stethoscope, or even a length of hose placed up to your ear and moved methodically around the engine, can help you isolate the source of a noise indicating a potential problem. Here's what you might hear.

TRAILER WHEELS GRINDING Jack up your trailer and spin the wheels. Hear grinding? Check the bearings and brakes.

CHIRPY BEARINGS A high-pitch chirp often indicates a bad bearing. Listen to rotational accessories like alternators, pulleys, and shaft-driven pumps. Rebuilding or replacing is much easier than getting towed in.

MYSTERIOUS ENGINE NOISES Got an engine noise that's driving you crazy? Narrow down the culprit by removing the belts from accessories like alternators one by one. When the noise stops, you've found the offending part.

AN UNHAPPY STERNDRIVE When out for a run, listen carefully for a grinding or whining noise from a sterndrive while trimming up and while turning. This indicates that a gimbal bearing needs replacement—the sooner the better.

A LESS THAN IMPRESSIVE HORN Sound signaling is important, especially in restricted visibility. Toot your horn. Often, a weak horn can be revitalized by applying spray lube to its diaphragm. Carry an air horn for insurance.

192   FEEL YOUR WAY AROUND

Get hands-on with these systems to ensure all is well.

WATER TEMPERATURE An outboard's telltale stream shouldn't be hot. Check the water pump and thermostats.

PRIMER BULBS A primer bulb should remain firm when the engine is running and drawing fuel. If it doesn't, and after checking for leaks in the fuel line, replace it—and buy extras for spares.

TRAILER TIRES With your trailer jacked up, grab the tires top and bottom or side to side and alternately push and pull. If they rock or wobble, service the hub and bearings.

BATTERIES According to the American Boat and Yacht Council, batteries must withstand a force of 90 pounds (41 kg), or twice their weight, without moving more than 1 inch (2.5 cm) in any direction. Eschew strap hold-downs in favor of those using threaded rods and locknuts.

HOSES Squeeze hoses. Those that are soft and mushy (as well as cracked, checked, discolored, or shedding) can collapse under suction, starving the engine of cooling water, failing and flooding the boat, causing fuel leaks, and more.

RAILS Grab rails should never come off in your hand. ABYC specifies rails must withstand 400 pounds (181 kg) of force. As a test, hang from them to make sure they hold your weight.

THE RUDDER Lift a rudder to determine end play. Then rock it port to starboard to determine side play. Excessive movement presages sinking.

BELTS If a belt deflects too much under hand pressure between pulleys, either it needs replacement or the equipment needs to be repositioned and retightened, or both.

REFRESH YOUR BOTTOM

If barnacles, slime, and plant growth gain a foothold on your boat's bottom, performance will suffer. Your best line of defense: antifouling paints. These come in a variety of types to suit different applications and budgets. For most boats, we recommend an ablative or self-polishing paint. But even within that niche, there are variables to consider, such as your location, how much you use your boat, and how fast it is. Like most jobs, the key to success in applying antifouling paint lies with understanding the whole job and doing the right prep work. If you've got a new boat, or at least one that's never had its bottom painted before, your prep routine is going to be a little different, but most of the steps remain the same. Don't be tempted to skip refreshing your paint because the current coat looks good enough. "Good enough" is probably not really good enough with such an important task.

194 MOD YOUR CAN

What's more frustrating than having a supposedly sealed can of paint tip over and spill everywhere? How about a can you stashed last season to do some touch-ups and finding the paint dried to a brick over the winter. If the can rim got clogged with paint the last time you used it, it might not seal properly. To prevent clogged rims, punch some holes in the can's rim before you pour the paint into the roller tray.

195 GET A CLEAN START

Assuming you've just pulled a boat out of storage or are putting it away for the winter (as compared to giving a n boat its first paint job), your first task is to clean off all th gunk—paint, slime, plant matter, barnacles, and so forth

WASH UP Start with a thorough pressure washing, which will take care of not only weeds and slimy stuff, but much of the paint as well. You can rent a machine if you don't own one. You'll want to use a tip with a 20-degree or greater spray radius for best results.

BLAST BARNACLES These tough little hitchhikers aren't going to hose off easily; you'll probably need to use a scraper and some elbow grease. Many pros use an oscillating tool to make barnacle removal a lot easier. Yo can spend hundreds of dollars on something marketed as a barnacle remover, or pick up a basic corded or cordless model at your local home improvement store for a little over a hundred bucks.

STRIP DOWN Now it's time to get rid of any and all loose or flaking paint that the pressure washer didn't take care of. Slap on some coveralls and a dust mask or respirator, since this is going to be messy and maybe even toxic. Spot-clean with a scraper or, if you've got a ton of paint to remove, use a chemical stripper. A process called soda blasting is more environmentally friendly, but needs to be done by a professional.

196 PAINT A NEW BOAT

If your boat is new or has never been bottom-painted before, you'll need to do some prep work before getting down to the business at hand. The good news is, this won't be as time-consuming or expensive as prepping a boat that's spent a season in the water. But you can't skip your prep work or the paint won't take, and you'll feel like an idiot. We don't want that.

STEP 1 The boat's bottom is probably coated with wax or some other protectant that you'll need to remove with the proper solvent. Soak a rag and wipe it off. Make sure you fold the rag frequently to avoid reapplying the wax you've just removed.

STEP 2 Suit up for safety in protective clothing, including a respirator and safety glasses. You do not want to end up coated in fiberglass dust.

STEP 3 Scuff the bottom with 80-grit sandpaper. You may be able to adapt a sander by removing the dust bag and using a hose clamp or duct tape to attach a vacuum hose. Be sure to keep the sander moving at all times. If you hold it in one place, you run the risk of sanding right through the gelcoat.

STEP 4 After you finish sanding, give it another thorough once-over with the recommended solvent, followed by a soap-and-water wash. After the bottom has dried completely, you're ready to get your paint on.

197 CLEAN CAREFULLY

Your gelcoat is only paper thin, so clean it with care. Don't use products with bleach, as found in many of the brown-waterline or rust-stain removers. Products with solvents such as acetone and toluene can clean almost anything, but also can wipe out the gelcoat's plasticizers. Abrasives are natural no-nos, too. To protect the high-quality finish on your boat, look for cleaners with chelating agents that get into the gelcoat on a molecular level and carry the dirt out as you rinse.

198 WAX POETIC

Gelcoats contain plasticizers that keep them shiny and supple. Over time, these plasticizers leach out, making the gelcoat dull and brittle. To slow the process, use carnauba—the hardest natural wax. Carnauba isn't reflective, so the product you use will also need silicone, oils, other waxes, and solvents to produce that jaw-dropping shine. Don't pay extra for waxes that claim to be 100 percent—anything more than about 30 percent would be rock hard and impossible to apply.

199 COMPOUND YOUR INTEREST

Do you need a mechanical buffer? Probably not, but it sure makes life easier. Just be sure you get the right one, and use it properly.

PICK THE MACHINE Inexpensive random-orbit polishers wax okay but don't do diddly when compounding. Professional-grade sander/polishers are great in experienced hands. These circular rotating machines require a knowing touch, since they can "burn" the surface and/or leave nasty swirl marks if not used properly. Perhaps the best choice for most boaters is a variable-speed, dual-action polisher that combines the user-friendliness of a random orbit with the power of a circular polisher.

CHOOSE THE SPEED When compounding, if the speed is too high, the aggregate gets used up faster and loses its ability to remove oxidation. Stick to 2,500 to 3,200 orbits per minute (OBM). Waxing and polishing can be accomplished at between 3,900 and 4,600 OBM. Higher speeds are useful when removing paint defects

and swirls. Wax and compound makers often specify a machine speed, so check the label of the product you're using.

CUT WITH A PAD Compounding is best accomplished with a wool pad since it has the right properties for "cutting" or removing surface oxidation. A pliable foam pad is great for waxing and polishing. For a slicker-than-slick finish, simply top a foam pad with a microfiber bonnet.

WEAR PROTECTION Wear a dust mask and eye protection, especially when compounding. If you are working while the boat is in the water, make sure you plug in to a ground-fault, circuit-interrupting receptacle (GFCI).

KNOT THE CORD Tie the polisher's cord and the extension cord into a square knot where they connect to prevent pulling the plug as you move around the boat.

200 RESTORE THAT SHINE

To keep your boat looking its best (and at the same time, protect against damage), get in the habit of waxing it regularly—routinely waxed gelcoat can retain its gloss for 15 years or longer. As your boat ages, or if you didn't quite keep up on the maintenance, or both, you'll need to add to your arsenal.

POLISH IT Gelcoat polish is a very fine abrasive that lets you gently rub away pitting and other minor flaws. Using a soft cloth, apply polish to a small area, rubbing with a circular motion, until it gets its glassy sheen back. Then, move on to the next spot. Follow up with a coat of wax when you're done.

USE RUBBING COMPOUND If your gelcoat is so weathered that polish doesn't do the trick, you'll need the stronger abrasives found in rubbing compound (be sure you choose one made for marine gelcoat). To be sure the compound goes on evenly, remove any and all wax from the area you're treating.

APPLY CAREFULLY Sweep a rag saturated with dewaxing solvent or toluene briskly across the surface. Sweep in one direction quickly; do not rub it back and forth. Once you're done, apply the compound like polish, one small area at a time, rubbing until it's glassy in appearance. Don't rub any one spot too long, and stop if the gelcoat starts looking transparent—a sign you've removed too much.

FINISH THE JOB Once you're done with the compound, follow up with polish, a coat of wax, and a thorough buffing.

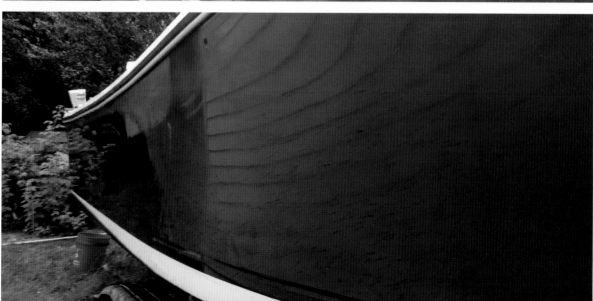

201 FILL A HOLE

If you need to repair a hole that had been drilled in your gelcoat at some time in the past, you'll need to take special care. It's likely that the gelcoat's surface might have become elevated from the upward pressure of an old fastener. To address this, use a countersink bit or rotary file on your power drill to carefully grind away the swollen perimeter. Once it's flush, scrape away any old sealant and clean the whole area up with acetone. Then, proceed with the instructions detailed in item 203.

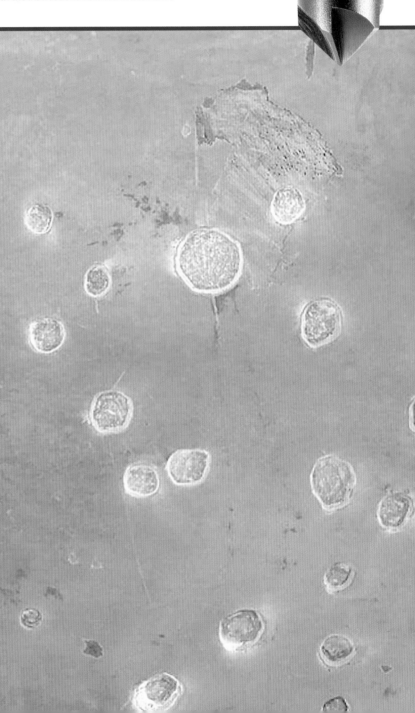

202 PREVENT THE POX

Gelcoat's microscopic pores can allow water into your hull's underlying laminate, where it may react with the resins and cause small bubbles in the coating. Almost every boat ends up with at least some tiny blisters of this sort over time, and they're generally just a cosmetic issue. The jury is still out on whether "boat pox" can actually cause structural damage eventually, but there's no question that they reduce your resale and trade-in value. So it just makes sense to minimize blistering. Here are some ways to do just that.

GO SKIN DEEP When you buy your boat, ask whether the builder used a barrier layer in the skin coat, which is the layer behind the gelcoat. If so, you're starting off with built-in protection.

GUARD THE SURFACE You can also apply a barrier coating over your gelcoat for increased water resistance.

CHECK UP Every year when you get your boat ready for a new season, carefully inspect the hull bottom for chips, dings, and star-shaped spiderwebbing cracks. It can be hard to see these signs through antifouling, so you may want to strip the paint for a good look at haul-out.

PUMP IT Keep your bilge dry by recaulking seams and replacing O-rings on hatches and deck plates frequently, as needed. Make sure your bilge pumps are mounted as low as possible.

203 REPAIR GELCOAT

Own a fiberglass boat long enough, and you'll end up with a scratch, nick, or gouge in the finish. It might be from a muffed landing, a dropped pair of fishing pliers, or just a hole drilled in the wrong place. You can usually fix these yourself. It takes a bit of patience, but do it right and few will notice.

Complications occur when there's damage on a textured surface like diamond nonskid or on a multitone finish. For these, call in a pro. Also, deep gouges may need structural fiberglass work or filler before you repair the gelcoat. On horizontal surfaces, liquid gelcoat works, but for vertical surfaces, a paste is easier to apply.

MATCH THE COLOR You might be able to buy gelcoat from a dealer, but if your boat has weathered at all, it may no longer be a match. Companies like Evercoat and Rayplex offer handy kits consisting of a neutral base and a range of colors that you can add slowly (A) until you have exactly the right tone.

SMOOTH OUT Use a rotary grinder to smooth the edges of the flaw to a 45-degree bevel (B), being sure to eliminate any loose material.

TAPE IT OFF Carefully mask around the edges of the repair area with 2-inch (5-cm-) wide painters' tape. Give yourself $\frac{1}{16}$ of an inch (1.5 mm) of unmasked margin around the damage (C). Mask off any adjacent areas or items to protect them from inadvertently applied gelcoat or errant sanding. Clean up the repair area with acetone.

MIX IT UP After you have color-matched the amount of gelcoat needed for the repair, you're ready for your catalyst (aka hardener). Different gelcoat resins require different catalysts, so make sure you are using the proper formula, as well as the right ratio (e.g. four drops of catalyst per teaspoon of resin). Mix the two parts thoroughly with a stir stick to ensure that the entire batch will cure at the same time (D). You should have about 10 to 15 minutes adding the catalyst before it starts to harden, so work carefully but quickly.

APPLY YOURSELF Use a small wood or plastic putty knife to spread the gelcoat smoothly over the prepped area (E). Fill the repair slightly higher than the surrounding surface to allow for sanding (if you don't plan to sand, go ahead and make it flush). Either way, spray the patch with a PVA curing agent and let it stand for 24 hours, or as indicated in the product instructions.

SAND IT Once the PVA has dried completely, go ahead and peel it off. If you don't plan to sand the area, just apply a coat of wax and you're done. Most patch jobs will require sanding, however, to look seamless. Wet-sand the cured gelcoat with 320-grit wet/dry paper on a soft sanding block (F). Confining work to the immediate repair area, continue wet-sanding with 600-grit paper until nearly even with surrounding gelcoat. Finish wet-sanding with 1,000-grit paper; then buff out with rubbing compound followed by a coat of wax.

A

B

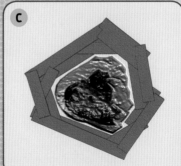

C

D

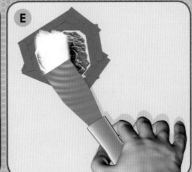

E

F

204 RESTORE A NONSKID DECK

Most modern boats have nonskid decks that rely on a diamond pattern formed into the deck mold. However, many older boats still in service, and a few new ones, rely on a grit-type traction additive in the gelcoat for deck safety. The problem is, the grit wears down with use and the deck eventually becomes slippery when wet. That's no good. You can bring the boat to a boatyard and pay a pretty penny to have someone else fix this problem or, if you are handy and have a weekend, you can do it yourself and put the savings toward boat enjoyment. Here's how we did it, using a product called Interlux that's based on a durable two-part epoxy paint. It's available in a variety of colors, so you can be safe and stylish.

STEP 1 Wash your deck with a mild detergent to remove dirt and grease. Allow it to dry, then lightly sand the surface using a random orbit sander loaded with 60-grit to level and scuff the old surface. Finish with 120-grit, vacuum up any dust, and wipe down the surface with a rag and a fiberglass solvent cleaner, replacing the cloth as it picks up residue.

STEP 2 Carefully mask the area to be coated with a premium painter's tape. Make clean, straight lines, and take special care with curves and corners. During a recent restoration, I used small paint cans and various-size flat washers to round corners with a razor knife, and the finished job was a knockout. Look around to see what round objects you have that match up perfectly.

STEP 3 Mix up a batch of Interlux Epoxy Primekote 404/414 per the directions on the can and apply using a roller with a solvent-resistant cover. Coat the old surface with a thin layer of primer and allow it to dry, noting that drying time can vary with temperature and humidity. Then lightly sand the surface using the orbital sander and 220-grit paper just enough to rough the surface.

STEP 4 Pour Intergrip into a baker's sifter or poke holes in the top of the can. Apply Interlux Perfection with a roller. While it is still wet, shake on enough grit to mask the gloss. One pound (0.45 kg) will cover 450 square feet (42 sq m). The grit will swell up in reaction to the paint. Allow it to dry and then vacuum up any loose grit.

STEP 5 Roll on a final coat of Perfection and allow at least two days for the entire system to harden before use. The finished nonskid surface will be safe and durable, enhancing your boat's look and safety.

205 TRY A KIWI TRICK

An alternate option for refurbishing your old nonskid deck is a unique product that has been used on racing sailboats and work boats in New Zealand and Australia for well over a decade now. It is a water-based acrylic polymer that comes ready to use in a 1-gallon (3.7-l) can and is 10 times thicker than paint, giving it the consistency of pudding. It comes with a special open-cell roller body that you use to add texture—no grit or other additives required.

For most boats under 26 feet (7.9 m), you can prep, tape, and paint the entire deck in a day, and it will be ready for use in 36 to 48 hours. KiwiGrip has excellent durability and can even fill minor imperfections in the deck surface. The product performs best when applied in a shady area or on a cloudy day because direct sunlight accelerates the drying process. Here's how.

PREP Wash the deck with detergent and allow it to dry. Using an orbital sander and 60-grit paper, scuff the entire area to be painted to remove any gloss, vacuum up the residue, rinse, and let dry.

TAPE Carefully mask the working area, as described in item 204.

PAINT KiwiGrip can be applied with a trowel or a large, stiff nylon paintbrush. When you complete an area, go over it with the open-cell roller to apply the texture.

FINISH Allow the paint to set up for an hour or two, then remove the tape for a clean edge. (If you wait until it dries completely, the tape will be more difficult to remove.) Cleanup can be done with soap and water. Allow at least a day before using the deck.

GET EXTRA PROTECTION

If the constant cycle of oiling and cleaning teak is too much for you, consider sealing or varnishing your wood. It's not "old school," but if you value ease over tradition, these can be reasonable solutions.

	WHAT IT DOES	**CONSIDERATIONS**	**MAINTENANCE**
SEALER	Seals out moisture and dirt, seals in natural oils and resins	Older teak may need to be restored before application. Clean and bleach the wood to a uniform color, then oil it thoroughly (see item 208). Wait at least two weeks before applying the sealer.	Maintain sealed wood by washing it and applying a fresh coat of sealer every two to three months.
VARNISH	Coating protects wood from moisture, drying, dirt, and grease	Teak doesn't hold varnish as well as other woods due to its oil content, and varnish can be fussy. You'll want to make sure wood is ivory smooth, have warm and dry conditions, and use a light hand with the brush. Plan on applying at least six coats.	Varnish alone doesn't protect wood from the sun, so you'll probably want to choose a varnish with UV filters. And understand that it may need to be redone if the wood darkens due to the sun essentially cooking the wood's oils.

207 CLEAN TEAK ON THE CHEAP

If your boat has teak surfaces that have gone grey, it's time for some TLC. You can pony up for a special marine solution to get it clean and ready for oiling if you really want to. Just know that what you're really paying for is that pretty picture of a boat on the bottle. Which is to say that the active ingredient in that bottle is oxalic acid, and a bottle of Bar Keepers Friend has the same ingredient at a much more reasonable price.

Fill a bucket partway with water, then add enough Bar Keepers Friend to make it suds up. Using a soft scrub brush, clean any and all teak surfaces, always working with the grain. Figure on about 3 minutes of scrubbing per square foot (0.09 sq m) of teak. Don't worry if the wood turns black; it's only the dirt coming out. When you're finished, thoroughly hose off the wood and all surrounding surfaces to get rid of all traces of acid. If the wood's grain appears raised, gently rub it with No. 00 (fine) bronze wool.

208 GO FOR THE GOLD

Teak is a beautiful wood that adds a rich feel to any boat—but also needs a fair amount of maintenance to keep its shine. Oiling teak, despite what you may have heard, doesn't actually do much to preserve it. We do it anyway to intensify the golden color and distinctive grain that make teak so desirable.

PICK AN OIL Teak oil is a base of either linseed or tung oil, with some resins added for durability. Linseed is markedly cheaper, but can darken the wood's color. Tung oil has less of a tendency to darken and is also more water resistant.

KNOW YOUR OPTIONS A wide range of formulations are available that claim to address these issues with added pigments, UV filters, and mildew retardants. So many factors affect what works best in local conditions that it's best to seek out boat owners from the area whose boats are well maintained and ask what they use.

PAINT IT ON You'll need to apply multiple coats as the wood really soaks up oil. Thin your first coat with mineral spirits (about 80/20) for deeper penetration. Apply the oil to your teak with a paintbrush, being careful to not get any on your gelcoat or painted surfaces, because it will stain. If you do have any "whoops" drips, wipe them up immediately with a rag soaked in mineral spirits.

KEEP GOING The wood will likely "drink" up the first and second coats. By the third, the wood may be saturated in some places. Wipe up excess oil with a cloth as you go, and keep brushing and blotting until the wood is totally saturated. Your finished product should be matte in appearance, with no shiny spots. If it is shiny, wipe further.

209 COMPREHEND CORROSION

Corrosion is complex and mysterious, and a constant threat to a boater's happiness, like an annoying and uninvited dinner guest. You might try to get that guest to fill up on bread and stay away from the roast beef. With corrosion, the unwelcome guest gets electrons instead of baguettes, ready to eat in the form of sacrificial anodes. Corrosion eats the anode instead of your sterndrive, prop shaft, or raw water through-hull because anode metals dish out electrons more freely. With each electron taken, a minute bit of the anode's metal is consumed, instead of some of your boat or drive's metal.

Most boaters call sacrificial anodes "zincs," because zinc has been used for a long time. But there are others—aluminum, magnesium, and alloys with various trade names. Non-zincs often outperform actual zinc anodes depending on the type of metal you need to protect and the nature of the water in which the metal is immersed. The higher the anode's voltage, the more freely it gives up electrons and the more able it is to feed corrosion. We are talking about negative voltage here, so wrap your mind around the concept of "more negative voltage."

210 FEED THIS BEAST

Anodes create electrical current by setting up a difference in electrical potential. More is better in that your guest, corrosion, will devour the anode readily. But suppose you run out of snacks? Magnesium has a low current capacity and is quickly eaten away. Zinc and aluminum have higher capacity, so they last longer. Magnesium offers more protective electrons faster, but it protects for only about one-third the time of zinc, and just one-fifth that of aluminum. In a hypothetical situation, where zinc would last 150 days, magnesium would last but 50 days, while an aluminum anode would have corrosion chewing away for 225 days.

Additionally, the high rate of electrons served up by magnesium can create too much current—i.e., overprotect—when used to protect a metal that itself is already very active, like aluminum, especially one used in more conductive waters such as salt water or polluted fresh water. If you take a freshwater boat protected by magnesium anodes to the coast and put it in a slip for a week, you'll have a catastrophe on your hands.

211 GET GALVANIZED

Galvanic corrosion occurs when two dissimilar metals are immersed in an electrolyte (water) and are electrically connected. When immersed and connected, they create a cell, like a battery's, and the current produced can be measured. Corrosion of the more noble metal (the cathode) will be reduced at the expense of the less-noble metal (the anode), which will corrode more rapidly. Basically, zinc, aluminum, and magnesium anodes are fastened to marine metals because they are more noble and will corrode first, sacrificing themselves to save your pricey equipment. Any boat needs some protection from galvanic corrosion, since most have at least some dissimilar metal fittings or equipment. The question is how much? The consequences of too little protection are obvious: corroded equipment. But too much protection, "over-zincing," can cause failure of antifouling coatings and other problems. A multimeter and a reference anode can tell you if your boat is properly protected against galvanic corrosion.

212 TEST YOUR METAL

How do you choose which anode type to use on your boat? Cost helps answer the question. Magnesium is more expensive than zinc, and zinc is more expensive than aluminum. Additionally, comparing zinc and aluminum, besides their carrying capacities, which bear on your length of season, zinc forms an insulating oxide film over itself, especially in fresh water, that stops it from working. In fact, if you have an anode that seems never to have worn away, it's probably oxidized and not doing its job! By mixing iridium and other metals with aluminum, alloys are created that don't form aluminum oxide.

There are other considerations. For example, if your boat is connected to shore power, and thus connected to all the other boats at the dock, you may choose "weaker" zinc over aluminum to minimize the electrical activity. But if your boat has a galvanic isolator, or you're not plugged in, the more active anode might be a better choice.

Confused? Here's the takeaway.

The principles presented should have raised your anode awareness. They give you the basis to ask the right questions. Seek out a mechanic with ABYC "Marine Electrical" or "Marine Corrosion" certification and have the conversation. Don't just buy an anode kit because it has your engine's brand on it.

214 USE A MULTIMETER

A multimeter is an indispensable tool that can easily sniff out a range of electrical problems on a boat. Most people know to use this device to check if fuses, wires, or circuits are working, but you can also use it in your battle against corrosion.

While your boat is out of the water, use the resistance function of the multimeter to check out the integrity of your bonding circuits and sacrificial anodes. For instance, if a through-hull has current running through it, it's better to find out now than after it crumbles to dust and sinks your boat once you've launched for the season.

Set the meter to the ohms function and place the probes on any two pieces of equipment connected to your boat's bonding system (the green wire). If the reading is less than 1 ohm, all is well. Continue through the bilge, checking each leg of the bonding circuit. Next, place the probes on a zinc and the metal it's intended to protect. A reading of 1 ohm or less means it is okay.

213 DON'T TAKE IN STRAYS

Stray current corrosion occurs when electric current escapes from its intended path, which is normally through the wiring, and uses your boat, or its underwater fittings, as the new path. Even a moist surface can carry stray current. It can occur due to poor connections, failing insulation, improper support of wires, and improper original installation. This is a more severe kind of corrosion than galvanism and causes very rapid metal loss. Stray current corrosion can and does sink boats by corroding through-hull fittings. And it can do so in less than a week. The stray current can come from your boat or from a neighboring boat. It occurs because of faulty wiring, and even the wiring of your marina or waterfront residence can be to blame. A reference electrode and a multimeter can tell you if your boat is undergoing attack by stray current corrosion.

215

CHOOSE THE BEST

When selecting a multimeter for boat work, a model with an audible continuity alert is best, as you are often working in a tight area where seeing the display is impossible, but hearing a beep or buzz is easy. Need more reach? You can extend the length of the probes with simple jumper wires fitted with alligator clips.

216 SNAP TO IT

To replace a snap, follow the instructions in item 222. You may find that, with a less expensive boat, the snaps may be riveted in place. To change the snaps, drill out the rivets and replace them with a screw stud. To keep the gelcoat from cracking when drilling, use a countersink bit to flare the hole's edges, inhibiting cracks.

217 DEAL WITH RIVETS

If the hole around the snap isn't yet too large, you can do a temporary fix by placing a stick-on patch behind the hole. That said, a sewn-on patch is better and more durable.

218 PATCH A HOLE

If there's a small hole that you want to patch, seal it off with a carefully wielded cigarette lighter or soldering iron, and then sew a patch over it. Use a sewing machine whenever possible.

219 REPLACE GROMMETS

A grommet is a reinforced metal ring about the size of a quarter in a cover or T-top. It's used to pass cords through. Much like on a snap, you use a die to press a grommet into fabric. If you're only replacing a couple, you can press it into the cover by placing the die in the fabric and positioning it on a block of wood. Then you pound it with a hammer to close the grommet around the material. If you're replacing a series of grommets in a T-top or similar application, have a professional do the work. The best grommets are corrosion-resistant stainless steel.

220 CARE FOR A BIMINI TOP

To make your Bimini top last longer, make sure it's dry, retract it at the end of the day, and store it in the zippered boot. Additionally, use the same protectants for your cockpit and bow covers on the Bimini top. Finally, upgrading to quick-release "grenade" pins in the deck hinges does away with thumbscrews and makes removal easier.

221 UNSTICK SNAPS AND ZIPPERS

For both snaps and zippers, apply a light coat of Teflon lubricant to keep scale and corrosion at bay. You can also use a crayon to "draw" a waxy protective film onto the snap or zipper. Make this part of your spring commissioning and fall layup regimens.

222

REPAIR CANVAS SNAPS

Snaps pulling out from boat covers and tops are a common event, especially in autumn when dropping temperatures cause fabrics to contract and stress the snaps. Take heart! In many cases you can repair the snap yourself. Here are basic steps for replacing the female snap on the canvas using the simplest, least expensive tools.

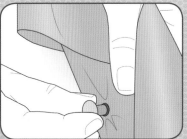

STEP 1 Insert the post of the "dome" through the hole. If the hole has become overly large, sew a patch four times the area of the hole onto the back of the canvas first so that the backing doesn't just slip straight through.

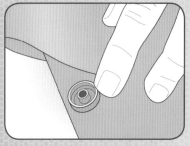

STEP 2 Place an anvil or die on a flat, stable surface that won't give under the blow from a hammer. A scrap piece of plywood laid on the ground will work. Place the dome head-side down on the surface, with the post sticking up.

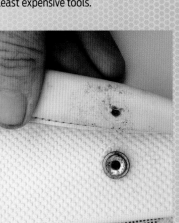

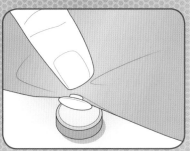

STEP 3 Place the female section of the snap onto the post of the dome. Smooth out any wrinkles or puckers in the canvas around the snap.

STEP 4 Place a snap- or grommet-setting punch or "set" onto the post and, with a firm rap (but not a mighty blow), hit the punch and deform the post down onto the dome.

223
REPLACE A BUNGEE

Bungee-style fasteners use tension to secure
canvas. The bungees hook over small studs mounted to the back of the boat.
The studs install just like the male half of a snap. The bungee half of the equation consists of
the bungee fastened to two plastic halves that go through a hole in the cover. After about three
years, the bungees stretch or break from weather exposure. To remove the broken bungee, pry off
the backing piece with a screwdriver. Expect to break it. To replace, sandwich the canvas between
the two halves and press the barbed male side into the female side. Just make sure you position it
correctly, because you can't get it apart (without destroying it) once it snaps closed.

224 REPAIR A SEAM

You can repair split seams on your canvas, but your
sewing machine has to be up to the task. The key to
canvas repair is a UV-resistant thread. Use the biggest
gauge your sewing machine can handle. The best seam
is a flat felt stitch, in which one of the two stitches is
hidden from exposure to the sun.

225 CARE FOR YOUR COVER

A boat cover will protect your valuable investment from the elements and from other potential damage or wear and tear. However, you also have to protect and care for the cover, or it won't be able to do its job as well.

PROTECT THE COVER To help a boat cover resist ultraviolet rays, use a fabric guard. Wait about a week and then apply waterproofing to improve a cover's resistance to water. When you're putting away any cover for winter storage, make sure it's dry, because a wet cover will promote mildew growth.

CLEAN IT RIGHT You can clean a canvas cover by hand with warm soap and water or a commercial canvas cleaner. You can also put it in your washing machine with a small amount of laundry detergent and clean it on the gentle cycle. Hang out the cover to dry.

226 FIX A ZIPPER

If the slider tab that you pull up to close the zipper breaks, cut off the last tooth on the zipper, slide off the old tab and slip on a new one. Then melt the last tooth of the zipper or crimp a zipper stop over it to keep the new tab from sliding off. Zipper parts are available from general sewing supply houses as well as specialty marine retailers. For anything more difficult, you'll need to see a pro (see item 227).

227 TAKE IT TO A PRO

There are some crucial pieces of canvas on your boat that you should not attempt to fix on your own. This could be because doing the repair properly requires highly specialized equipment, or perhaps it's just one of those things that will be really expensive to fix if you mess it up. Below is the skinny on those items, so you'll know what to do when things go awry—and what you're risking if you decide to ignore our hard-earned wisdom!

REPLACE A ZIPPER Once a zipper separates behind the slider, it's done. The plastic teeth on the zipper are shaped like a mushroom, and that expanded shape holds the seam closed. As the plastic teeth degrade, they lose their grip and the zipper needs to be replaced (A), which requires stitching capability beyond what most folks have access to.

REPAIR A SPLIT Where vinyl is concerned, even a short split-seam repair is more difficult to do than an otherwise identical repair to an all-fabric seam (B). It's harder to stitch the vinyl because it's thicker, so this one should be left to the yard. When the clear vinyl comes into play, it takes a stronger machine to punch through the thicker vinyl of the windows.

REPLACE HIGH-TECH FASTENERS Common-Sense and Lift-the-Dot fasteners are high-tech snaps that are used in places where the conventional stud and female combination won't hold (C). They are both installed similarly to a snap, and a layman could handle them, but the press/pliers cost about $300, which would make it cost-prohibitive. Take it to the pros.

REPLACE CLEAR VINYL Many boaters have watched their clear vinyl (D) become foggy or brown over time. Most boaters don't even realize that a shop can sew new clear vinyl panels onto the existing canvas, which can save a lot of money. This requires an industrial-strength sewing machine to punch through the canvas along with the two layers of vinyl. Have access to one? Start by pinning down the new vinyl to maintain the windows shape properly. Once the new vinyl is in place, cut out the old cloudy stuff and you'll see clearly again.

228 DIAGNOSE A DEAD ENGINE

There are few things worse than wanting to get out on the water only to find your boat won't start. If you know what to look for, and you know how to fix those problems, the day may not be lost. Here are the top 25 reasons your boat's engine won't start. Check through this list methodically, and you may be able to find and fix the problem yourself. Even if you can't, you'll have a lot of data for a mechanic, which will make their job easier and save you time and money in unnecessary diagnostics.

- Loose or broken wire or frayed insulation somewhere in the electrical system
- The fuel tank is empty, either because you burned more fuel than expected or developed a catastrophic leak
- Fuel tank air vent not open
- Fuel lines kinked or severely pinched
- Water or dirt in fuel system
- Clogged fuel filter or screens
- Too much/too little choke on start
- Pump primer bulb leaky or damaged
- Carburetor adjustments too lean (not allowing enough fuel to start engine)
- Timing and synchronizing out of adjustment
- Manual choke linkage bent (auto choke out of adjustment)

- Spark plugs improperly gapped, dirty, or broken
- Fuel tank primer inoperative
- Ignition points improperly gapped, burned, or dirty
- Reed valves not seating or stuck shut
- Weak coil or condenser
- Cracked distributor cap or rotor or shorted rotor
- Loose fuel connector
- Poor engine or ignition ground
- Faulty ignition or safety switch
- Low cranking speed
- Low voltage to ignition when cranking
- Low compression
- Safety lanyard/kill switch disconnected
- Drained battery (if engines won't start and you don't stop cranking the ignition!)

229 INSTALL SPARK PLUGS

Today's fuel-injected marine engines run so clean that plugs need changing less often than in years past. But that day will come. For those with a mechanical jones, or with older engines, here are some helpful tips.

PLUG PROPERLY "Close enough" won't do. A plug that is too long or with the wrong heat range can cause engine damage. Our money's on the dealer for the accurate information; ask him if the engine manufacturer has issued any service bulletins advising of a new spark plug—or of one for a special application, like extended trolling.

WRENCH IT RIGHT Spark plug sockets have foam inside to protect the plug's porcelain snout. A standard socket may crack the porcelain. In many applications, the plugs are buried deep, requiring a careful touch, a socket extension, and a tight gripping socket, so as not to drop or lose the plug during removal and installation.

GET TRUE TORQUE When reinstalling spark plugs, don't use the old mechanic's joke specification, "goodentite." Use a torque wrench adjusted to the proper specification according to the engine manual. Typically, 18 to 20 foot-pounds (24.4 to 27 Nm) is as tight as any spark plug needs to be. Overtightening is a huge mistake; if the threads are stripped, the cylinder head will have to be removed and rethreaded. That can mean a huge repair bill, especially with a four-stroke engine. Buy a torque wrench; it's cheaper.

230 KEEP CARBS HEALTHY

When "ethanol-induced" varnish deposits start to clog the carb's jets, less gas gets into the engine. Your now lean-running carb can run hotter, making the aluminum pistons expand and causing cylinder scuffing and the loss of compression. Or the engine simply seizes up. Spray the intake with a carburetor cleaner. Do this when you first crank over the engine each spring, and then again every third fill-up. Also, add a stabilizer containing fuel-system cleaner to the tank regularly throughout the season.

231 EASE BOLT ACTION

Remove the bolts that hold the lower gear case one at a time, brush on some nonhardening gasket sealer near the heads, and then torque each one back into place. The sealer will prevent water from getting on the threads and rusting them in place, plus bolts will be easier to remove when you service the water pump.

232 KEEP CABLES SLICK

Your engine controls and steering cables will last a lot longer if you keep them well lubricated. Here's a quick-and-easy DIY method—it shouldn't take more than an hour, and you should do it every other season.

STEP 1 Cut a bottom corner off a plastic sandwich bag, forming a hole just big enough for a cable sleeve to slide through.

STEP 2 Disconnect one of the cables you plan to work on at its cockpit end.

STEP 3 Tape the bag to the sleeve and hang the cable up by the bag.

STEP 4 Pour some cable lube (I use graphite and WD-40) in the bag and let it sit while the lube seeps into the cable.

STEP 5 Repeat for all of your control and steering cables, and make a note of the date so you can repeat the process in two years.

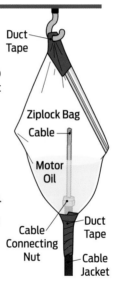

Duct Tape

Ziplock Bag

Cable

Motor Oil

Cable Connecting Nut

Duct Tape

Cable Jacket

233 LUBE & GO

For a super-fast lube job, take a lesson from your friendly local motorcycle mechanic and use a cable lubricator. This handy little tool clamps onto your cable and directs lubricant straight from your spray can down the cable housing. Give it two long squirts, move the cable back and forth to spread the lube, and you're done. Some people complain that it can be a little messy, with the lubricant leaking out if you're not careful, so don't perform this little task on your best Persian rug.

234 KEEP CABIN AIR FRESH

Sad to say, but our boats sit unused and sealed up most of the time—a perfect environment for mold, rot, and corrosion, all of which can be prevented by circulating fresh air throughout sealed areas. Ideally, you want to completely replace all of the air in your cabin every hour. To get a sense of the task at hand, the cabin of a typical 30-footer (9.1 m) holds about 800 cubic feet (22.5 cu m) of air. In other words, this is a big job, and you can't rely on natural ventilation to get it done.

The solution is to use solar-powered fans, one for intake and another for exhaust. To reach all parts of the boat, drill vent holes at the tops and bottoms of lockers and any other closed-off areas.

235 KNOW THE ANSWERS

So you've done the diagnostics and troubleshooting you're comfortable doing, and the darn thing still won't start. At this point, the smart thing to do is call your technician—after all, DIY is a great way to save money right up until you get in over your head and become "that guy." Don't be that guy. Instead, be prepared with detailed notes that will help your marine tech figure it out. If time is money, having the answers to these questions will help keep your wallet in good shape. You might want to copy or scan this form and have it filled out and in front of you before you dial. Studying this list before a problem occurs should help train you to become more observant, and thus catch some problems earlier.

☐ How long ago was it that you first noticed the problem?

☐ Did it happen over a period of time or start suddenly?

☐ Did anything specific or noteworthy happen before the problem started?

☐ What audible alarms sounded (if any)?

☐ What were your gauges reading at the time? Did the "check engine" light come on? Did the engine overheat?

☐ What were your fuel and oil levels at the time?

☐ When was the last time you used the boat prior to the problem?

☐ When and where did you last fuel up, and how much fuel did you put in the tank?

☐ Did you change the prop to a different pitch or have any other prop work done recently?

☐ What the weather was like?

☐ Does the problem occur only when the boat's in neutral, or when it's in gear?

☐ How fast you were traveling, and/or what was your rpm at the time?

☐ Is the problem limiting you to a specific rpm? (As in, you can't go above a certain rpm; you're stuck in "limp home" mode.)

☐ Was the boat at full capacity, and/or did you have more people on board than usual?

☐ What you were doing at the time (cruising, towing a wakeboard, pulling a skier, etc.)?

☐ Did you hear noises, see fluid leaks, sheen in the water, etc.?

☐ Who was operating the boat when you first noticed the problem, and was that person operating it any differently than normal?

☐ Have you recently modified the boat (new transducer, through-hull fittings, etc.)?

☐ When was the last time you replaced your batteries and performed the recommended routine, scheduled maintenance (fuel- and oil-filter changes, etc.)?

☐ How many hours are on the motor?

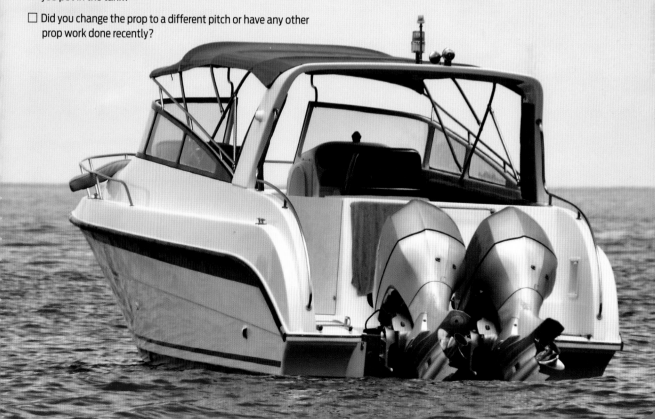

236 TAKE CHARGE

Whether you're just looking to extend the time between charges to keep your bilge pump running or intend to go hybrid and use some combination of internal combustion and electricity to propel your boat, you'll find this primer helpful. Regardless of the battery technology you choose, electricity remains the same. Here are some rules to live by. I call them the "great eight."

RULE 1 Cold cranking amps (CCA) are rated at 0º F (-18º C).

RULE 2 Marine cranking amps (MCA) are rated at 32º F (0º C).

RULE 3 An amp-hour is the reserve capacity, stated in minutes, that a battery can withstand during a 25-amp draw before requiring recharge.

RULE 4 Two batteries wired in series double the voltage.

RULE 5 Two batteries wired in parallel double the ampacity.

RULE 6 Double the voltage, and amp draw is halved.

RULE 7 Never draw batteries below 50 percent charge.

RULE 8 Base your battery bank size on 50 percent of battery capacity: If you need 200 amp-hours to run your stuff, install a 400 amp-hour battery bank. Make that 500 amp-hours, just to ensure the most reliable service. Reliability is the main feature we need from our batteries. (NOTE: According to ABYC standards, a battery should never be installed below a connection in a fuel line.)

237 FACE UP TO FAILURE

It's never fun to have a battery fail—whether we're talking about your car refusing to start up on a cold morning, a flashlight conking out during a blackout, or a cheap toy failing to wow us on Christmas morning. In the world of boating, however, battery failure can be much worse than annoying or inconvenient. it can be downright deadly. And that's why even those boaters who failed every science class in high school turn just a bit nerdy when it comes to understanding how batteries work. Here are some things to keep in mind when trying to figure out why a battery might fail. Short answer? It's probably a matter of chemistry. Longer answer? Likely caused by under- or overcharging.

UNDERSTAND THE CHEMISTRY Batteries depend upon a chemical reaction of sulfuric acid with lead plates to create direct electric current. As the reaction proceeds, sulfates are deposited on the plates, reducing their ability to produce current. Recharging the batteries puts the sulfate back into the solution, which in turn gives the battery the potential to provide electricity once again.

BEWARE OF SULFATION There are a number of reasons that sulfuric acid crystal may build up on the batteries plates; a common one is running the battery infrequently, and recharging after light use. The tricky thing is that the battery will test as okay, but run out of power quickly. If a battery is serviced early, sulfation can often be corrected. In fact, some chargers have a setting to temporarily boost the charging voltage for a brief period of time, causing a mixing of the electrolyte and dissolving the crystals. The process is called equalization and can be done—depending on the manufacturer—about once a year. This should only be done on wet cell batteries as it can destroy other types.

DON'T OVERCHARGE Didn't we just talk about overcharging as a cure for bad batteries? Yes, but that doesn't mean it's generally a good idea. In fact, overcharging a flooded battery can cause the fluid to boil away, exposing the plates to the air, which will ruin them. In worst case scenarios, the battery can burn, or even explode.

MAINTAIN IT Proper battery maintenance includes checking your terminal connections for corrosion or frayed wires, and fixing or cleaning immediately. The charge can slowly leak out through conductive paths made by dirt or spilled water, so keep that battery case clean. Finally, be sure that wet-cell batteries are topped up with distilled water and have their vent caps in place.

238 VISIT THE TERMINAL

Keeping battery terminal connections clean is Boating 101. But don't forget the battery charger's terminals as well. Here's how to keep them clean and shiny.

STEP 1 Disconnect the nuts that secure the terminal's lugs.

STEP 2 Clean the terminals with degreaser.

STEP 3 Use fine sandpaper to polish off any corrosion.

STEP 4 Lightly coat all the parts with grease.

STEP 5 Reinstall the nuts and torque them down tight.

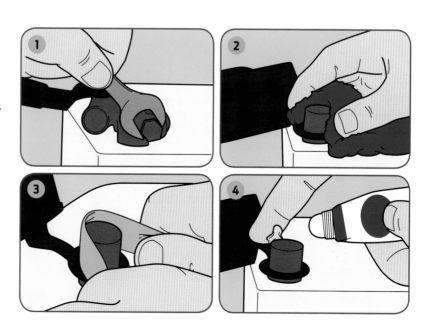

239 GET THE DROP ON VOLTAGE

Voltage drop is one of those concepts it's important to understand when doing wiring. Wires carrying current always have inherent resistance to the current's flow, which is called "impedance." Voltage drop is defined as the amount of voltage loss that occurs through all or part of a circuit due to impedance.

Excessive voltage drop makes everything work harder trying to deal with the substandard current, causing lights to flicker or burn dimly, heaters to give off less heat, and motors to burn out.

You want to keep voltage drop to 3 percent or less, for any critical application affecting the safety of your boat or passengers, such as bilge pumps, navigation lights, electronics, etc. This means using the right wires, which requires some complex math to do correctly. You can find detailed tables online by searching "3 percent voltage drop." If you have any uncertainty at all, consult an electrician or other expert, as this can literally be a matter of life and death.

240 PREDICT FAILURE

Most electrical failures occur on the positive leg of a circuit because there are so many switches, fuses, and connectors, unlike the negative leg, which goes straight to ground. The best way to detect potential problems is with a "voltage-drop" test. Connect the negative probe of a multimeter set on 12 VDC to the battery. You'll need a long jumper wire to reach. Switch the ignition to "on" and touch the positive probe to the positive contact point of the lamp, pump, or whatever you're checking. If the meter reads within a few tenths of a volt of the battery, then that circuit's good. If it's substantially lower, there's trouble.

Work back toward the battery using the positive probe to test all connections until you find full voltage. You'll now know that the fault is down-current of this point.

241 IMPROVE YOUR CONNECTION

If you're finding faults when you do voltage-drop testing, the cause is more than likely to be corroded connectors. These are circuit killers if the condition is not improved or allowed to worsen, but easy to fix once found. The usual way to clean connectors is with bronze wool pads, which work well on flat surfaces but are difficult to use on panel screws, female connectors, and hard-to-reach spots. I've seen my auto mechanic go right for a can of oxidation solvent. Spray it on to remove oxides, sulphide residues, oils and dirt, while leaving a protective film. He also checks if the wire itself is corroded under the insulation. If you can't expose clean strands, replace the wire.

242 SET UP AN AUTOMATIC CHARGING RELAY

Automatic Charging Relays (ACR) share charging current for all of a boat's batteries and protect the starting battery from discharge. Managing all of your batteries while boating is a cinch with an automatic charging relay system. Such a system allows charging current to flow to both starting and house batteries automatically, without your having to remember to throw a switch. But it also prevents inadvertently draining the starting battery while using house loads (stereo, fish finder, plotter, etc.), which might leave you dead in the water. While there are a number of ACR configurations, here's how to set up a basic two-battery system on a single-engine boat.

STEP 1 Make sure you use marine wire and fuses sized to handle the engine's alternator output and starting requirements. Check the owner's manual to determine the amperage output and draw, and follow the recommendations rigorously. If you're not sure, check online.

STEP 2 Choose a location close to the batteries to attach both main components. It should be dry and well ventilated. Use stainless-steel fasteners to install them securely, and check behind bulkheads for wires, hoses, and tanks before drilling any holes. You will need access to the back of the battery switch to connect wires, so don't mount it until after step 3.

STEP 3 Connect the starting battery positive to the ACR stud A and the house battery positive to stud B, with fuses for both. (You always want to connect the positive first in 12-volt systems.) Connect the house and starting batteries' positives to the lower studs 1 and 2 on the battery switch, respectively. Finally, connect the switch panel positive with a fuse to the upper stud 1 and the outboard starter/alternator positive to the upper stud 2.

STEP 4 Connect the negative terminals of both batteries to the negative bus bar. Next, connect the terminal marked GND on the ACR to the negative bus bar. Install a fuse in the ACR ground wire. Make sure all terminal connections are crimped firmly, tightened properly, and coated with dielectric grease.

STEP 5 Turn the dual circuit plus battery switch to "on." The SI-ACR will manage the charging of both batteries when underway and when plugged in to a charger. In case you need the house battery to start the boat in an emergency, turn the switch to "combine batteries." Rotate the battery switch to "off" when you leave the boat.

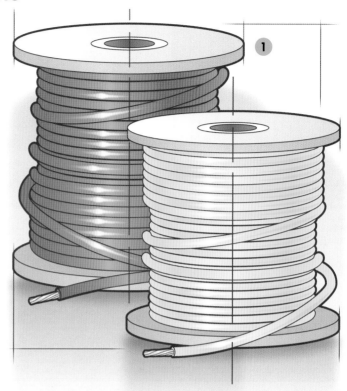

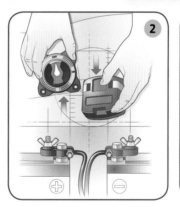

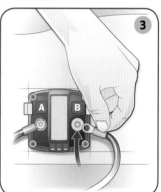

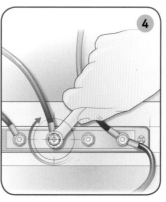

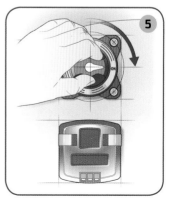

243 INSTALL A MARINE DUAL-BATTERY SYSTEM

If you have a boat with just one battery, it's wise to add another, giving you twice as much battery capacity in case, for instance, you inadvertently drain a battery with the stereo while the engine is off. You can use the second battery to start the engine and then switch to the low battery to give it a charge while you're running.

Adding a battery is an easy project using a dual-battery selector switch. When properly installed, these switches let you choose one of the two batteries, combine them, or disconnect both with the turn of a dial. More complex systems incorporate automatic charging regardless of switch position, but this setup is simple and upgradable and gets the job done.

STEP 1 Make sure you buy a selector switch designed for two batteries (some are simple on/off switches, which won't work for this application) that will handle the amperage when starting the engine. A rating of 250 amps continuous is sufficient for most outboards and gasoline inboards. You can also buy switches with locks for security against boat theft, and some have field disconnect circuits to protect the alternator in case you turn the batteries off while the engine is running.

STEP 2 Choose a marine battery that meets the engine specs. Installation should comply with Coast Guard and ABYC standards. Wet-cell batteries should be secured in a battery box. Absorbed glass mat batteries don't need boxes. Both need tie-downs or brackets, and the positive terminals should be covered with nonconductive boots.

STEP 3 Selector switches have a 4- to 6-inch (10–15-cm) wide footprint, so pick a surface where you have enough space. ABYC standards dictate that the switch be as close to the batteries as possible and readily accessible. Some can be flush-mounted for a cleaner look abovedecks, but make sure the switch is protected from spray. Hold off on final installation until after you have connected the positive cables to the posts in the back.

STEP 4 Cables should have "marine cable" stamped on the insulation. Size 2/0 cable handles most outboards and gasoline inboards. Connect the positive terminals of batteries 1 and 2 to the corresponding posts on the back of the switch, and then connect the positive cable from the engine to the output post of the switch. Also connect the positive accessory wire to the output post.

STEP 5 In order for the dual-battery system to operate properly, you need a crossover cable between the negative terminals of the two batteries. Also, connect the negative cable lug from the engine/ground and the negative accessory wire to either of the negative battery posts, and make sure all terminal nuts are tight (we like to replace wing nuts with locking hex nuts).

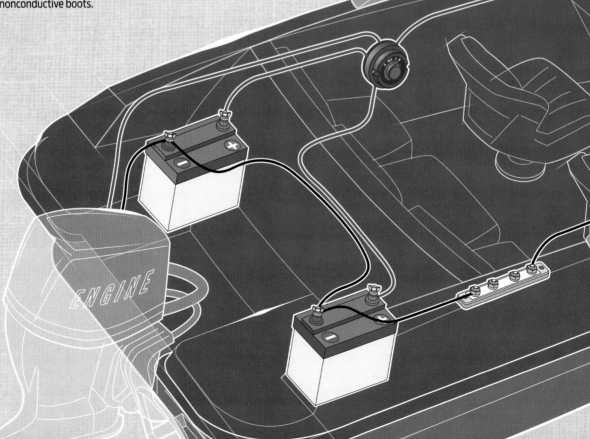

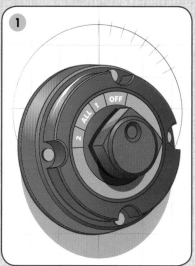

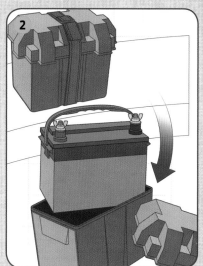

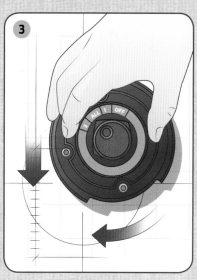

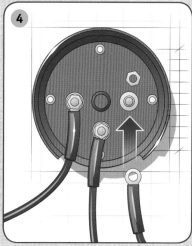

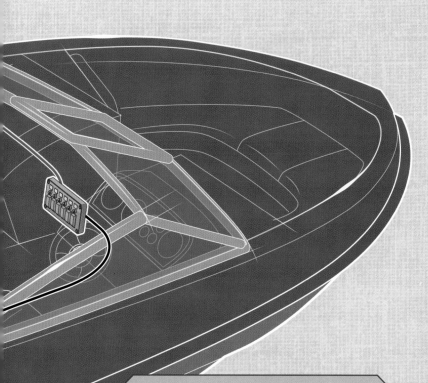

244 KEEP IT TOGETHER

Try to install the batteries and selector switch together and as close to the engine as possible. This will keep the cable runs short, saving you money and making it easier to route the cables. It will also minimize the amount of voltage drop you need to deal with (see item 239).

245 BELT IT OUT

As a general rule, belts should not deflect much when you press on them between pulleys. If you find a loose one, it may mean a worn belt or a loose pulley. Check it out before you end up calling a tow boat. Keep a universal "no-tools" replacement belt stowed aboard.

246 LIGHT 'EM UP

Before buying a new light fixture, clean the socket and contacts using 220-grit sandpaper wrapped around a stick. You can also purchase replacement sockets if they've gotten really corroded otherwise damaged. If you do replace the fixture, consider upgrading to energy-saving LED lights.

247 FLOAT YOUR GEAR

All you need is an inner tube, an old garden hose, and a scrap of plywood to make this handy mini-raft. Think of it as an extra companion that can follow you around and carry supplies from boat to shore, or for wade-fishing or snorkeling.

STEP 1 Measure a car or truck inner tube's interior diameter, and add 10 percent to get the diameter of the deck.

STEP 2 Tie a bit of string around a pencil, then measure out half the length you just calculated above. Drive a nail through the other end of the string and use it to draw a circle on a piece of plywood.

STEP 3 Cut out the circle with a jigsaw. Sand the edges.

STEP 4 Paint the disk, making sure to coat the edges.

STEP 5 Slit an old garden hose along its length and slide it onto the edge of the deck to create a seal between the deck and the tube.

STEP 6 Drill four evenly spaced holes through the hose.

STEP 7 Put the tube on the floor with its air stem down, and push the deck into the tube. Next, tie the deck in place through the holes with nylon line.

STEP 8 Tie on a yellow polypropylene tow rope. Now you're ready to float!

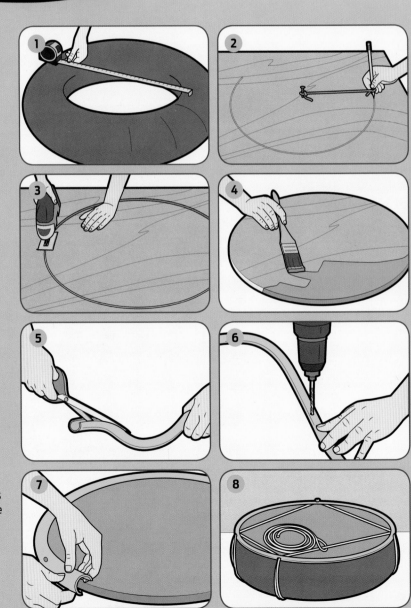

248 DO A MIDSEASON CHECK

Once your boat has been out on the water and in use for a few months, take the time to do a thorough evaluation of how it's going, and to tune up, do repairs, and replace or add components where necessary. Keep a logbook handy for notes on what service was done when (things like filter changes, pump rebuilds, and the like). Also, note your impeller numbers, fuse sizes, bulb types, filter elements, and other parts. Here's a list of the basics.

LOOK AT THE PROP Assess your prop (A) for damage and look for line that may have wound around the shaft.

DRY IT OUT On a dry, windy day, open the hatches (B), pry off deck plates, and let the boat breathe to reduce moisture and the chance for corrosion and mildew.

MONITOR SEACOCKS Open and close seacocks (C) regularly to keep them in shape and ensure any problems are caught early. Once a year, fully disassemble and lubricate them.

CHECK ZINCS You never know when your marina's wiring or your neighbor's boat has developed an electrical problem, and stray current can eat up underwater metals quickly. Check your zinc anodes (D) for corrosion regularly to avoid nasty surprises.

REVITALIZE CANVAS A hot day, right after washing the boat, is the perfect time to freshen up your canvas (E) with a new layer of waterproofing.

LUBRICATE GENEROUSLY Thoroughly lube grease fittings and linkages; also, spray engine (F), fuse blocks, and ground buses with products, like a corrosion blocker, that dry to a waxy film. Spray lubes that stay wet attract grit, making more of a mess.

CHECK YOUR FUEL FILTER It's easy to check filters (G) visually—just drain the filter's contents into a clear glass jar or bowl. Water and gas will layer, so you can assess how the filter's doing at a glance. When you get a fuel filter serviced, mark the date on the outside with a grease pencil for quick reference.

TOP OFF BATTERIES Pop the caps off flooded cell batteries (H) and check the electrolyte levels. Use distilled water, not tap water, to top off low cells.

TIGHTEN UP Gather your tools and tighten every fastener (I) properly. Check windshield fasteners, bow rails, and the screws securing seats to the cockpit sole as well as engine-mounted accessories (alternator, filter brackets, etc.).

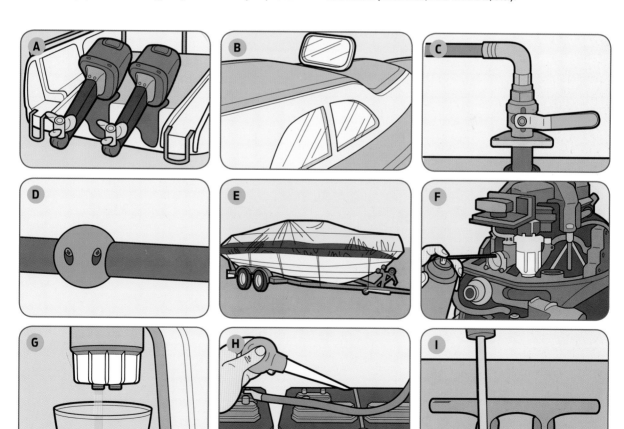

249 MAKE A HOLE SAFELY

Besides docking on a windy day with a new boat in front of an audience, drilling holes is one of the most dreaded tasks for a do-it-yourself boater. But boats are full of holes, from antennas on the hardtop to transducers on the bottom. So why do we fear them?

Probably because, on some level, we know water isn't our element. Despite our boat blessing us with the ability to visit a different realm, a special place reserved for the members of our rank, its primary purpose is to keep the water out.

There's merit to this fear. According to marine survey firms, leaks at through-hulls are estimated to be the cause in 18 percent of sinkings while underway. The numbers are worse at the dock, where failures of fittings below the waterline account for a full 50 percent of sinkings. Insurance claims back up the data. According to Boat U.S. numbers, fittings cause 44 percent of dockside sinkings and 16 percent while underway. But, if you want conveniences like a head or livewell, or even an extra cleat, you've got to drill holes.

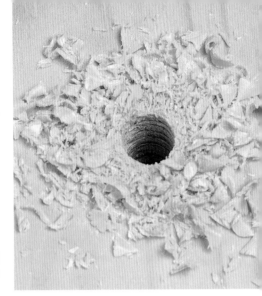

250 KNOW THE RISKS

From bowriders to express cruisers, boats have dozens, possibly scores, of holes. There are holes for water pickups, drains, and transducers, and above the waterline for bilge outlets, air conditioners, and exhaust. And the deck? Fresh from the cut-and-grind booth, it looks like Swiss cheese: There are holes for cleats, tow eyes, grab handles, speakers, lights, and more—and that's on a brand-new boat. Why should you fear drilling one or two more?

Well, problems can happen when good holes go bad. We've cited the serious consequences, but there are other risks. Gelcoat can spider-crack or chip; electrical wiring can be damaged; you may even accidentally drill right through the hull side.

"Measure twice and cut once," cautions Regal plant manager Mark Vahle, echoing an age-old construction adage. "Verify what's behind the hole you intend to drill," Vahle says. "You don't want to think you've got 2 inches (5 cm) before you hit the hull side and discover you've only got 1 inch (2.5 cm). Fiberglass repair costs a lot of money!"

251 DRILL, BABY, DRILL

What are the proper tools for making holes in your boat? You need two: a drill and a jigsaw. Standard bits will do for holes under 1 inch (2.5 cm) in diameter; for larger cutouts, use a bi-metal hole saw. Use sharp, fine-tooth blades. Coarse blades will grab and chip the gelcoat. Masking tape provides good protection. Use it to cover the boat's surface at the area to be drilled or cut.

PLACE CAREFULLY Many items, like cleats, may come with a paper or cardboard template to follow. Clamp your jig in place, and critical alignments are virtually guaranteed. If not, make one of your own, or use the piece you're installing to carefully mark the hole pattern. To ensure that your bit stays put at the center of a hole when starting the drill, punch a small nick in the surface with an awl first. It prevents the bit from skipping.

CUT IN STAGES Rather than drilling through the entire depth of the material, drill partway through, and then stop to pop the "plug" from the cut out of the saw, continuing when clear. This prevents "plugging up" the hole saw, a problem that plagues home mechanics.

SQUARE UP Cutting a square hole? Use your jigsaw. Mask the area to protect the gelcoat. Rounded corners prevent stress cracks, so drill the four corners and then use the jigsaw to connect the dots. If you must cut a right angle, use a knife to score an arc around the corner first. Should you start a crack, it won't spread beyond that line. Likewise, countersink screw holes to avoid starting a crack.

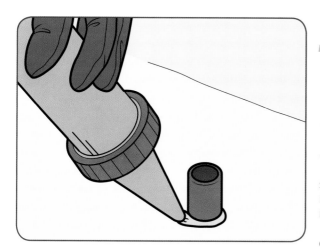

252 SEAL THE DEAL

Cutting or drilling is just the start. To finish the job, you must properly bed the fitting with sealant. Start by cleaning the surface with adhesive remover or acetone. Above the waterline, silicone sealants are often acceptable. For below the waterline, or for additional bonding strength, use a urethane-base sealant. Place a generous bead around a fitting's flange, so that sealant evenly oozes out around the perimeter of the hole as you push it into place. If additional screws are required to secure the flange, squeeze a bead of that same sealant into each hole before installing them. Inside the hull, run a bead of sealant around the interior of the hole, and then snugly tighten the collar or nut.

Urethane sealants often yellow when exposed to the environment, so keep that in mind.

Working neat with sealant can be tough. Use a plastic scraper, or scrap of Formica, to remove most of the excess. Avoid razor blades; it's too easy to damage the surface. A scrap of foam rubber with soapy water wipes away the final filmy excess better than paper towels do.

If the hole is through cored fiberglass, you'll need to seal out moisture. Many coring materials don't readily absorb water. Wood cores, however, require added attention. To properly seal a wood core, use epoxy resin, and brush it onto the exposed surface to thoroughly wet out the exposed end grain of the wood. Allow the epoxy to soak in. Recoat several times. Some pros suggest preheating the area with heat lamps or a heat gun, allowing the resin to penetrate even deeper.

Don't forget post-project common sense. If you're drilling through the bottom of your boat, check that it's watertight before you go offshore.

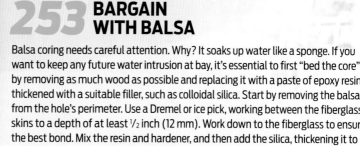

253 BARGAIN WITH BALSA

Balsa coring needs careful attention. Why? It soaks up water like a sponge. If you want to keep any future water intrusion at bay, it's essential to first "bed the core" by removing as much wood as possible and replacing it with a paste of epoxy resin thickened with a suitable filler, such as colloidal silica. Start by removing the balsa from the hole's perimeter. Use a Dremel or ice pick, working between the fiberglass skins to a depth of at least $1/2$ inch (12 mm). Work down to the fiberglass to ensure the best bond. Mix the resin and hardener, and then add the silica, thickening it to a paste. Next, use a tongue depressor to work the goop into the void, moving in one continuous direction to eliminate trapped air bubbles. A single session should do it. For depths deeper than $1/2$ inch (12 mm), allow one layer to cure to avoid building up excessive heat that cracks the resin. Once cured, sand the edges and add the next layer. Lastly, sand the edge back to the shape of the original hole.

254 PUT A SHOWER IN THE COCKPIT

Nothing beats showering in the cockpit after a swim, or when it's so hot you need a refreshing rinse. Single-valve cold shower assemblies take the least space. If you have a water heater, or think you might be installing one in the future, you might as well install a dual-valve hot/cold shower. This installation assumes a pressurized, cold freshwater system plumbed with reinforced PVC tube.

STEP 1 Create the master plan. Lay out the piping from the freshwater source to the shower valve assembly to ensure clear passage. Avoid hot engine parts, protruding fiberglass, hull-to-deck screws, and other obstructions. The showerhead comes with 10 feet (3 m) of hose; when selecting the transom or bulkhead location, there must be enough clear space behind and below the enclosure for the hose.

STEP 2 Cut out the opening. The enclosure requires a cutout of 5 inches by 8 inches and 6 inches of depth (12.7 x 20.3 x 15.2 cm). Using the provided template, drill a ½-inch (12 mm) pilot hole for the jigsaw and cut the opening. Slide the enclosure into place, mark the mounting screw positions, and drill ⁷/₆₄-inch (2.7 mm) pilot holes.

STEP 3 To tap your water line, find a convenient place in the pressurized side of the cold-water supply line. Cut the line, insert a T-fitting, and run the piping to the shower enclosure. Apply two stainless hose clamps to all three sides of the T and support the piping every 18 inches (45.7 cm) with cable clamps. If your boat has quick-disconnect plumbing, use that instead of clamps.

STEP 4 To connect all the pieces, start by screwing the supplied female adapter to the threaded inlet on the shower body, and connect to the piping. Push the shower hose through the enclosure, thread the supplied thread-to-barb adapter to the outlet, slip the hose over the barb, and secure with the supplied stainless hose clamp. Cap off the unused hot-water inlet.

STEP 5 To slide in shower unit, turn on the pump and check for leaks. Test-fit the enclosure, and push the shower hose in to be sure it goes in and out without any problems. Apply a thin line of sealant around the mounting flange and slide the shower unit into the opening. Secure with the supplied screws.

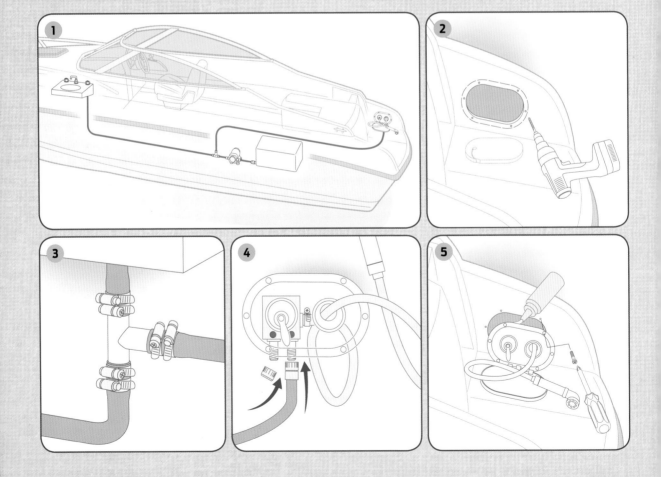

255 CHECK YOUR HEAD

When you feel back pressure while pumping your marine toilet, stop pumping! It's probably a blocked holding tank vent that's pressurized the tank. Continuing to pump can blow a hose or crack the tank. Clean the vent's screen with a toothbrush once a season to keep it open. And never use household toilet-bowl cleaners or any products with bleach, pine oil, or petroleum. They'll destroy internal rubber parts. Use white vinegar, mixed with 1 cup (237 ml) to 1 gallon (3.7 l) of fresh water.

Rub rails cover a boat's hull-to-deck joint, hiding the seam and fasteners connecting the two. Rub rails don't replace competent close-quarters handling, but they do protect against abrasion and mild bumps. Eventually, they need to be replaced. Fortunately, you can find complete kits and factory-matched rub rails, making it easier for DIY boaters.

This installation involves a semirigid rub rail, because it's quite common and the steps involved are illustrative of other types. Before starting, you need to remove the old rub rail. Remove the end caps, pull out the insert, remove the screws or drill out the rivets, and scrape off excess sealant. Then fill the old holes with an epoxy paste.

TAPE IT Apply masking tape (A) above and below the rub rail location to make a neater job of using sealant. Make marks for fastener holes above or below the location of the rub rail every 6 inches (15 cm) around the entire boat. A helper to hold the rail while you drill will help speed things along. If the vinyl rail is bent on being bent, a heat gun helps straighten the coiled rail out.

SET IT To ensure a "natural" location for the end caps, start at the middle of the transom (the flat, back end of the boat) or at a transom corner (a back corner of the boat). Unroll 3 feet (0.9 m) of the coiled rub rail (B) and bore holes through the rail and boat, countersinking the hole through the rail. Apply sealant to the back of the rail and the fastener threads, and install the fasteners.

HEAT IT Continue around the boat in the same fashion. At corners or the bow, wave the heat gun (C) over the rail to soften it to take the bend. If you use up one coil of rub rail, leave the last foot (0.3 m) loose and start with the new coil, leaving its first foot (0.3 m) loose and overlapping the first coil by $1/8$ inch (3 mm).

SCREW IT When you reach the starting point at the transom or transom corner, go back and pull together the splices left dangling and install a screw 1 inch (2.5 cm) in on both sides of the joint (D). Trim excess at the transom clean and mated with the transom angle, using a hacksaw. Install the end caps.

SEAL IT With a gloved hand, use your finger to smooth squeezed-out sealant above and below the rub rail (E), cleaning your finger frequently. Pull the masking tape up and away from the upper edge, down and away from the lower edge.

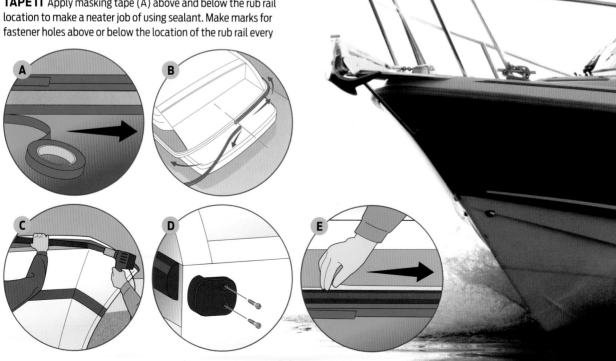

257 CHOOSE YOUR MATERIAL

Rub rails can be made of a variety of materials with various benefits and issues. Here's a quick and easy chart to help you determine the right rub for you!

MATERIAL	FLEXIBILITY	IMPACT ABSORPTION	IMPACT RESISTANCE	INSTALLATION	DURABILITY	PRICE
Aluminum	Low	Low	High	Difficult	Highest	High
Stainless Steel	Low	Low	High	Difficult	Highest	High
Rigid Vinyl	Moderate	High	Moderate (may require heating tools)	Moderate (may require heating tools)	Higher	Low
Semirigid Vinyl	Moderate	High	Moderate	Moderate	Higher	Low
Flexible Vinyl	High	High	Low	Easy	High	Low

258

DO THE MATH

Because of the curves involved, you'll need more rub rail than just double your boat's overall length. Add your boat's length to its beam and then double the sum to ensure you order enough rub rail to complete the job.

259 INSTALL GUNWALE ROD HOLDERS

Extra rod holders can really add to your boat's utility and enhance your fun out fishing. Here's how to make the most of the space you have to work with. Keep in mind that a 30-degree rod holder often won't fit inside the gunwale if oriented at 90 degrees to the boat. You may have to rotate the holder or use a 15-degree holder instead.

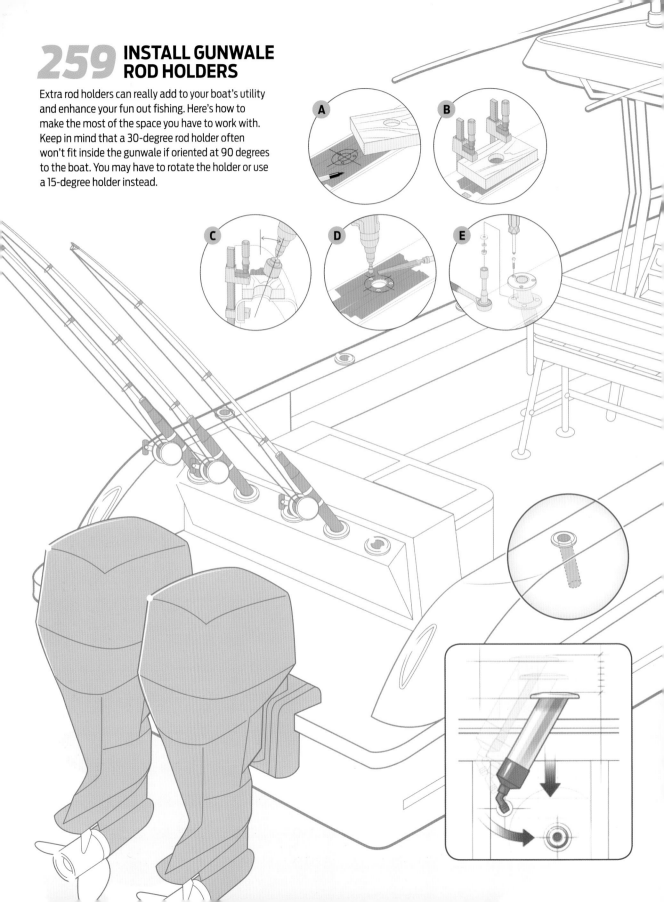

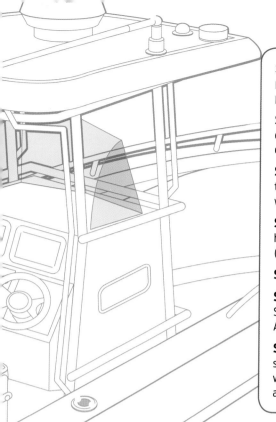

STEP 1 Mask the area with a good painters tape to reduce chipping and protect the surrounding gelcoat, and then mark the center of the rod holder position (A) using the template that came with it.

STEP 2 Make a simple jig (B) with a 1-inch (2.5-cm) scrap of wood wide enough to clamp in place over the gunwale. This will guide the hole saw to establish the proper angle of the cut.

STEP 3 With the jig clamped over the template, guide the hole saw into the jig (C). Begin slowly, apply pressure carefully, and the hole saw will cut without binding.

STEP 4 Drop the rod holder in place, align it, and check and mark screw holes. Then, remove the holder and drill the screw holes with the 1/4-inch (6-mm) bit. Countersink the screw holes slightly (D) so they won't crack.

STEP 5 File or sandpaper the center hole's edge, then remove the tape.

STEP 6 If the coring is wood, seal it with epoxy resin using a paintbrush. Seal nonwood coring with 3M 4200 or other polyurethane-based sealant. Allow it to cure.

STEP 7 Apply a bead of 3M 4200 sealant to the rod-holder flange and the screw holes. Put the rod holder in place; install the screws, backing plate, washers, and locknuts (E), and tighten. Use a damp-gloved finger to remove any excess sealant and allow it to cure. Now go catch some fish!

261
CHOOSE THE RIGHT ROD HOLDERS

If you use your boat for fishing—and stats show 80 percent of us do sometimes—it usually doesn't take long to realize that you never seem to have enough gunwale rod holders. Adding a couple extra "guns" to the armory is a fairly easy weekend project that can be accomplished with basic tools if you are fastidious about measuring and not queasy about cutting holes.

When choosing flush-mount rod holders, be aware they come in various angles from 0 to 30 degrees. The steeper the angle, the more space is required under the gunwale, so make sure a 15- or 30-degree rod holder will fit the available space. Also, be certain no other gear, rod storage tubes, plumbing, electrical wiring, or hydraulics are in the way. You can check out what's behind the coamings and under the gunwales by opening access plates, removing stereo speakers, or even taking out tackle boxes.

Choose open-bottom holders if you're OK with rainwater draining through them. Some models have drain tubes that can be routed to the cockpit if it drains overboard. Once you've made that decision, you should pick whatever model best matches your boat's existing rod holders and hardware.

260 DRAIN IT RIGHT

Full-liner, foam-injected hulls help make small boats hard to sink. Yet they create issues when it comes to installing flush-mount gunwale rod holders. Spray and wash-water can pour into the rod tubes and accumulate inside the gunwales, soaking the foam, adding weight, and promoting mold and mildew. Also, cup holders can drain into wiring, causing shorts and corrosion. The solution is to install drains, allowing any water that enters to quickly exit.

A few manufacturers sell aftermarket drain caps that you can fit into the bottom of your holders, then fit with drainage hoses. Installing and fitting the hoses properly should take about an hour per holder and is easy if you have intermediate DIY skills. Look for tutorials online, including from *Boating* magazine.

262 TOW THE LINE

Despite the name, a tow tower is less like a tower and more like a sturdy cage arching over your boat. It's there to serve as an attachment point for towing a wakeboarder, waterskier, or perhaps a float tube or other floating object. Here are a few things to consider when looking to add towing to your on-the-water capabilities.

STYLE Towers may be functional, but form still rules. Before anyone gets into details like fit and construction, the first factor you should consider is style. Modern designs can rake backward or forward, so you can choose the option that best complements the lines of your boat. Your boat's windshield design and location will have the most influence on what looks and works best. Cockpit clearance is another consideration.

CONSTRUCTION Towers endure a ton of torque. Look for beefy construction that will minimize motion. When installing your tower, be sure to add a backing block to make your tower even more solid. You want something sturdy such as aircraft-grade anodized aluminum for your safety. Other alternatives include stainless steel, in polished or brushed finishes. Colors are becoming increasingly popular, but with powder coating, insist on marine-grade polymers that will better resist corrosion, particularly in salt water. Chunky, threaded knobs and handles will make taking the tower down for storage and travel a much simpler process.

MOUNTING Tower feet should mount to the top of the gunwale (ideal) or the hull sides (if necessary). However, not all decks have a flat surface for mounting. Manufacturers use rubber pads between the mounting feet and deck to adapt to sloping contours. Swivel fittings or heim-style joints, situated between the tower legs and base brackets, will allow the necessary play.

263 BACK IT UP

The sturdier your tower is, the safer it is. Always use a backing block because it makes the tower sturdier. Use 1/4-inch (6-mm) or thicker composite or rot-resistant plywood, as big a piece as possible. Taper the edges to ease the localized stress.

264 BLING YOUR BOAT

What else to consider to optimize your boarding experience? Board racks offer the most bang for the buck because they offer extra space. Styles that can swivel into the boat may be more costly, but they make it easier to load and unload. Many tower designs will interfere with a conventional top, so you might want to consider a bimini. Going for the bling factor? Tower-mounted speakers are a popular addition, but avoid tower lights, which may tempt you to ride after dark. It's illegal.

265 MOUNT YOUR TOWER

The exact details of how to mount any given tower will vary depending on the manufacturer and model, but here are some basics to keep in mind.

GET PROTECTION Protect your boat's gelcoat by placing thick rags over the area where the mounting bases and arch might make contact.

CHECK IT OUT Before you drill any holes, plan out the entire installation in advance, and check thoroughly to be sure that your installation won't require drilling into areas where you might damage speaker wires, control cables, hoses, foam flotation, or conduits under the gunwales.

MOUNT UP The most secure place to mount the tower's bases is on top of the gunwales, but sometimes a side or angle mount is necessary. You need access to the underside of this location so you can reach the backing plate and tighten the nuts. This may mean removing a panel, speaker, or cup holder.

GO BY THE BOOK Follow the manufacturer's instructions closely as to the correct order in which to assemble and attach each piece. This is not a time to cut corners, as you could damage your tower or your boat—and even worse, put your passengers at risk.

266 TOW SAFELY

Even if you're not doing serious watersports like wakeboarding or waterskiing, you need to think seriously about safety. Here's a few thing to know before you tow (an inflatable craft).

GIVE 'EM ENOUGH ROPE Your tow rope should match the capacity of your towable, so be sure to check manufacturer specs closely; they'll vary widely from what's safe for a single-rider towable, six-person tubes, and everything in between. Many higher-end towables feature a quick connection point that makes it easier to hook up to the boat.

GET TO THE POINT While towers or center-mount pylons are perfectly suitable for pulling wakeboarders or skiers, never attach your tube's tow rope to either of these points. If the tube became submerged while towing, the amount of stress on the boat would be tremendous and potentially damaging. Attach your tow rope to the transom ski tow or use a bridle.

PUMP IT UP Towables should be inflated to their maximum air pressure. An underinflated towable can lead to a loose cover, which can catch on the water instead of skimming over it. All tube valves are easy to use and allow for quick inflation or deflation from either a manual or electric pump.

BE SAFE It goes without saying that boat drivers and all participants in towed watersports need to be constantly aware of other boats, buoys, and other large floating objects. This doubly applies to towables, which do not have the same maneuverability as wakeboarders or water-skiers. Be extra cautious when pulling someone on a towable.

267 POP IN SOME POP-UP CLEATS

Retractable cleats eliminate snags and stubbed toes, and preserve a boat's sleek lines, but are quickly accessible. Pop-up cleats are spring-loaded; pull-up versions are manually lifted, with detents to keep them in position. A downward push tucks both cleat types virtually flush with the deck. Nearly all are stainless steel and come in a variety of styles. Most require a larger hole than conventional cleats, as well as drain cups to keep water from leaking below deck.

STEP 1 If replacing conventional cleats, select the same size cleats or larger. The footprint might help cover holes left from the previous cleat; otherwise patch the old holes. Ensure the mounting studs or bolts are long enough and that you have access to the cleat's underside.

STEP 2 Use the supplied backing plate as a template to mark the mounting holes and central cutout (clear the underside of wires or hoses before you start). Cut the mounting holes with a drill motor and $3/8$-inch (1-cm) bit; use a 1-inch (2.5-cm) hole saw and jigsaw for the central cutout. If the underside of the deck is plywood, apply a light coat of catalyzed finishing resin to the exposed wood to seal it from moisture, and let cure before continuing.

STEP 3 To mount the cleat, mask off the area, bed the mounting surface generously with a marine sealant, and position the faceplate. Some cleats have welded mounting studs; others bolt up through the faceplate. Position the drain cup and backing plate on the underside, and then the washers and locknuts. Tighten the locknuts. Once the cleat is snug, clean up the excess sealant and remove the masking tape.

STEP 4 The drain cup is attached last, or with the cleat. Attach $3/8$-inch (1-cm) inside-diameter vinyl tubing to the hose barb at the bottom of the cup, then route the tubing to a suitable drain location. For the drain fitting, use a T-H Marine $3/8$-inch (1-cm) push-in impact drain. Most fishing boats won't require one, since the gunwales are open to the self-bailing cockpit.

268 GO LONG

Allow 1 inch (2.5 cm) of cleat horn length for each $1/16$ inch (1.6 mm) of rope diameter. This provides enough room for the rope to make a gentle curve without pinching, which weakens the line.

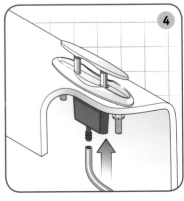

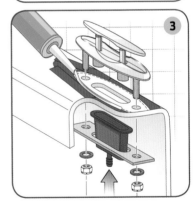

269

INSTALL AN ANCHOR WINDLASS

An electric windlass can save your back when you need to drop or haul anchor. You have two options: a horizontal-gypsy model, fully enclosed abovedeck, or vertical-gypsy concealed belowdeck. Both feed line and chain into the rode locker. Models with free-fall function let you drop anchor more quickly and precisely than "power-out" models, but you'll need a deeper locker to avoid tangles. The gypsy also needs a rope-to-chain splice; you can buy premade windlass rode, or make your own (see item 273).

270

MOUNT UP

A bow-mounted windlass needs to be able to let the rode drop right into the anchor locker while keeping the gypsy in line with the anchor roller. (You need a minimum anchor-locker depth of 12 inches (30 cm) to the top of the rode pile.) Cut holes per your template to feed the rode and accommodate wiring and mounting studs. If necessary, level the deck with fairing blocks on top and underside, and consider a backing plate made of aluminum or plywood. Secure studs inside the windlass with thread-locking compound, and fit a rubber gasket seal between the windlass and mounting surface.

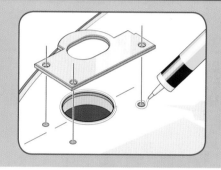

271

MAKE THE SWITCH

An up/down contactor (A) relays 12-volt power from the battery to the windlass and allows for multiple control switches, from the helm and on the bow. Install it vertically in a dry area (for example, through-bolting to a bulkhead in the bow), and connect the wiring from the windlass to the output studs on the contactor.

A windlass requires heavy-gauge cable from the battery to the contactor for both positive and negative feeds. The positive cable needs to go through a breaker switch, which also let you cut power to the windlass.

To install the helm switch (B), use its template to cut a mounting space, and drill holes for the screws. Attach its wiring to the switching studs on the contactor.

Your best choice for the bow switch (C) is a hard-wired, waterproof, hand-held model with a coiled cord; when not in use, it can be snapped into a vertical bracket—perhaps close to or inside the anchor locker—or unplugged and stowed.

272

SQUARE UP

The transoms of many boats are angled some 15 degrees. Side decks and cabin sides are often sloping. When installing accessories, it is important to drill the hole and install the fastener square to the mounting surface—not at a "dead level" 90 degrees. Drill guides are available at tool stores to help you achieve this. Doing so ensures the head of the fastener and the base of the fitting will sit flush, making for a structurally sound, easy-to-seal, cosmetically appealing installation.

A

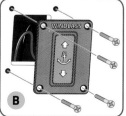

B

C

273 CONSTRUCT AN ANCHOR RODE

To the newbie, anchor tackle may seem rather mundane. Experienced boaters know better: Proper tackle means convenient, efficient, safe holding. Set things up correctly, and your craft will stick fast, even in strong currents or windy conditions. Do it wrong, and you could find trouble in short order. The core of your anchoring system, besides, of course, the anchor itself, is what's called the "rode," the rope and (usually) chain that, well, anchors it to your boat.

START WITH ROPE While straight chain is often used on bigger boats, the anchor rode on most recreational craft is generally comprises rope with a trace of chain. Nylon—either three-strand or a double braid—is best, because it is elastic, strong, and easy to handle. Always cleat the bitter end in the anchor locker (A).

MEASURE CAREFULLY A general rule of thumb is to use 1/8-inch- (3-mm) diameter rope (B) for every 9 feet (2.7 m) of boat length. Running a 36-footer (11-m)? You'll some need $\frac{1}{2}$-inch (12-mm) diameter rope. When building an anchoring system, keep in mind that prudent seamanship demands a scope of 7:1 for holding in the worst conditions. For every foot (30 cm) of water you'll be anchoring in, 7 times that amount of rode is generally required, plus the height of the bow cleat above the water. You'll need about 455 feet (138.6 m) of rode on most craft to hold through the worst in a wide range of conditions.

GO DEEP if anchoring in fairly deep water, say 60 feet (18 m) or more, you might consider running a slightly thinner-diameter rope in the upper zone (C) of the rode. This will reduce drag and make hauling much easier. The two ropes can be easily secured via a strong loop-to-loop connection.

SPLICE IT Fasten the top end of the chain to the anchor rope (D) with an eye splice. A crown splice can be woven into the chain, or use a thimble eye splice connected to the chain via a shackle.

CHAIN IT All anchoring systems should have a boat length of stainless steel or galvanized chain (E) separating the rope and the anchor, to prevent chafing and abrasion. Its weight also keeps the anchor's shank horizontal, allowing the flukes to better bite the bottom.

FINISH RIGHT Shackle the lower end of the chain to the anchor (F). The shackle should be larger than the chain links, and it's wise to wire the pin (known as mousing) to keep it from coming undone. You might also consider using an Anchor Saver (a device designed to help handle anchor problems) when connecting the chain to the anchor.

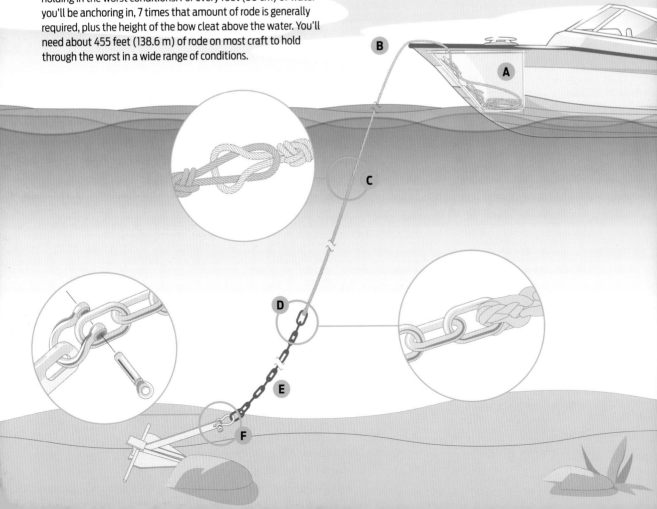

274 PIN ME

In an emergency, the integrity of your ground tackle may be the only thing that's keeping you off the rocks. You can "mouse" a shackle using stainless-steel wire, or by running a tie wrap through the hole in the pin and around the shackle. Periodic ground tackle inspection is good seamanship regardless of the method you choose.

275 MASK IT

To resist corrosion, use tinned-copper marine wire and marine-grade connectors with heat-shrink nylon sleeves. Also, enclose all connections with heat-shrink tubing.

276 SAVE YOUR ANCHOR

A stuck anchor means a tug-of-war. Once the windlass starts groaning in protest, we all groan and vow that it will never happen again. But we know it probably will unless we get proactive.

FLOAT ALONG An anchor float typically slides onto the rode, using a sliding bolt as a cam. The cam action prevents the anchor from sliding back through the tube once the anchor is free and floating at the surface, and also lets it serve as a marker buoy. An anchor ring can't do that, but can be clipped on the rode at any angle.

GET WIRED If you take risks in pursuit of fish, or need to anchor over "sticky" bottom while cruising, try trip-wiring. Many anchors have a hole in the forward part of the shank; drill a hole above the crown if yours doesn't. Shackle the bitter end of the chain here, and then run it back along the shank, wiring a link to the normal shackle point using thick copper wire or nylon tie-wrap. If you foul the anchor, the wire or wrap breaks under enough pressure, allowing you to pull it out by the crown. Re-rig with extra wire or wraps.

TRY A NEW ANGLE Try retrieving a fouled anchor from different angles. Try not to foul the anchor line in a prop as you reposition, and be careful not to swamp the cockpit if you're backing into seas.

USE SOME RUBBER This strategy should only be tried in calm conditions and only with relatively light, three-strand anchor lines that you can manhandle. Be sure to put on a pair of gloves before you begin, and to avoid wrapping the line around your hands. Pull on the fouled line, stretching it as tightly as possible, like a rubber band, and then let go. The sudden recoil often shoots the anchor away from the snag.

CUT YOUR LOSSES If you foul the anchor in rough conditions, the best bet is to cut your line and head back to the harbor. Things can go wrong quickly in heavy seas, especially in a small boat; have a sharp knife handy so you can immediately cut free. New ground tackle is relatively inexpensive, especially compared with the safety of your crew.

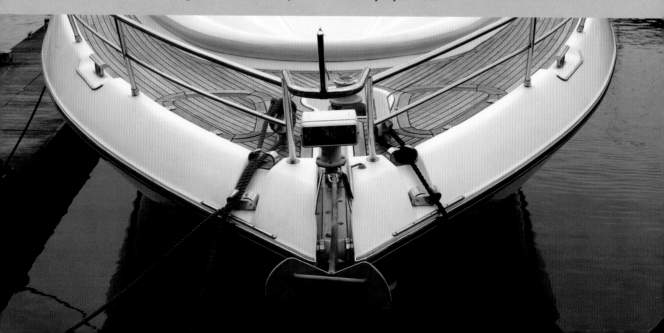

277 GET THE MOST FROM YOUR BOATYARD

A lot of folks think of their friendly neighborhood boatyard as the place to go for repairs that are too tough to DIY. And, in fact, that's the main service boatyards provide—professional repairs by certified technicians and experts. But your local yard may well offer more, which may be particularly relevant once you start thinking about winterizing. If you have the option in your area, definitely shop around. Most yards have a specialty, either the type of work they do or the type of boats they work on, so find one that deals with your needs the best. They may have a fantastic reputation for working with diesel engines, but nobody on staff who does fiberglass repairs. That kind of thing. Also, of course, do your due diligence by reading online reviews and asking around. Here are some things to look for above and beyond the repair shop.

DIAGNOSTICS Why wait until something breaks to fix it? Some boatyards will run diagnostics on your boat to let you know what has the possibility of failing in the next year or two, what needs immediate attention, and what is functioning at full capacity. This can save you a lot of money if you do the preventive maintenance before disaster strikes.

WORKSPACE Some boatyards offer you the space to work on your boat yourself if you have the skills. And if you find you don't—hey, the repair shop is right there!

SHRINK-WRAPPING Boatyards have the skills, tools, and, perhaps more importantly, insurance to shrink-wrap your boat for you, which is a great option for winterizing.

BOAT STORAGE Boatyards might have an advantage you don't: space. Many boatyards offer services to store your boat in a barn for the off-season. Save money and time by having the boatyard repair, winterize, and store your boat!

278 PREPARE FOR WINTER

You've had your summer fling and now it's time to settle in for the winter. Tucking your precious boat away for the winter, or for the off-season if your locale doesn't quite have a winter, is vital to your boat's well being. "Winterization" refers to the process of preparing your boat for a few months of latency. Winterization includes filling your tank, adding stabilizer to your gas, adding antifreeze, parts removal, covering, and many other tasks. You do have a few options for how to store your boat.

WET You can store your boat in the water, but know that this is considerably more work than storing it on land. If you choose to go this route, you'll need to seal all below the waterline through-hulls and pipes after draining them. Any water that gets in to the through-hulls or pipes has the potential to freeze, expand, and damage the boat. In areas that freeze, have high winds, or torrential rains, you are probably better off avoiding this option.

DRY Even if you don't have a serious winter where you live, getting your boat out of the water for maintenance and to let it dry out is a good idea. You can paint the bottom, do routine maintenance, or bust out some DIY upgrades. You can store the boat on your own property, but you might want to look into getting space at a yard that might offer addition services such as shrink-wrapping and maintenance. Not to mention, the yard probably has a large, covered shelter to put your boat in to help protect it from sudden cold snaps!

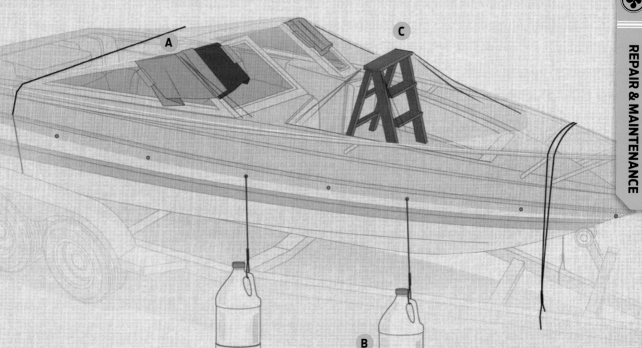

279 BE TARP SMART

A good tarp, properly tied down, is in most cases your boat's main line of defense against the elements. If this is the case for you, you'll want to be sure you do a thorough job. To make sure your tarp stays in place without damaging your boat all winter, follow these tips.

PAD IT Sharp edges, corners, and protrusions can wear holes through tarps in no time flat. Prevent this problem by covering those sharp edges with strips of old carpet remnants or rags (A), and use duct tape to secure them in place. Common problem areas include windshield frame corners, burgee poles, rocket launchers, and antenna mounts. Stretch an XL cotton T-shirt over outboard cowls to protect their glossy finishes against abrasion from fluttering tarps.

WEIGHT IT To keep your tarp from migrating south for the winter, you can cross lines under the boat or lash them to a trailer. However, this makes getting into the boat for winter projects troublesome. An alternative method that maintains easy access is to fill 1-gallon (3.7-l) jugs (B) with sand and hang them from the tarp's grommets. When you need to get inside the boat, just lift a jug or two to remove the tension and duck under the cover.

KEEP IT UP A tarp needs propping up in low spots, or it'll hold water, sag, and rip. You could build a frame, but that's overkill for many boats. Telescopic poles work well to prop up small areas, though you may need to reinforce with duct tape or the like in order to prevent the tarp from ripping. Another solution is to place a stepladder (C) on the deck to support the low spot. Still other boaters use a tow tube to support the tarp, storing a bulky toy

and helping to protect their boat in one fell swoop. Make sure the tarp has good ventilation, or mildew can become a problem.

CRANK IT A battery-powered AM radio left playing and tuned to an all-talk station will deter critters from moving in for the winter.

280 GIVE YOUR PROPULSION A PRE-WINTER CHECKUP

After you haul your boat out, but before winterizing, give your propulsion system a thorough inspection. If you spot anything awry, you'll have plenty of time to replace parts or make repairs over the winter, saving you the hassle next spring when you're anxious to get on the water. The following entries include key areas that warrant inspection on the boat's drivetrain, be it an inboard, outboard, or sterndrive power system.

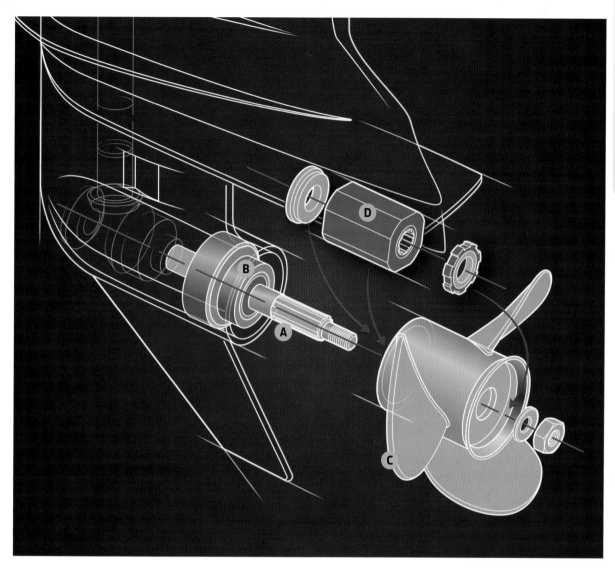

281 PREPARE YOUR PROPS

Even if everything else is working well, your boat won't budge if its props are out. Here's what to look for.

GEAR CASES On outboards and sterndrives, remove the propellers and check the lower-unit seal (A) for damage or leaks. Check for cracks in the case itself. Look at the skeg (a rudder that moves only up and down) too, to see if it needs a coat of paint. If bent, chipped or snapped off, remove the lower unit and take it to a shop to have a new skeg welded on.

PROP-SHAFT SEALS Inspect and replace or rebuild this vital component (B) of an inboard's running gear, if necessary. Look for fishing line on all shaft seals.

PROPELLERS Inspect props (C) for damage such as dings or bent blades. If in doubt, ask a prop shop to check them out and, if needed, repair or replace the wheel(s).

PROP HUBS If your outboard or sterndrive prop is more than five years old, have the hub (D) replaced as preventative maintenance in the off-season.

282

SEAL IT ALL UP

Once you're done checking over your propulsion, seal the exhaust outlets on the hull and air filters on the engine with heavy plastic and duct tape. This will prevent moist air from finding its way into the combustion chambers via open exhaust or intake valves while your diesels are enjoying some well-deserved downtime.

283 INSPECT PUMPS AND FILTERS

While you're pre-winterizing your boat, take the opportunity to give every single pump and connection in the drive a good look.

FUEL LINES Look over the vent lines, fuel-line connections, fuel-tank connectors, selector/shut-off valves and primer bulbs. Replace any rubber lines that are more than five years old. Any upgrade should meet the latest evaporative emission standards.

RAW-WATER AND CIRCULATING PUMPS Pull these off your inboard or sterndrive and look inside the pumps for wear and tear. Replace or rebuild them, if necessary.

GEAR-CASE WATER PUMPS Remove sterndrive and outboard lower units and replace the water pump. It's cheap insurance. Since it's off, this is a good time to have the gear-case pressure- and vacuum-tested for leaks.

STERNDRIVE BELLOWS Remove the drive and carefully check the drive and shift bellows for aging, wear, damage, or marine growth. If the flexible bellows—which serve in the critical role of keeping water out of the boat—are more than two years old, replace them.

WATER-SEPARATING FILTER Winterization dictates a fresh water-separating fuel filter element before the boat goes into storage. Don't forget to inspect the filter head too, especially if it is a painted aluminum version. As the paint ages, it can slough off the mating surface with the filter, allowing the aluminum to corrode and create air leaks in the fuel system. If the filter head is less than pristine, replace it.

SECONDARY FILTERS Most outboards have one or more secondary filters under the cowl. Check your owner's manual to see if you're due for new ones.

EXAMINE EVERY CONNECTION

Every electrical, hydraulic, and physical linkage should get careful consideration.

SPARK PLUGS Remove the engine spark plugs and clean and re-gap them. Replace them if your owner's manual says to do so.

ENGINE ZINCS Replace them if they are more than half gone. Also check the zinc ground cables as these can corrode or break.

BATTERY CONNECTIONS Pay particular attention to connections between the engine and battery. Make sure the connections are tight and free of corrosion. If the battery cable feels stiff or brittle, the wires inside might be toast. Replace the entire cable and brush the connections with dielectric grease. Toss the wing nuts; secure cables to battery terminals with nylon-locking nuts instead.

CABLE STEERING Replace the cable if you see any corrosion, a damaged or cracked sheath, or sense any binding or difficulty turning the wheel.

HYDRAULIC STEERING Inspect the hydraulic steering rams and caps. Also, check hydraulic hoses and connectors for wear and leaks. Rebuild or replace system components as needed. Grease the Zerk fittings.

POWER-ASSIST STEERING Inspect the power-assist pump for corrosion, especially around the wires providing electrical power to the pump. Check the fluid level and top off as needed.

POWER TILT AND TRIM Inspect the power tilt and trim system on your outboards or sterndrives for corrosion damage or hydraulic fluid leaks around the pump and rams. If you find trouble, have the system rebuilt over the off-season. Grease the Zerk fittings and coat the rams with waterproof grease.

THROTTLE AND SHIFT CABLES Check the insulation for cracks that can lead to corrosion. Make sure the cables operate smoothly and easily. If there's any binding, install new ones.

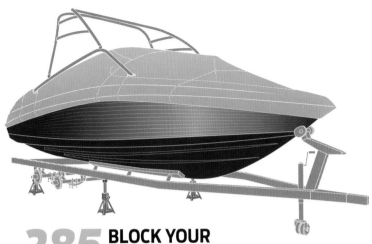

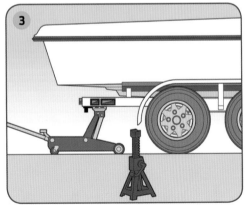

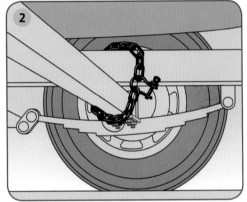

285 BLOCK YOUR TRAILER

If you plan to keep your boat on a trailer for winter or other long-term storage period, it's a good idea to block up the trailer. This takes the strain off the suspension system and deters tire rot and flat-spotting, saving you money and extending the longevity of your trailer and its components, whether you store your boat trailer on a paved surface or not. It also thwarts would-be thieves, who'd have a hard time stealing your boat and trailer without wheels.

Blocking the trailer is a relatively simple process, provided you have the right tools and equipment. Here's how to get it done, using a tandem axle holding a 25-foot (7.6-m) deck boat as an example.

STEP 1 Select a spot that's level (fore to aft and side to side) and does not block any areas you might need to access. Avoid overhangs that might dump snow, water, or ice on the boat cover. The trailer will be supported at five points with four jack stands and the tongue jack. Make sure the ground under each point is firm enough to support each jack. Give yourself enough room to work on both sides. Chock the wheels, disconnect the tow vehicle, and level the trailer with the tongue jack.

STEP 2 If your trailer has a leaf-spring suspension system, chain each axle to the trailer frame with the same amount of slack at each end. Use shackles to secure the chains. Be careful not to run the chain directly across any brake lines or trailer wires, which might be pinched or cut by the chain when it grows taut. This support will prevent the trailer axles from sagging excessively when you jack up the trailer frame. This step is not needed if your trailer has torsion-axle suspension. Slightly loosen the lug nuts.

STEP 3 Start about 4 feet (1.2 m) aft of the rear axle. Use a sufficiently rated floor jack to lift the frame until the rear tires are 1 to 2 inches (2.5 to 5 cm) off the ground. You may need to use blocks with the jack to get sufficient height. Place a jack stand under the frame with a 2-inch- (5-cm-) thick piece of solid wood underneath for support and lower the floor jack. Then move the floor jack to a spot about 4 feet (1.2 m) ahead of the front axle and do the same thing. Repeat the process on the opposite side. Readjust the trailer level with the tongue jack.

STEP 4 Use a star wrench to spin off the lug nuts, then remove the wheels/tires. Before you roll them into your garage or shed for winter storage, inspect the tires for cracks or damage to the sidewalls (both sides), treads, and valve stems. Check the wheels for bent rims or excessive corrosion, especially around the center, spokes, and outer rim. Plan on replacing worn or damaged wheels and tires before next season. Don't forget to do the same with your trailer's spare tire. Check the air pressure before reinstalling next spring.

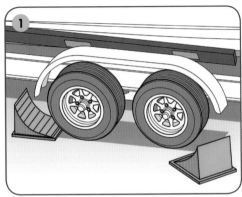

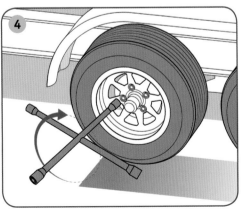

286 KEEP YOUR TRAILER HAPPY

Once you have your the trailer's wheels removed and the frame safely up on jack stands, don't just say "see you next spring" as you walk away. This is the perfect time to do a basic inspection and determine what's needed in the way of maintenance and repairs. Here are some of the critical items to check.

CORROSION Use a wire brush to remove spots of rust, then thoroughly clean with denatured alcohol and apply two coats of corrosion-inhibiting primer. Finish off with a coat of paint that matches your trailer.

LIGHTS Check and replace any wires or connections that look frayed or corroded. If there are multiple repairs, it might be easier to run an entirely new wiring harness. Now is also a good time to replace any burned-out lights.

BEARINGS Pull off the wheel hubs and inspect the bearings and seals. If in doubt, replace them. Repack with fresh grease.

BRAKES Check the brake pads and replace them if they have less than $1/8$-inch (3 mm) of useful life left. Have drum brakes turned. If disc brakes are scored, have them turned as well.

COUPLER/SURGE ACTUATOR Make sure the coupler is in good condition and that the surge-brake actuator operates properly and is free of leaks. Check the brake lines for leaks too, and replace any that show excessive corrosion or look faulty. Top off the system with brake fluid.

BOW WINCH Check the winch's functionality to make sure it is operating properly. In addition, inspect the winch strap or cable and bow hook to be sure they're in good condition.

287 STAND UP FOR YOUR BOAT

Placing a boat on blocks can be dangerous to you and your boat, if done wrong. While a boat can be blocked properly on cement blocks, jack stands (aka "boat stands" or "poppets") are the pro's choice. Some boat manufacturers recommend positioning for blocks and jack stands, so check the owner's manual or with the builder. Generally, keel blocks should be positioned under internal bulkheads to avoid stressing the boat. Improper blocking can lead to gelcoat stress cracks, damaged stringers, misaligned engines, and other problems. Check for proper blocking under your boat or that new one you're considering. Remember that even a small boat is heavy enough to kill you should it fall. Be careful, and call in a pro if you have any doubts.

GET GROUNDED Find a nice patch of solid and reasonably flat ground. Regardless of the surface, place the stands on plywood bases to spread the load and prevent the stands from settling. Even asphalt will give way, especially if it gets hot.

CHOOSE YOUR BLOCKS In all cases, 12-by-12-inch (30-by-30-cm) blocks are acceptable. Use wood blocks; barrels and cinder blocks should not be used for keel blocking.

SUPPORT YOUR KEEL The keel takes all

the weight, so it gets supported first. You can use concrete blocks with wood on top, but special poppets called keel stands with threaded rods are more convenient. Keel-stand pads screw up flat. A minimum of two stands will enable you to level the boat fore and aft. Use one stand or pile of block for every 10 feet (3 m) of length along the keel. Have a helper tip the transom onto the blocks as you gingerly pull forward until the boat is supported by the trailer forward and the blocks aft. Stack blocks along the keel and aft of the stem to a height that allows the cockpit to drain. Pull the trailer out from under.

BALANCE Position one adjustable jack stand every 8 feet (2.4 m) with a minimum amount of threaded rod exposed. The boat's manufacturer may have recommended places to place the jacks. If not, identify areas where bulkheads are installed and place them there to help distribute the load. The base should be parallel to the waterline and as far out from the keel as possible, generally tucking the pad into the chine. Thread the pads up, one side at a time, and finish when they are secure against the hull and the boat is level abeam.

288 DON'T FREEZE UP

To avoid freeze damage and corrosion, plumb the intake pumps to draw propylene-glycol antifreeze from a bucket, and run each engine until the solution exits the exhaust. This action displaces any standing water and coats the water jackets and heat exchanger with a corrosion inhibitor, while also distributing a coat of the fresh, clean oil that you put in earlier to help prevent internal rust during storage. Once the engine is off, immediately shut down the supply of antifreeze to prevent siphoning liquid into the combustion chambers and hydro-locking the engine. Because antifreeze can swell some rubber materials, remember to replace the intake-pump impellers next spring as part of recommissioning. If your engine has closed cooling, check the recommended maintenance schedule to see if you need to change the antifreeze in these systems as well.

289 PURGE COOLING SYSTEMS

Open all drain plugs to purge the raw-water cooling systems. Plug locations vary by manufacturer, so check your manuals. Use a stiff wire to clear any sediment from drains. Also, bump the ignition to turn over each engine (without starting it) to clear water from the pumps. If your boat stays afloat all winter, you can drain the systems by first closing the seacocks for the raw-water inlets and then removing the inlet hoses and intake-pump covers as well as all drain plugs. After clearing the raw-water systems, replace the drain plugs. If you removed the intake-pump covers, give each impeller a light coat of petroleum jelly and replace the covers.

290 STABILIZE YOUR FUEL

Unless properly treated, anything less than a full tank of diesel—especially the newer biodiesel and low-sulfur fuels—can grow stale, develop bacteria, and contract fungal infestations while

in storage, resulting in sludge and sediment that can plug filters. These create engine turnover problems and damage engines. Conversely, an empty fuel tank invites condensation, and over time, this results in water collecting in the bottom of the tank, posing a serious problem for diesel engines. Fill up and stabilize your diesel before long-term storage to help prevent any of these maladies. After treating the fuel, install new primary and secondary fuel filters, and then bleed the fuel lines to eliminate any air pockets.

291 REPLACE OLD OIL

Used diesel engine oil contains acids and other contaminants that can eat away at metals over the winter. So, ditch the old oil now. To change the oil, run the engine for a few minutes to warm up the oil. If the boat has been hauled, you'll need the proper motor flushers for the engines (or plumb the intake pumps) to supply cooling water from a garden hose. Installing a flush kit makes this job easy. Then shut down and drain or pump out the old oil. Change the oil filter and fill the crankcase with fresh oil (per the manufacturer's specifications). It's a good idea to change the oil for the transmissions at this time as well.

UPPER LEVEL

LOWER LEVEL

292 CHECK BATTERIES ON LAND

Batteries are often treated more like stray cats than family pets. They're attended to only when they're being loud and annoying. One reason is that many boat batteries are installed in cramped, nearly inaccessible locations making servicing a pain. But make no mistake, they need care and feeding to provide reliable long-term service. If you notice weak starting performance, check everything out now! Otherwise, once you've got your boat on the land for winter, check everything, whether you think it needs attention or not.

POWER UP Charge the battery, and then remove the negative cable. Let it rest for several hours before verifying its status.

CHECK SPECIFIC GRAVITY Each cell should have a specific gravity (see item 294) of between 1.21 and 1.28, if you are using a hydrometer.

GET A CHARGE A fully charged battery should read 12.5 volts; a good voltometer is a great tool to have.

BE VIGILANT Use a trickle charger/maintainer or check the charge monthly so you don't start the spring with a flat battery.

TOP OFF Check the electrolyte level of flooded batteries and top off with distilled water—just enough to cover the plates.

GET BENT Give each cable a gentle bend. If it resists and crackles, you've found a problem.

293 KEEP CHARGED IN THE WATER

If you've decided to store your boat in the water, you'll likely be doing less maintenance, but there are some vital steps you can and should take.

POWER DOWN Switch off all breakers except the one(s) for the bilge pump(s).

MAKE ROUNDS Check the boat weekly, more frequently in rough weather and during power outages.

KEEP IT UP Plug in to shore power and keep the battery charged with your installed charger or a regulated battery maintainer.

294 USE A METER

You can use either a hydrometer or a voltmeter to test how strong the charge is in any given battery. The hydrometer measures specific gravity (often abbreviated as SG), which corresponds to the weight of the sulfuric acid in the battery, while the voltmeter (as you might guess from the name) measures volts.

A hydrometer will give you a more consistently accurate reading because things such as weather or storage conditions do not affect it. However, it is a slightly more involved method than the voltmeter, and some folks prefer ease over accuracy.

295 KNOW YOUR ENGINE TYPE

There are four main types of boat engines: outboards, inboards, sterndrives, and jet boats. Cleaning and maintaining your boat properly means knowing what type you have. Some engines might require special cleaning or a few extra steps. Let's shed some light on the matter. Along with various engine types, there are different types of fuel delivery systems, including direct fuel injection (DFI), electronic fuel injection (EFI), and carbureted fuel systems. Regardless of the type you have, they will all need maintenance.

OUTBOARD An outboard engine (A) is a self-contained engine (comprising the engine, gear case, and propeller) that attaches to a boat's transom. Although two-stroke engines used to be the norm for outboards, four-stroke is quickly becoming the new standard. A tiller or steering wheel attached directly to the engine swivels the whole engine, including the rudder.

INBOARD If you can't see your boat's engine at all, you have likely have an inboard model (B). These models are typically four-stroke engines mounted inside the hull of the boat. They use a steering wheel to change the position of the propeller.

STERNDRIVE Also referred to as an I/O (inboard/outboard) model, the sterndrive (C) take aspects from both inboard and outboard engines. A sterndrive engine's body is mounted inside of the transom, as opposed to an outboard that's placed against the transom and hangs off of the end of the boat, or an inboard that remains entirely unseen. These engines are driven with a drive unit that swivels much like an outboard motor.

JET BOARD Another type of "invisible" engine, the jet board is available in both outboard (D) and inboard (E) options. Both work by propelling the boat forward by using an engine that sucks up water and pushes it back out with great force. The nozzle that pushes the water back out swivels, which is how you turn a boat using this system. When the boat isn't in motion, there's no way to steer since there's no propeller.

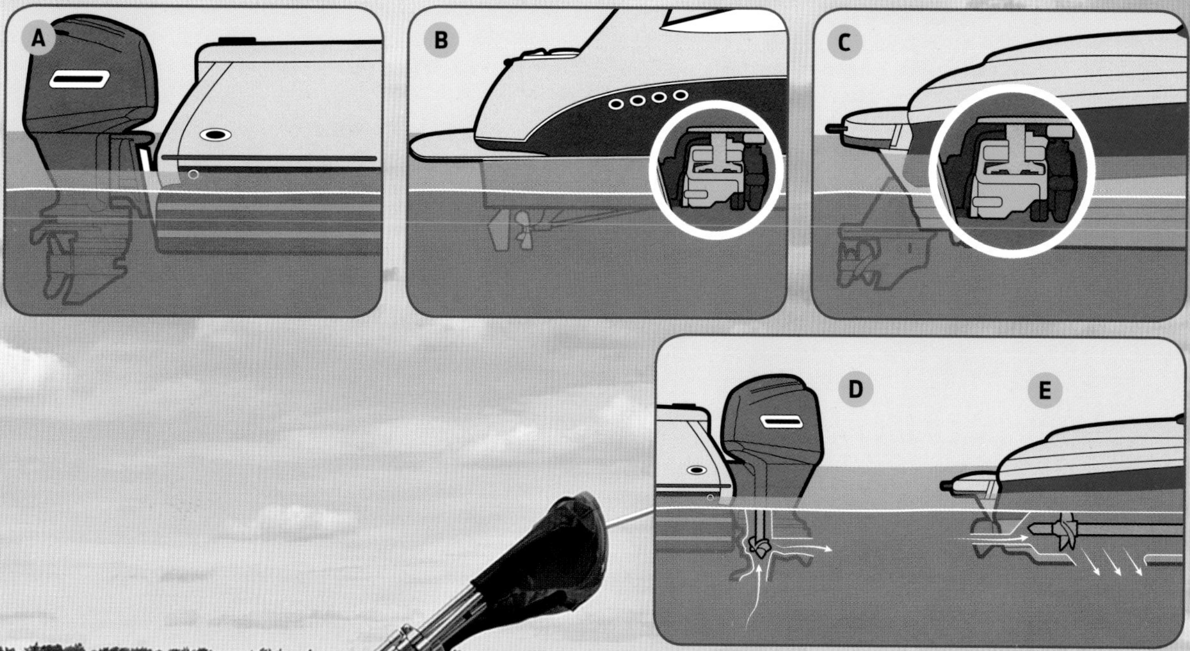
A
B
C
D
E

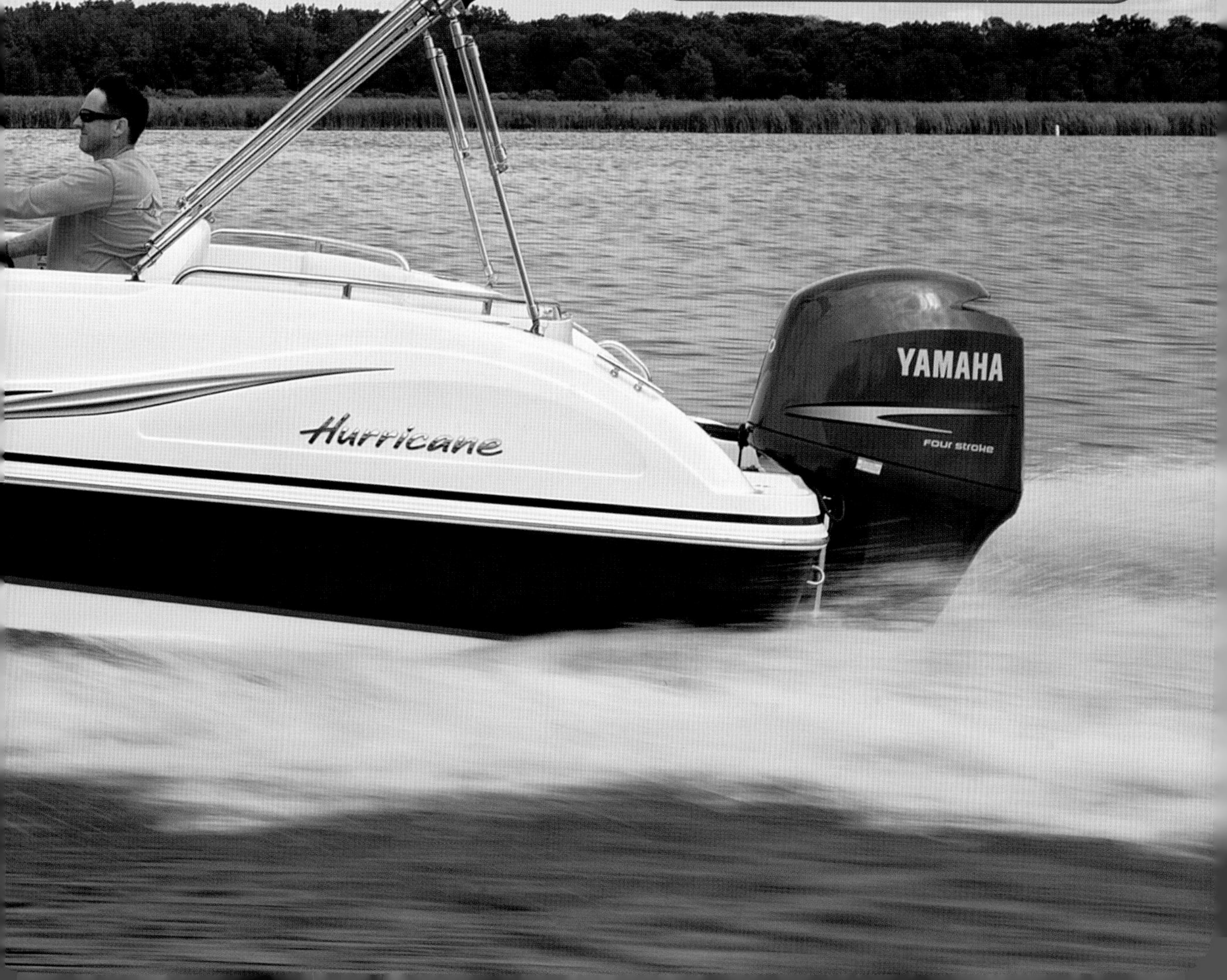
YAMAHA
FOUR STROKE
Hurricane

MAINTAIN YOUR COOL

There are two basic engine cooling systems: closed (or freshwater) and raw water. In a closed cooling system, the engine has a tank that holds fresh water, antifreeze, or a mixture that the system continually circulates through itself to stay cool. In a raw-water system, the engine draws from the water you're boating on and pumps it into the engine to keep it cool. For both types of systems, beware any water left in the hoses because it might freeze, expand, and crack the cooling system components.

STEP 1 Fully drain the raw-water side of a closed-cooled engine, including the manifolds, seawater pump, and heat exchanger. Drain-plug locations vary by engine; check your manual to find yours. Next, disconnect the raw-water inlet hose, and then remove the drain plugs. Use a stiff wire to clear any sediment blocking the drain. Finally, bump the ignition key just enough to crank the engine—without starting it—to purge the seawater pump.

STEP 2 The closed-cooling side of the system doesn't need to be drained since it's filled with an antifreeze-and-water solution, though it should be flushed and refilled according to the engine's maintenance schedule. Drain the rest of the system; many engines offer air-activated drainage using a supplied hand pump. Lock it onto the actuator fitting and pressurize the system until the green indicators extend. (There's no need to remove drain plugs; the air should purge the water. If not, drain as described before.) Next, crank the engine without starting to purge the seawater pump. Remove the hand pump.

STEP 3 Replace the plugs after draining. Fill with a propylene glycol antifreeze containing rust inhibitors to protect nooks and low spots where raw water might sit. Place a motor flusher ("earmuffs") over the water pickups, plumbed to draw the antifreeze from a bucket. Run the engine on your winter-mix fuel tank until the pink antifreeze solution exits the exhaust.

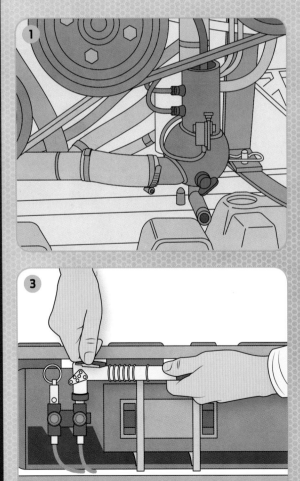

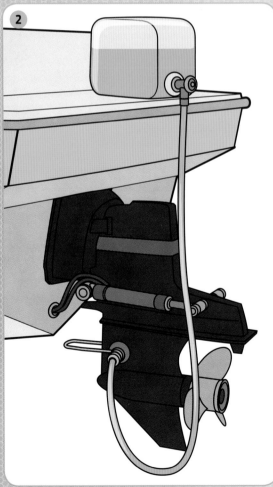

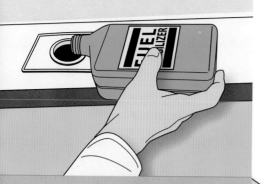

298 SWEAT THE SMALL STUFF

Once you've done everything we've recommended, you're probably not really done. Consult the owner's manual for any other suggested maintenance. Give the engine, drive, steering, and tilt-and-trim systems a thorough inspection. Check the belts, wires, shift cables, exhaust manifolds, and hoses, and bellows for wear, cracks, corrosion, or other damage. Check the hydraulic fluid levels in the power steering and trim pumps. Inspect the fuel hoses and replace if necessary.

297 FOG YOUR ENGINE

Keeping your engine lubricated is an important part of winterizing. First, add fuel stabilizer to the tank and run the engine so the treatment circulates. Shut it off and let it cool. Then, fog your engine: apply lubricating oil to cylinders and pistons while the engine is running. "Fog" the engine from a 6-gallon (22.7-l) remote tank. Add 5 gallons (19 l) of gas, 2 quarts (1.9 l) of two-stroke oil, and 5 ounces (29.5 ml) of fuel stabilizer. Disconnect the hose from the main tank at the filter. Connect the remote tank and run for five minutes at 1,300 rpm. Shut down and replace the oil, filter, and fuel filter.

298 SAVE YOUR POWER

Leaving batteries in your boat over winter is a sure-fire way to waste them. Remove the batteries from the boat and give them a charge. If they don't hold a charge, wait until spring to replace them (watch for sales over the winter). Clean the terminals with a wire brush using water and baking soda to neutralize acid; coat with light grease; check the battery cables for cracked insulation and corrosion, and replace if they show signs of wear and tear.

300 WINTERIZE YOUR STERNDRIVE

When it comes to a sterndrive engine, one of the most important winterizing steps is to remove the drive, and then inspect the bellows, universal joint, gimbal bearing, shift cable bellows, water intake hose, and exhaust run. Once it's apart, replace the bellows as well as any O-rings and gaskets, install a new water intake hose, align the engine and drive, and lube the U-joint.

301

CHECK 'ER OUT

Inspect the steering and tilt-and-trim components for wear. Replace anything that shows damage. Check the hydraulic fluid levels in the power steering and trim pumps. Inspect all of the sacrificial zinc anodes and replace them if less than 70 percent is left. Use zinc-chromate primer and touch-up paint on any scratches or chips on the drive. Give all grease fittings a shot of fresh marine grease. Wait until you're ready to launch in the spring before rebuilding the water pump, because the pump's impeller vanes tend to take a set during off-season storage.

302 DRAIN YOUR HOSE

With the boat on a trailer or blocked level, trim the drive down fully and turn it dead astern to drain any water. Crank the engine slightly (but don't start it) to purge any water from the pump. Keeping the drive down and straight will keep rainwater and snowmelt out of the exhaust hub during winter, as well as helping to extend the usable life of the flexible rubber bellows that seal drive components from water intrusion. Insert a small wire repeatedly into the various accessible vents and drain holes to ensure that all water drains from the drive.

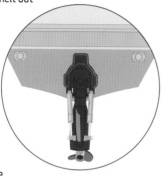

303 FILL 'ER UP

Propylene glycol antifreeze with a rust inhibitor, mixed to the manufacturer's instructions, should be used in sterndrive raw-water passages in areas subject to freezing temperatures. Attach a flush device (aka "ear muffs") to the drive's water pickups, but plumb it to pick up the antifreeze solution from a 5-gallon (19-l) bucket. This will feed the solution through the water pickups into the raw-water systems of both the drive and engine. Run until the pink-colored propylene glycol solution comes out of the drive's exhaust. Turn off the engine.

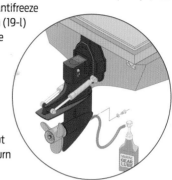

304 REVITALIZE YOUR LUBE TUBE

Drain your gear fluid by removing the lube drain/fill and vent plug screws. Put new gaskets on the plug screws. If you also have a remote gear lube reservoir (in the engine compartment), remove and drain it; then clean, dry, and reinstall the reservoir. Pump fresh lube into the drive from the drain (bottom) hole until fluid appears out the vent (top) hole. Install the vent screw, which creates a partial vacuum. Quickly replace the drain/fill screw. The vacuum created doesn't allow fluid to drain very quickly. Don't forget fill the lube reservoir to the proper level.

305 PROP UP YOUR SHAFT

Make it part of your winterizing routine to remove the propeller and inspect the shaft seal for fishing line. Remove any line you find; if it was there for a long time, it may have cut the seal. If the seal seems damaged or gear lube appears to be leaking from the prop shaft seal, have the seal replaced, the gears and bearings checked, and the gear case pressure-tested. Otherwise, grease the shaft and send the prop out for reconditioning.

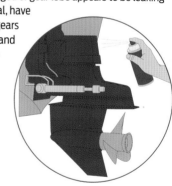

306 KNOW THE COLOR CODE

While you're at it, pay attention to how the gear lube looks and smells. If you diagnose any of these issues, be sure to tackle the appropriate remedies.

 WHITE STREAKS
Water in the lube. Solution: Pressure-check the gear case.

 COLOR OF COFFEE WITH CREAM
Another sign of water. Solution: Pressure-check the gear case.

 BLACK LUBE
Too long between changes. Solution: Adhere to maintenance schedule.

 FOUL ACRID SMELL
Water in the lube. Solution: Pressure-check the gear case.

 METAL SHAVINGS
Another sign of water. Solution: Pressure-check the gear case.

 GRAY MUDDY COLOR
Too long between changes. Solution: Adhere to maintenance schedule.

INDEX

PLEASE NOTE *Numbers refer to tips, rather than pages.*

ABOUT THE AUTHOR

Kevin Falvey is an award-winning journalist, speaker, and author of the heralded *Falvey's Guide to Fishing Long Island*. He has been writing about boats, boating, and the outdoors since 1982. Falvey oversees a steady stream of informative content at his post at the helm of BOATING, celebrated for helping boaters buy the right boat, teaching them to maintain their craft, and instructing them on how to operate their boats reliably, confidently, and safely. He lives and boats with his family on the waters of eastern Long Island, New York.

ABOUT *BOATING*

BOATING is the largest and most popular content provider serving recreational boaters. Founded in 1956 as *Popular Boating*, *BOATING* today produces video, magazines, and books, as well as publishing several monthly enewsletters. *BOATING* reaches almost 2 million people per month via boatingmag.com and social media. *The Total Boating Manual* joins this portfolio, delivering the same high-quality information about boats, their maintenance, operation, and navigation that boaters have come to expect from *BOATING* for over 60 years.

ACKNOWLEDGMENTS

Before man walked on the moon, before color TV was common, and long before the Internet, my parents sat me in a small, outboard skiff and handed me a fishing rod. The fish were biting that day, but it was I who was hooked. I thank them both for setting me off on a lifelong adventure involving boats and the sea, which has resulted, among other things, in the writing of this book.

I also have to thank my staff at BOATIING for the guidance, dedication, and inspiration they deliver each day. In particular, Sue Whitney and Ryan Swanson spent many extra hours helping to bring this book to fruition.

Finally, let me thank the staff at Weldon Owen, and, in particular, my editor Mariah Bear. Mariah, you maintained a steady hand on the helm and, like a compass, you always showed the way.

PHOTOGRAPHY CREDITS

Photographs courtesy of Shutterstock Images, with the following exceptions: Airman Technology Group: 076; Avon: 093 (lotion); Jim Barrett Photography Inc.: 264, 266; Christian Brecheis: 106; Chris-Craft: 001 (cuddy cabin); Eric Colby: 226, 227; Columbia Sportswear: 085 (shirt); Costa Del Mar: 088; Crevalle Boats: 039; Cruisers Yachts: 001 (express); DieHard: 052 (left); John Digsby: 186; Bill Doster Photography LLC: 009, 011, 020, 027, 056 (A), 073, 085 (shoes), 089, 096, 144, 165, 175, 191, 207, 212, 284, back cover (cabin cruisers, fishing couple); Doug Dukane: 295; Drawtite 19; Ebbtide: 001 (bowrider); Kevin Falvey: 082, 158, 200, 211, 253, back cover (man in hatch); FLIR Systems: 147; Fluke: 214; Four Winns: 001 (midcabin); John Frazier: 199; Furuno: 069 (screenshots); Greg Galuba: 283; Garmin Ltd.: 146; Grady-White: 001 (dual console); Jim Hendricks: 070, 075 (fisherman), 084, 269; Hummingbird: 069 (sensor); Hurricane Boats: 001 (deck boat); Interlux: 202; Interstate Batteries: 237; JimBuoy: 037 (horseshoe, ring); Richard Johnson: 069; Steve Karp: 035, 203; KCS International/ Cruisers Yachts 118; Tom King: 018, 28, 093 (pool noodle), 102–104, 201, 251; KiwiGrip: 205; Josh Letchworth: 019, 021; John Linn: 227 (closeups), Chapter 3 Closing Image (Bayliner); Lowrance: 074, 077 (transducer); Magellan: 056 (B); Mallory Marine: 283 (bottom); MasterCraft Boat Company: 155; Maxwell Marine International Ltd.: 124; Pete McDonald: 210; Mercury Marine: 075 (motors); Minn Kota: 075 (I-Pilot); Mojo Sportswear: 085 (shorts); Polk Audio: 056 (D); Proline Boats: 001 (walkaround); Ravenol: 297; Raymarine: 077 (green image); RC Pet Products: 184; Tom Reid: 060; Scarab Jet Boats: 153; Tom Schlichter: 196; Sea-Doo: 001 (PWC); Sea Ray: 001 (flybridge); Si-Tex: 056 (C); Grafton Marshall Smith: 142, 216; Stamas: 001 (center console); Star Brite: 225; StayPut: 223; Richard Steinberger: 053 (courtesy Meridian Yachts), 188, back cover (lake); Stingray Boats: Chapter 3 Closing Image; Zach Stovall: 045, 234; Rick Strand: 013, 015; Thomas R. Wilson / Cobalt Boats LLC: 227 (boat), back cover (pontoon boat); John Tiger: 289; Tilley: 085 (hat); Trojan Battery Company: 052 (right); USCG / Chief Petty Officer Chuck Chavtur: 176; USCG / Petty Officer Shawn Eggert: 048 (figures in water); USCG / Chief Petty Officer Albert Michell: 042; USCG: 157, 170, 173; Randy Vance 90, 93; WestMarine: 052 (middle), 072; John Whittle: 290. The publisher made every effort to reach rights holders and regrets any omissions.

ILLUSTRATION CREDITS

Illustrations courtesy of Conor Buckley, with the following exceptions: Tim Barker: 007, 032, 043, 046, 081, 094, 107–109, 111–113, 122, 124, 125, 128, 130, 134–135, 140, 154, 168, 174, 181, 204, 222, 242, 243, 254, 256, 259, 260, 267, 270, 271, 273, 279, 281, 285, 287, 296, 299–310; Tim Eggert: 127; Marine Retailers Association of the Americas: 010; Christine Meighan: 097; Steve Sanford: 114; Pete Sucheski: 059; Lauren Towner: 031, 248, 249

weldon**owen**

President & Publisher Roger Shaw
Associate Publisher Mariah Bear
SVP, Sales & Marketing Amy Kaneko
Finance Director Philip Paulick
Project Editor Robert F. James
Associate Editor Ian Cannon
Creative Director Kelly Booth
Art Director Allister Fein
Illustration Coordinator Conor Buckley
Production Director Chris Hemesath
Production Mananger Michelle Duggan
Director of Enterprise Systems Shawn Macey
Imaging Manager Don Hill

Weldon Owen would also like to thank Brittany Bogan, Kate Forristall, and Jan Hughes for editorial assistance and Kevin Broccoli for the index.

DESIGN BY CAMERON + COMPANY
Publisher Chris Gruener
Creative Director Iain R. Morris
Designer Suzi Hutsell
Design Assistant Amy Wheless

Boating and Weldon Owen are divisions of

BONNIER

Library of Congress Control Number on file with the publisher

ISBN 978-1-68188-045-7
10 9 8 7 6 5 4 3 2 1
2016 2017 2018 2019 2020
Printed in China by 1010 Printing International

BOATING
WORLD'S LARGEST POWERBOAT MAGAZINE

Group Publisher Glenn Sandridge
Publisher John McEver
Editorial Director Sean Bean
Editorial Director, Boating & Watersports
Group Kevin Falvey
Managing Editor Sue Whitney
Deputy Editor Pete McDonald
Electronics & West Coast Editor Jim Hendricks
Senior Digital Editor Brian Daugherty
Creative Director Jerry Pomales
Art Director Ryan Swanson

460 N. Orlando Avenue
Suite 200
Winter Park, FL 32789
www.boatingmag.com